Duncan McDonald

Flathead Indian Reservation Leader
and Cultural Broker

1849-1937

Duncan McDonald.

Duncan McDonald
Flathead Indian Reservation Leader and Cultural Broker
1849-1937

by
Robert Bigart
and
Joseph McDonald

published by
Salish Kootenai College Press
Pablo, Montana

distributed by
University of Nebraska Press
Lincoln, Nebraska

2016

Cover illustrations: Top: Toole Archives, Mansfield Library, University of Montana, Missoula, photograph 82-61a. Bottom: Manuscripts and Special Collections, Holland Library, Washington State University, Pullman, Wash., McWhorter Papers, PC85, box 3.1, folder 45.
   Frontispiece: Duncan McDonald, 943-624, Montana Historical Society Photograph Archives, Helena.

Library of Congress Cataloging-in-Publication Data:
Names: Bigart, Robert, author. | McDonald, Joseph, 1933- author.
Title: Duncan McDonald : Flathead Indian Reservation leader and cultural broker, 1849-1937 / by Robert Bigart and Joseph McDonald.
Description: Pablo, Montana: Salish Kootenai College Press, 2016 | Lincoln, Nebraska: Distributed by the University of Nebraska Press, 2016. | Includes bibliographical references and index.
Identifiers: LCCN 2016004248 | ISBN 9781934594155
Subjects: LCSH: McDonald, Duncan. | Salish Indians--Biography. | Salish Indians--Montana--Biography. | Flathead Indian Reservation (Mont.)--Biography.
Classification: LCC E99.S2 B539 2016 | DDC 978.6004/9794350092--dc23
LC record available at http://lccn.loc.gov/2016004248

Distributed by University of Nebraska Press, 1111 Lincoln Mall, Lincoln, NE 68588-0630, order 1-800-755-1105, www.nebraskapress.unl.edu.

Table of Contents

Foreword

Duncan McDonald, 1849-1937, of Ravalli, Montana, was the physical and cultural embodiment of tribal societies in the Old and New Worlds. On his father's side of the family, Duncan was heir to centuries of conflict between the Highland Scottish tribes or clans and their Lowland cousins allied with the English. In the nineteenth century, many McDonalds worked for the London based Hudson's Bay Company. Duncan's ancestors on his mother's side had battled Plains Indian tribes for over a century to protect their access to the Great Plains of North America and their right to hunt buffalo.

As a man of two worlds, Duncan prospered and became a leader in the Indian and white communities of western Montana. His ability to operate in both the Indian and white societies opened up new opportunities for him, but his intermediate position also weighed on him. In 1928, Duncan wrote that he was "in the same box" as the early twentieth century German Kaiser, Wilhelm II, who had a British mother and a German father. The Germans criticized Wilhelm as "too much of pro British because his mother was british and the british hate him that he was too much of a German — because his father was German. This is my predicament."[1]

During the Roman Empire, Scotland was just outside of Roman control. After the Romans withdrew, invasions of Irish settlers and Viking raiders continued to make Scotland a hard place to earn a living. Over the centuries, however, the biggest conflict was with England, and the McDonalds fought on the Scottish side. Foreign enemies did not prevent the Scottish clans from fighting amongst themselves. By the end of the seventeenth century, McDonalds fought a losing battle against the Scottish Campbell clan and the English. After their defeat, the McDonalds integrated themselves into the English economy and society.

Many members of the family entered the employ of the Hudson's Bay Company. This London based fur trade company had a royal charter giving them exclusive rights to the fur trade in much of northern North America.[2]

The eighteenth century ushered in an era of change among the Native American tribes of the Northern Rocky Mountains and northwestern Great Plains of North America. The Nez Perce, Pend d'Oreille, and Bitterroot Salish tribes that most influenced Duncan's life had homes in the Rocky Mountains and neighboring valleys that later became part of the Pacific Northwest of the United States. They intermarried and cooperated in hunting buffalo on the Great Plains and in the Rocky Mountains. The eighteenth century introduced the tribes to the horse, which greatly widened the range and resources the tribes could utilize. Using horses for transport made it possible to expand their seasonal buffalo hunts on the plains and permitted much larger cargos of buffalo meat and leather products to be hauled west to their homelands. The later eighteenth century also assaulted the tribes with virulent disease epidemics, especially the 1780 smallpox epidemic. These new diseases greatly reduced tribal populations and challenged their ability to defend themselves against enemy tribes.

At the same time the tribes' mobility was being increased by the horse, and their population seriously depleted by disease, Plains Indian tribes such as the Blackfeet and Sioux were expanding into the northern plains. The Bitterroot Salish had to withdraw west from the Three Forks area, and plains buffalo hunts became hotly contested military operations. The early nineteenth century expansion of white fur traders into the area provided the tribes with new allies against the hostile plains tribes, guns and ammunition for hunting and defense, and metal tools to make the labors of daily life more productive.

The world in which Duncan McDonald grew up was a time of growth and challenge for the Nez Perce and Salish tribes. As a backdrop to Duncan's life story, the tribes faced assaults on their political independence and economic viability. In 1855 Washington Territory Governor Isaac I. Stevens negotiated a series of treaties with the tribes that committed them to share their land and resources with white men and gave the United States government a voice in tribal affairs. As a consequence of these agreements, during the second half of the nineteenth century, the tribes saw their political independence slowly lose ground to the growing power of the Flathead and Nez Perce Indian Agents. By 1900, the federal government controlled the tribal law and order machinery on the reservations.

The 1860s saw the beginning of a flood of white miners and farmers into western Montana. By 1900 the tribes of the Flathead Reservation were a minority in their traditional homeland. The loss of the buffalo and increased white competition for other resources undermined the economic base of tribal life. In 1850 the reservation tribes supported themselves with hunting and gathering supplemented by a few livestock. Fifty years later, the tribal economy was based on livestock and farming — primarily grain — supplemented by hunting and gathering in western Montana.[3]

The economic transition was made with only minimal government assistance. The tribes of the Flathead Reservation were basically economically self-supporting during the nineteenth century. Unlike the plains tribes which relied on government rations after the buffalo herds were exterminated, the Flathead Reservation tribes fell back on their herds and farms on the reservation. In the 1880s, rations only provided subsistence during short term adjustments after families relocated to the reservation. General ration support was limited to the sick, indigent, and crippled.[4]

Duncan McDonald entered this world of wrenching cultural, economic, and political change in 1849. Drawing on the cultures of both of his parents, he embarked on a long life as a cultural broker. In the course of his career as a fur trader, historian, hotel owner, farmer, stockman, political leader, and sage,

Duncan spent years helping white people understand western Montana Indians. He also struggled to secure fair treatment for Indians in the new order.

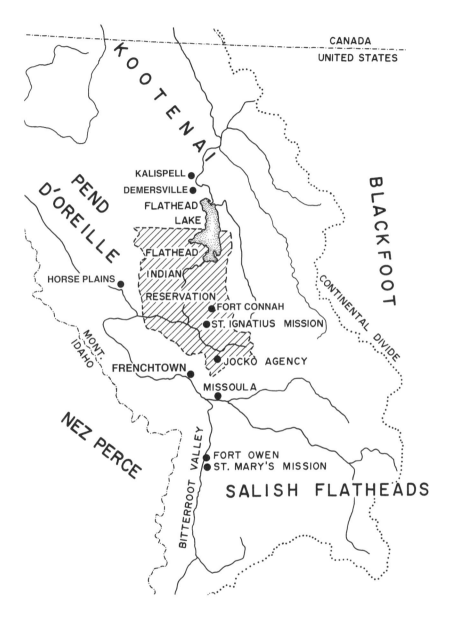

Flathead Indian Reservation
Showing Tribal Territories and Surrounding Towns

Map by Marcia Bakry, Smithsonian Institution, Washington, D.C., 1973

Chapter 1

Family
and Childhood

1849-1867

Duncan McDonald's parents were Angus and Catherine McDonald. Angus was descended from the McDonald clan of warriors who had fought the British for generations. He was born in Scotland in 1816, and in 1838 he followed many other McDonalds into the employ of the Hudson's Bay Company. In 1869 an awestruck young woman described Angus riding on a British Columbia trail: "a solitary horseman, the most picturesque figure I had ever seen. He rode a superb chestnut horse, satiny and well groomed...[Angus] wore a beautifully embroidered buckskin shirt with tags and fringes, buckskin pants, embroidered leggings and soft cowboy hat."[1]

Duncan's mother was Catherine, a half Nez Perce and half Iroquois-French Canadian lady. As a young woman in about 1841, Catherine had traveled with her father and other traders on a long and adventurous journey to the mouth of the Colorado River in Mexico. A year later in 1842, she married Angus at Fort Hall. Catherine lived half of the year in her Hudson's Bay Company house but spent the rest of the year wandering around the countryside with her relatives and friends because she "could not be much in-doors."[2] In 1847 the couple moved to the newly relocated Flathead House, also known as Fort Connah. In 1852 Angus received a promotion and the family moved to Fort Colville, where Duncan spent most of his childhood. By 1853 Angus became chief trader in charge of Fort Colville and surrounding trading posts including Flathead House.[3]

Duncan McDonald's parents.

Top: Angus McDonald.

Bottom: Catherine McDonald.

Sources: Toole Archives, Mansfield Library, University of Montana, photographs 77-289 and 83-96.

Fort Colville was the head of a Hudson's Bay Company district that covered the upper Columbia River Basin. It was located near Kettle Falls on the Columbia River northwest of present-day Spokane, Washington. The chief trader in the district was responsible for the Fort Colville trading post and a number of subsidiary establishments. Two of the smaller trading posts that were under Fort Colville management were Flathead House and Kootenay House. The Colville District of the Hudson's Bay Company was not typical of other Hudson's Bay Company operations. Fort Colville and Flathead House traded for furs, but much of the business involved the "country produce trade" which provided supplies needed by other Hudson's Bay Company trading posts in the course of normal operations. In 1830, for example, the Flathead Post traded for 670 large beaver pelts, 492 small beaver, 2 black bear, 2 brown bear, 2 grizzly bear, 14 fishers, 4 red fox, 18 lynx, 1 mink, 5 martens, 180 muskrats, and 18 otter pelts. But that same year the Flathead House also traded for 47 deer hides, 7 elk hides, and 16 buffalo robes. That year the post traded for 6,684 pounds of dry buffalo meat, 150 buffalo tongues, 84 pounds of buffalo tongues split, and 336 pounds of grease or tallow. Flathead also got 270 appichimons or saddle blankets made of buffalo-calf skin, 105 parfleches, 114 pack saddles, 240 pounds of pack cords, 81 pounds of another kind of cord, and 7 tipis.[4]

Fort Colville in the middle 1840s consisted of a stockade and eight buildings that served as a trading hall, employee residences, and storage buildings. Auxiliary functions such as a kitchen, a blacksmith's shop, a carpenter's shop, a meat house, a bake house, a poultry house, a pigeon house, and a root house were in separate structures. There was a flour mill, several pigs' houses, a stable, a barnyard, and a cattle yard. There was also a farm and livestock ranch nearby. In 1846, a total of 28 men were employed at Fort Colville.[5]

The trade goods stocked by the Hudson's Bay Company emphasized arms for self-protection and warfare and metal and cloth products of European manufacture that made tribal members more productive workers. During the 1830s and 1840s, the returns from Colville District were usually more than double the company's expenses. In 1831 the post returned over three times the company's outlay, but in 1851 the return dropped to 175% of their costs. The Fort Colville District sold mostly guns and ammunition; tobacco; metal traps, tools, and household utensils; and blankets. Metal items included fishhooks, traps, knives, axes, awls, kettles, and thimbles. Colville stocked bells, beads, buttons, brass rings, and mirrors for personal adornment.[6]

An Englishman named John Keast Lord visited Fort Colville in 1861 and left a description of Duncan's boyhood home. Angus' home as chief trader was described as a "primitive mansion." The main room was lit by two small windows and furnished with chairs and a large table. The table covered a trapdoor which let to a cellar where alcohol and valuables were stored. The room was always occupied and was where the chief trader slept, preventing pilferage. A large fireplace provided light and heat. Behind the chief trader's house was a large fenced in courtyard where the furs were baled for shipment to London.

The Fort Colville trading room adjoined the chief trader's house. The trader stood behind a large counter while bargaining. During the bartering, the Indian customer expected payment for each skin separately. If an Indian customer "had fifty marten skins to dispose of, he would only sell or barter one at a time, and insist on being paid for them one by one. Hence it often occupies the trader many days to purchase a large bale of peltries from an Indian trapper." The unit of trade for all transactions was the beaver pelt. If an Indian wished to purchase a blanket or gun, he would need to trade say three silver fox furs, twenty beaver pelts, or two hundred muskrats, depending on their relative value at the time. Indian workers were also paid in beaver skin units for labor of various kinds.[7]

Duncan McDonald was born on March 31, 1849, at Fort Connah, the Hudson's Bay Company trading post on the Flathead Reservation, to Angus and Catherine McDonald. He was their second son and third child. In 1852, when Duncan was about three years old, the family moved to Fort Colville in Washington Territory. Angus and his wife had a number of children and Duncan grew up in a large family. By 1864, when Duncan was 15 years old, he had eight brothers and sisters with more to follow. Angus and Catherine communicated in French at home, but Duncan and his siblings were also exposed to English and several Indian languages in the Fort Colville community.[8] Few contemporary sources have survived documenting Duncan's childhood years at Fort Colville. Fortunately, however, Duncan included occasional childhood reminiscences when he was interviewed by various historians and newspaper reporters. The most valuable source for Duncan's childhood years was a 1929 interview of Duncan by William S. Lewis which was published in a Spokane, Washington, newspaper.

In 1861, Lt. Samuel Anderson of the British Army visited Fort Colville while helping survey the Canadian-American boundary through the Columbia Valley. Anderson described the sleeping arrangements of Angus' brood of seven children at Fort Colville:

> About nine o'clock the eldest girl [Christine] appeared perfectly enveloped in blankets, thrown over head and shoulders, and this burden she deposited in one corner of the room. She made several dives into the adjoining room, and appeared each time with a load of blankets some between her teeth, and others in her hand, till at least about 15 blankets were brought out and placed in different portions of the room. The boys were then told to go to bed, which was as quickly done as said, for they went straight off to the different corners of the room, rolled themselves, dressed as they were, in one blanket and then lay down on two others and were soon asleep.

According to Anderson, the McDonald children spoke broken English because their parents conversed in French. Anderson did complain about what he felt was the children's "want of cleanliness."[9]

The McDonald family had visitors from the Indian tribes living in the Fort Colville area. Duncan later told of an elderly Indian woman who in the 1850s visited his mother Catherine and shared traditional weather lore. The lady visited, was fed, and told Catherine that if the hair lice struggled vigorously then it would be a hard winter with a lot of snow. The lady's weather forecast proved accurate.[10]

For Duncan as a child, life at Fort Colville must have been busy with numerous playmates and frequent holiday celebrations. Charles Wilson, the secretary of the British Boundary Commission surveying the 49th parallel, described the 1860 Christmas feast and holiday at Fort Colville. There was beef and plum pudding accompanied by many toasts with port wine. Songs, Scottish reels, and Highland flings were topped off with a "capital sword dance" by Angus and "an amateur Indian war dance & song."[11]

Sam Anderson described the New Year's celebration at Fort Colville which included many of the local Indian chiefs. Angus began to play a Scottish reel and the celebrants, Indian and white, took up the dance energetically. Food, alcohol, song, and dance flowed freely at the celebrations at the fort. Anderson described a sword dance performed by Angus one winter evening in 1861:

> After that we had two or three dances in which the ladies joined, and after that Mr. Macdonald from the Fort favoured us with a dance called the Gilli-callum or Sword Dance. Two swords are placed on the ground, the blades crossing one another at right angles and the dance consists in dancing in and out between the blades of the swords without touching them, and Mr. McDonald tho more than 40 seemed as nimble about it as he could well be.

Some of the galas lasted all night and broke up at daylight the next morning. Presumably the children were restricted to just observing the adult parties, but the celebrations must have livened up the social life for all of the post residents.[12]

In later life, Duncan's memories of growing up at Fort Colville suggested that he had plenty of freedom to explore and play with his siblings and other children at the fort. The fort

Fort Colville, Hudson's Bay Post, Washington.

Source: Toole Archives, Mansfield Library, University of Montana, Missoula, photograph 83-84.

had a pigeon house which Duncan and his friends climbed in order to pull feathers out of the pigeons' tails to use in making arrows. Duncan particularly remembered an employee named Custer who whipped and abused some of the local Indian people when Angus was away from Colville. One day when Duncan saw Custer whipping his oldest brother John, Duncan threw a stone at Custer. Custer chased Duncan into the kitchen where Duncan confronted Custer with a bow and arrow. Custer threatened Duncan and Duncan shot him in the thigh with an arrow. Custer retreated and never mentioned the confrontation to Angus.[13]

Angus made educational provisions for the fort children. He hired a teacher to run a school for the children during the winter season. During the winter of 1859-1860, when Duncan was about ten years old, a Frenchman named Emile Toulon taught school at Fort Colville for a season.[14] Later in the 1860s a teacher by the name of "Doc" Perkins conducted school for the McDonald and other children at the fort.[15] None of the surviving sources describe the subjects Duncan studied at school. His correspondence in his later life showed he had a good grasp of English grammar and spelling. Duncan was able to express himself in writing. His penmanship was readable but not beautiful.

There was also considerable time for Duncan to travel with his father around the northwest. In 1855 when Duncan was about six years old, he traveled with his father and older brother to the Pend d'Oreille placer gold mines at the mouth of the Clark's Fork River. They camped near the mines, and, the next morning before he left for the mines, Angus warned Duncan and his brother John about a poisonous plant:

> "Look at that, [Angus said] pointing to some plants growing among the sand and gravel. "Don't you touch it. It's a bad thing. If you touch it, it will poison you."
>
> He left us in camp. Soon after my brother began to warn me of the poison plant.
>
> "Oh, bosh," I replied, and disregarding father's warning, I deliberately pulled a bunch of the plants and

rubbed my face with them as hard as I could. Standing a little way from my brother I said:

"I think father was only fooling us. I don't feel anything but a little itch on my face."

"You fool," my brother answered, "you just wait awhile."

I continued to feel all right and went to bed. In the morning I was blind and my face was so swollen that they said I looked like a conquered pugilist. This is about all I saw and remember of the Pend Oreille mining excitement of 1855.[16]

According to Duncan's older sister, Christina MacDonald Williams, Angus sent his family to Montana in 1856 to keep them safe during the wars that broke out after the 1855 treaties negotiated by Washington Governor Isaac Stevens.[17] In 1858, when Duncan was nine years old, Duncan and Angus traveled through the Missoula Valley and Prickly Pear Valley, the present site of Helena, Montana. Duncan remembered seeing grizzly bears, deer, and antelope in the Prickly Pear Valley.[18] A year later Duncan visited the present-day site of the town of Dixon, Montana, when he was ten years old.[19] About 1863, when Duncan was 12 years old, he witnessed a foot race between Chief Charlo's father Victor and an unnamed tribal member. The race took place near Missoula, Montana, and Victor won "by a good margin."[20]

Duncan witnessed history at Fort Colville as a boy. In 1858, he overheard a conversation between his father and Chief Spokan Garry as Angus pleaded with Garry to stay out of the war between some of the interior tribes and the U.S. Army. Angus feared that the conflict would lead to a defeat or the "darndest thrashing" of the Indian warriors.[21] Spokan Garry was a famous chief of the Spokane Indians who had attended the Red River School in Canada in the 1820s. After Governor Issac I. Stevens' 1855 treaty councils, Garry struggled to find a way to keep the peace with the invading white settlers while also protecting the Spokane homeland. In 1857 Garry led the Spokanes on an extended buffalo hunt on the Great Plains to keep their distance from Pacific Northwest tribes who were fighting the United States Army. Despite Garry's best efforts to keep the peace, in May 1858 fighting broke out between the United States Army and the Spokane combined with neighboring tribes. In August 1858, the hostile Indians were defeated by Col. George Wright. Despite such setbacks, Garry and the Spokanes were successful in getting a reservation in their home territory.[22]

In the middle 1860s tragedy struck the McDonald family with the death of John, Duncan's older brother. He accidently cut himself with his pocket knife while doing tricks at a New Year's celebration. The wound became infected and proved fatal.[23]

In 1867, when Duncan was eighteen years old, he was traveling through the Thompson River country with Angus and two Catholic missionary priests. Two white men, Panama Pat and Mickey Hunt, had a cabin on the Thompson River. A party of about twenty Indians had come down from Hot Springs and camped with Panama Pat and Mickey Hunt. The combined group began to drink whiskey and a fight broke out. Mickey Hunt and an Indian named Chiri-ax-mi were killed. Shortly after the trouble, Panama Pat left the country.[24]

Chapter 2

Duncan McDonald, Trader

1867-1877

Duncan was still three months shy of his nineteenth birthday when he arrived at Fort Connah on Christmas eve 1867 and took charge of the Hudson's Bay Company post on the Flathead Indian Reservation in western Montana. He remained in charge until May 1872, when the Hudson's Bay Company closed its operations in the United States.[1] The surviving documentation about Duncan's life between 1867 and 1877 is spotty and leaves many questions unanswered. Almost no information has been found to document Duncan's operation of Fort Connah between 1867 and 1872. Over the years, Duncan related a number of incidents from his 1871 or 1873 trip to the plains with a Pend d'Oreille war party/horse stealing expedition. This trip to the plains in his early 20s was one of his most colorful adventures. During this period in the 1870s, Duncan was a frequent critic of Flathead Agency operations. His criticisms were mentioned in the government records, but the records often fail to give Duncan's viewpoint. In 1877 he was part of a group of tribal members and relatives who ran a Flathead Indian Agent out of office.

The only event recorded from Fort Connah during Duncan's tenure was a celebrated, but undated, poker game at Fort Connah. One of the post employees, Camille Dupree owed an overdue bill at Jack Demers' store in Frenchtown. Demers sent Missoula County Sheriff Mose Drouliard to Fort Connah in an attempt to collect the money from Dupree. Since it was getting late, Duncan invited the sheriff to spend the night. After dinner and whiskey, a poker game started. As host, Duncan observed

Fort Connah, Hudson's Bay Company Trading Post on Flathead Indian Reservation, Montana Territory, 1865, by Peter Peterson Tofft.

Watercolor on paper, original in color, Gift of Maxim Karolik for the M. and M. Karolik Collection of American Watercolors and Drawings, 1800-1875, 53.2464, Museum of Fine Arts, Boston, Mass. Photograph copyright 2016, Boston Museum of Fine Arts, Boston, Mass.

but did not play. Dupree, the sheriff, and Dave O'Keefe, a white neighbor, played. Luck was running against Dupree, but Duncan noticed that Drouliard, the sheriff, was cheating by pulling aces out of his shirt collar. Dupree lost eight dollars but could not pay. A fight broke out between Dupree and O'Keefe, with Dupree sustaining a blow to his stomach. Duncan helped administer first aid and insisted they stop the fight. Duncan noted: "The sheriff stood by in the attitude of an interested spectator only."[2]

In November 1868, Duncan and a white man named John McLean came across the body of a dead white man on the trail between the Big Blackfoot River and the Jocko River. Duncan was returning to the reservation from a visit to Helena. He estimated that the man had been dead for six weeks before being found, and he could not tell from the remains if violence had been involved in the death.[3]

A few months after discovering the body, Duncan purchased two cans of oysters and two pounds of crackers from Worden and Company in Missoula on January 28, 1869. According to one account, this may have meant Duncan was a loser in a game called freeze out. In 1869 the loser was expected to treat the other players to canned oysters.[4] The next day, January 29, 1869, and November 5, 1869, Duncan purchased violin strings at Wordens, but no record has been found to indicate who used them.[5]

Also in January 1869, Duncan applied to Montana Territorial Governor Green Clay Smith for a license to operate a ferry on the Flathead River at the foot of Flathead Lake. John Owen wrote Governor Smith in support of Duncan's application. According to Owen, Duncan was "a worthy young man & I would like to see his rights respected."[6] The Flathead Indian Agent, however, maintained that the license had to be issued by the Office of Indian Affairs rather than the territory. On February 4, 1869, W. J. McCormick, a temporary Flathead Agent, wrote to the Commissioner of Indian Affairs to request permission for Duncan to construct and operate a ferry at the foot of Flathead Lake.[7]

Two months later, on April 2, 1869, however, M. M. Mc-Cauley, the new Flathead Agent, objected to giving Duncan the ferry license. McCauley felt Duncan was "a most improper person to receive or exercise any privilege whatever." According to McCauley, Duncan should not get the license because he was a British subject and the agent for a foreign trading company. He also complained that Duncan was frequently at odds with the missionary priests at St. Ignatius. McCauley gave the ferry license to two mixed bloods from the reservation. One of them, Baptiste Ignace, operated the ferry for many years in the late nineteenth century.[8]

After the contest for the ferry license played out, on October 2, 1869, Duncan purchased two bottles of strychnine at Wordens. No information was located explaining what Duncan did with the strychnine.[9]

The next year, Duncan witnessed a murder on the streets of Frenchtown in May 1870. John Stanley and George Young were quarreling about hiring some men. Duncan was in T. J. "Jack" Demers' store when he heard a commotion in the street and went out to investigate. According to Duncan's testimony, Stanley was holding a knife and chasing Young down the street. Young grabbed a piece of wood, struck Stanley on the head, and ran towards a hotel building. As Young was running away, he looked back and ran into a hitching post. The collision knocked Young down, and Stanley jumped on him and stabbed him to death. Despite Duncan's testimony in the Missoula court trial, the jury was unable to agree and did not convict Stanley.[10]

On July 12, 1870, Duncan sent a large order to Worden and Company for $66.96 in merchandise that suggested someone was setting up a household. The order included wallpaper, wallpaper border, plates, cups, cotton cloth, broom, matches, glue, white lead, red lead, boiled oil, turpentine, and a paint brush. No evidence has been found explaining who needed the household goods.[11]

C. S. Jones, another Flathead Indian Agent, wrote the Commissioner of Indian Affairs on January 5, 1871, charging

that Duncan was trading at Fort Connah without a U.S. government license and selling liquor to Indian customers.[12] Nothing
came of Jones' complaint, but the Hudson's Bay Company soon
abandoned all its operations in the United States, and in May
1872 Duncan transported the Fort Connah records, documents,
and property to Fort Colville.[13] Duncan was out of a job.

On June 29, 1872, *The Pioneer*, a Missoula newspaper,
published an unsigned essay on the demise of the last of a band
of wild black horses in western Montana. The unknown author
of the piece referred to Duncan and another Indian lassoing the
last of this wild band, but letting the horse go free out of respect
for her independent spirit. In 1887, Duncan related a parallel
story of a band of wild black horses living on Wild Horse Island
in Flathead Lake. According to Duncan's story, in the 1830s a
Blackfeet war party drove the black horses off the island, but they
escaped into the hills before they could be captured. In the 1887
account, the last of the wild black horses from Wild Horse Island
were killed in about 1870.[14]

Later, during the fall of 1872, Duncan joined a posse of
white men from Missoula in November in pursuit of two black
men who were accused of stealing horses belonging to Judge
Dance. The posse captured one of the two men at an Indian
camp fifteen miles below Missoula. The second man was found
sleeping in a cabin below Frenchtown but escaped the posse in
an exchange of gunfire. The second suspect was later arrested at
Cedar Creek near Superior.[15]

One of Duncan's most adventurous enterprises was joining
a Pend d'Oreille war party/horse stealing expedition across the
Continental Divide in February 1871 or 1873 when he was 21 or
23 years old. No complete account of the trip has survived, but
Duncan did discuss events on the trip in different interviews over
the years. According to one account related by Duncan, Chief
Michelle was the leader of Duncan's 1871 or 1873 buffalo hunt-
ing/war party. Michelle was crippled in an accident in 1872, but
most of Duncan's accounts date the trip to 1873. Duncan never
reconciled the dating conflict for his first trip to the plains.[16]

"There's only one hold," says Dunc, "shorter than at tail hold on a buffalo — that of a bear."
Drawing by C. M. Russell.

Source: C. M. Russell, *More Rawhides* (Great Falls, Mont.: Montana Newspaper Association, 1925), pp. 29-31.

Apparently the party's horses were stolen by the Blackfeet while they were on the plains. They started out on foot from Marias River for the south fork of the Saskatchewan River after the horses. According to an 1894 interview, the war party headed east during bitterly cold February weather. The members of the party carried only one blanket apiece and could not light a fire for fear of being discovered. They had to live on the scanty frozen food they had taken with them out of the camp. Duncan wrote, "The dangers of being shot were nothing as compared to the dangers of freezing to death — but they enjoyed it."[17]

Early morning at one camp, one of the warriors painted himself and began to sing his medicine song. The singer told the rest of the party that they would also need to paint themselves or one of the party would be killed by the Blackfeet. At this point, all of the party painted themselves except Duncan and another man named Linlay. The Pend d'Oreille insisted that the last two paint themselves and join the medicine song. Duncan took part unwillingly. Before singing their medicine song, they said the Lord's Prayer and three Hail Marys. During the entire trip, the Christian prayers were faithfully recited morning, noon, and night. The party wanted to steal Blackfeet horses and take Blackfeet scalps, but the Pend d'Oreille were convinced they would "receive no punishment for so doing in the hereafter. In this connection I wish to say that Michael, the Pen d'Oreile chief, punishes severely to this day any member of his tribe who refuses to believe in his [Christian] creed."[18]

While camped on the Marias, Duncan had joined a small hunting party that killed two buffalo, but only brought the buffalo tongues back to camp. The women complained that they did not bring back more meat. At this point Chief Michelle stripped and painted himself to perform his traditional buffalo calling medicine.[19]

At some time during his winter 1871 or 1873 adventure, Duncan and a mixed blood companion came across a small band of buffalo. Duncan sneaked up to the buffalo and shot a cow which fell down. He laid his rifle on the ground and walked up to cut the cow's throat. When he reached the animal, he grabbed her tail and yanked, but she was not dead. She jumped up and tried to gore Duncan. Duncan held on to the tail and took a wild ride. After hanging on for as long as he could, Duncan let go and ran for his life. The buffalo charged after him, but she dropped dead before catching him. This episode was a favorite tale for Duncan in later years and was even immortalized in a Charles M. Russell drawing.[20]

Duncan and eight other Indians attempted to return west of the mountains led by Little Charlie. They camped in a saddle in the lowest pass through the mountains but were hit by a snowstorm in the morning. The leader feared snow slides and decided to retreat back towards the east. Duncan and two others started east and the rest of the party promised to follow. However, the others headed west instead, and two of them were buried in a snow slide: Octave Revais and Pierre Chilchimtu. Their three companions escaped the slide and dug out the two who were buried. Apparently all five survived.[21]

Beginning in the summer of 1873 and for at least the next five years, Duncan made large purchases at Worden and Company which could have been for resale. This might indicate when Duncan started his trading business, first as an itinerant trader, and then in a store at Flathead Agency. For example, on June 12, 1873, he purchased 25 pounds salt and 50 milk pans. On September 8, 1873, he got 7 pounds coffee, 3 pounds tea, 2 pounds powder, 10 pounds shot, and one pound tobacco. On September 15, 1873, he purchased 15 pounds of bacon, and on September 19, 1873, another 26 pounds of bacon.[22]

On August 25, 1874, Flathead Agent Peter Whaley wrote to the Commissioner of Indian Affairs that Daniel Shanahan, the previous agent, had given Duncan a plow that should have been given to Kootenai Chief Eneas. Whaley promised to get the plow back from Duncan, so it could be given to Eneas.[23] There is no record in the official correspondence, but presumably Duncan returned the plow and it was given to Chief Eneas.

In 1874, Duncan embarked on his long career as a cultural broker and interpreter presenting Indian viewpoints and grievances to white society. Duncan wrote a letter for Chief Arlee to the U.S. President on November 1, 1874, complaining about Flathead Agent Peter Whaley. According to Duncan's letter, Arlee complained that "our new Agent is not fit to hold this office he is lead by the Jesuite priests by the nose. Such Agent that is governed by priests we do not wish to have him around here whatever." Arlee wanted the six chiefs on the reservation to nominate an honest man for the Flathead Agent position. The President would appoint one of the nominees and could fire him if his work "does not suit you." Now the twelve or fourteen year old son of the agent, David Whaley, was paid $60 a month for "doing nothing only eating." Arlee also asked to be the disbursing agent for the $5,000 a year paid to the Bitterroot Salish who had removed to the Jocko Valley under the 1872 agreement with then-Congressman James Garfield.[24] Duncan's ally, Chief Arlee, had been a noted warrior in his youth and was elected second chief of the Bitterroot Salish in 1871. In 1872 he had signed the Garfield Agreement to move from the Bitterroot to the Jocko Valley, which earned him a lifetime of enmity from Chief Charlo and the majority of the Bitterroot Salish. On the Jocko or Flathead Reservation, he joined Duncan in frequent complaints about the operation of the Flathead Agency and the St. Ignatius Mission schools.[25]

While Duncan helped Chief Arlee present his views in Washington, D.C., Duncan was also active in the cattle business on the reservation. During the winter of 1874-1875, Duncan and his father Angus grazed a herd of cattle on Post Creek in the Mission Valley. That winter the weather was so severe that the trees turned yellow and lost their needles up to an elevation of 3500 feet on the Mission Mountains. The damaged trees recovered and grew new needles the next year.[26]

Duncan married Louise Quil-soo-see or Red Sleep in a religious ceremony on May 6, 1875. The ceremony was conducted by Father Joseph Bandini, S.J., in a tent on Camas Prairie on the

Top:
Duncan McDonald and
wife, Louise.

Bottom:
Mother of Mrs. Duncan
McDonald
at 80 years of age.

Sources: Toole Archives,
Mansfield Library, University of
Montana, Missoula, photographs
Carling Malouf Papers, MS 640,
box 18, folder 8; and 82-122.

reservation. They had previously been married by Indian custom for two years.[27] According to one account by Duncan, she was Salish/Nez Perce, but she was enrolled as full blood Pend d'Oreille. They remained married until her death in 1928.[28] According to family records, Mary McDonald, Duncan and Louise's first child, was born on May 6, 1875, on Camas Prairie, the same day as their Christian wedding.[29]

In 1875, Duncan's father Angus met Angus P. McDonald, his 14 year old son born of a Canadian Indian mother in 1861. The boy's mother died and Angus took the boy back to the Flathead Reservation. Catherine embraced the boy and accepted him into her family. Angus P. became a prominent Flathead Reservation cattleman and was adopted into the Confederated Salish and Kootenai Tribes.[30]

On July 28, 1875, Duncan purchased a gold pan at Worden and Company in Missoula. During the middle 1870s, Duncan's travels were for trading and prospecting.[31]

Duncan spent the winter of 1875-1876 at Fort Macleod in the Saskatchewan or Whoopup Country trading in furs and robes. He made the trip with Robert McGregor Baird, a part-time teacher, prospector, trader, and clerk.[32] In October 1876, Duncan and Baird rushed to the head of the Flathead River to investigate rumors of a gold discovery in the area.[33]

Between 1875 and 1877, Duncan joined T. J. Demers, a Frenchtown merchant; Chief Arlee, of the Salish; and Chief Michelle, of the Pend d'Oreille, to oppose Flathead Indian Agent Charles S. Medary. Most of the surviving historical documents give Medary's complaints, so Duncan's side of the story has not been preserved.[34] In 1876, Duncan started his trading post at the Jocko Agency, and Medary claimed to have assisted Duncan in launching the business.[35]

Medary had been nominated as Flathead Indian Agent by Charles Ewing, director of the Bureau of Catholic Indian Missions in Washington, D.C. Under President Ulysses S. Grant's Indian Peace Policy, the Roman Catholic church got to nominate Flathead Agents. Medary was a Civil War veteran whose father had edited a controversial Democratic newspaper in Ohio during the war. He had been selected because his family had long been influential in Ohio politics and most had converted to the Catholic church.

When Medary took charge of the Flathead Agency on July 1, 1875, he found "the Agency in a horrible condition" and suffering from years of neglect. He was determined to put things in order: "So I shall have a good many changes to make which will keep me busy for some time to come."[36]

Medary's efforts quickly ran afoul of concentrated opposition from Duncan and other tribal leaders. No sources have survived indicating how much of the opposition was directed by Duncan. The anti-Medary forces were likely financed and organized by Telesphore J. Demers, a leading merchant at Frenchtown, a local politician, and the husband of a mixed blood member of the Pend d'Oreille tribe. Demers operated a number of businesses in Frenchtown, ran pack trains to trade in Canadian mining camps and other outlying areas, and organized cattle drives from Texas and Idaho to western Montana. In 1875 he was elected chairman of the Missoula County Commissioners.[37]

Duncan's other ally against Medary was Pend d'Oreille Chief Michelle. Michelle agreed with Duncan and Arlee's complaints against the Flathead Indian Agency, but Michelle was a devout supporter of St. Ignatius Mission and the priests. In 1872 Michelle had been seriously crippled in an accident, and he lived in the Jocko Valley while most of the Pend d'Oreille lived in the Mission Valley to the north. During the 1880s, Michelle often served as spokesman for the tribes after councils had hammered out unified positions in answer to government negotiators.[38]

Agent Medary wrote to General John Gibbon at Fort Shaw, Montana, on December 7, 1876, pleading for troops to be sent to the Flathead Agency. Medary argued that the chiefs who opposed him were "mere tools in the hands of half-breeds [Duncan] and unprincipled white men [Demers]...It seems that a certain educated halfbreed is the main spring in all these movements."[39]

Top:
Chief Arlee, Salish.

Bottom:
Chief Michelle,
Pend d'Oreille.

Sources: Peter Ronan, *Historical
Sketch of the Flathead-Indians
from the Year 1813 to 1890*
(Helena, Mont.: Journal
Publishing Co., 1890), p. 78;
and National Anthropological
Archives, Smithsonian
Institution, Washington, D.C.,
08501400.

Whe - whtils - schay.

In December 1876, Chiefs Arlee and Michelle appeared before the U.S. Grand Jury in Deer Lodge. Duncan was their interpreter. According to the grand jury report, the chiefs complained that many of the promises the government made in the 1872 Garfield agreement and 1855 Hellgate Treaty had not been fulfilled. The testimony also charged Medary with being involved with the business of Duncan's predecessor as agency trader, Wm. Goodyer. Finally the chiefs accused Medary of financial improprieties in agency operations.[40] Medary was acquitted of the charges at trial, but he was nearly ruined by the expense incurred in his defense.[41]

In Medary's January 5, 1877, letter to the U.S. Attorney General in response to the grand jury charges, Medary agreed that some treaty provisions had not been fulfilled. Medary admitted that agency employees hired under the treaty to provide services to tribal members actually spent much of their time running the agency bureaucracy. This arrangement had, however, been endorsed by the Indian Department in Washington, D.C. Regarding his involvement with Agency Trader Wm. Goodyer, Medary argued that he merely turned Goodyer's stock and accounts due over to the new trader, Duncan McDonald, for sale and collection to cover bills owed to Goodyer's creditors in Missoula. In conveying any funds collected by Duncan to Goodyer's creditors, Medary was "acting simply as agent for all parties in the matter as a favor to them." And Medary maintained that he had used his own funds to pay for any services agency employees provided for him personally.[42]

On January 30, 1877, Duncan wrote to *The New North-West*, a Deer Lodge newspaper, publicly repeating his charges that the federal government had failed to fulfill some of the promises in the 1855 Hellgate Treaty to provide schools and services on the Flathead Reservation. Duncan also charged that some of the treaty employees had herded Agent Medary's private horses, cattle, and hogs.[43]

A few days later, on February 19, 1877, Medary wrote to the Commissioner of Indian Affairs requesting authority to remove Colville and Nez Perce mixed bloods from the Flathead Reservation. Medary stated he was particularly interested in forcing Angus and Duncan McDonald off the reservation.[44] In a February 21, 1877, letter to the Bureau of Catholic Indian Missions in Washington, D.C., Medary expanded his complaints about Duncan. Medary accused Duncan of falsely interpreting the chiefs' testimony at the Deer Lodge grand jury. According to Medary, Duncan "hates the whites worse than the pure Indians do, and is an enemy of the Church and the fathers, as well as of mine. He has been continually, of late, since he became *Trader*, stirring up the school question and trying to create disturbance. He is dangerous alike to the best interests of the Indians and the Government."[45]

By February 27, 1877, Medary learned he was being sued for having 191 head of personal cattle and horses grazing on the reservation. According to Medary, when the U.S. Grand Jury found in December 1876 that the chiefs objected to Medary grazing cattle and horses on the reservation "they *did not* in *reality* [object]. Duncan McDonald was Interpreter for them and this was his own personal complaint...The chiefs never requested me to take them [the cattle and horses] away nor did I ever hear of their offering any objections on the subject."[46]

Finally on March 28, 1877, Charles Ewing, the director of the Bureau of Catholic Indian Missions requested Medary's resignation as Flathead Indian Agent. The Commissioner of Indian Affairs had decided that the "alleged dissatisfaction existing among the Indians" required Medary to be replaced.[47] We do not have Duncan's side of the story, but the continued agitation by Demers, Duncan, and Chiefs Arlee and Michelle had forced a change of agents.

On June 1, 1877, Peter Ronan relieved Charles Medary as the new Flathead Indian Agent. Peter's wife, Mary, described Duncan in 1877 as "a handsome young man of twenty-eight" who conducted "a trader's store just outside of the [Jocko] agency square." Mary thought Duncan in 1877 "was not aware of the advantage of capitalizing on his Indian ancestry and inheritance.

He was anxious to appear to be a pure-blooded Scotchman like his father."[48]

Chapter 3

Nez Perce War Historian
1877-1880

The rumbles of war between the Nez Perce Indians and the United States Army in Idaho in 1877 set Duncan on a trajectory emphasizing his growing role as a cultural broker. Duncan's prominence as mediator between the Indian and white communities in western Montana made him a familiar and respected public figure, but also raised the risk he faced if the white community suspected him of supporting the Nez Perce who were fighting the U.S. Army — and some of the belligerents were his relatives.

The hostile Nez Perce heading west over the Lolo Trail during summer 1877 created serious problems for those Nez Perce who wanted to stay out of the war. For example, one Nez Perce chief who opposed the war, Eagle-of-the-Light, arrived at Flathead Agency in 1877. His band camped near Chief Arlee's home at Jocko for the duration of the war. The eleven lodges in his band professed their neutrality and friendship towards the white settlers, and they survived the hostilities safely.[1]

Since Duncan was half Nez Perce and half white, he was suspect in the eyes of some white Montanans. Indian runners conveyed word of the outbreak of hostilities to the Montana tribes, and Duncan relayed the news to Montana newspapers.[2] Especially risky for Duncan were rumors circulating in Missoula that he had sold ammunition to hostile Nez Perce warriors at his Jocko Agency trading post. Duncan related the story in his Nez Perce War history. Three Nez Perce were working as scouts for General Nelson Miles against Sitting Bull and the Sioux. When they learned that war had broken out in Idaho, they deserted Miles and attempted to get home to their families. They reached the Jocko Agency and learned that the hostile Nez Perce were on the Lolo Trail. The three men had a pack mule, but Duncan insisted it was "for their blankets and cooking utensils and not to pack cartridges." When the three found they could not reach their homes via Horse Plains, they returned to the Jocko Agency. Duncan advised Grizzly Bear Youth, the leader of the group, to go to Lolo and surrender to General O. O. Howard in order to keep out of the war. But when the three Nez Perce reached the Bitterroot Valley, they entered the Nez Perce camp and advised Looking Glass and White Bird to head north through the Flathead Reservation to Canada. Looking Glass and the hostile Nez Perce decided instead to head for the Yellowstone Valley where they could join the Crow Indians.[3]

Duncan's later description of his personal activities while the hostile Nez Perce were passing through Montana was a bit vague. On February 1, 1928, he wrote Lucullus V. McWhorter that, when the Nez Perce came down the Lolo Trail in late July 1877, he tried but failed to enter the hostile camp:

> I was about four miles West of Missoula when I met the volunteers going back to Missoula. I asked them where are the hostiles? They told me that they are out of the LoLo or Capt Rawns Fort an[d] moved up the Bitter Root Valley. In getting this information I changed my notion and returned to Missoula. I was calculating to go right into the hostile camp, since they got out LoLo, I quit.

He did not explain what he had intended to do if he reached the camp of the hostile Nez Perce before they entered the Bitterroot Valley. Duncan said he was home at Jocko Agency while the Battle of the Big Hole was being fought in August 1877.[4]

Duncan may have had more contact with the Nez Perce hostiles in 1877 than he wanted to admit publicly in later years. Both a McDonald family oral tradition and a Nez Perce tribal historian indicated Duncan met with the Nez Perce hostiles in

Top:
Chief Joseph,
Nez Perce.

Bottom:
Chief Looking Glass,
Nez Perce

Sources: Library of Congress,
Washington, D.C., USZ
62-49148; and National
Anthropological Archives,
Smithsonian Institution,
Washington, D.C., inv
01005001, photo lot 4420,
photo by William Henry
Jackson, 1871.

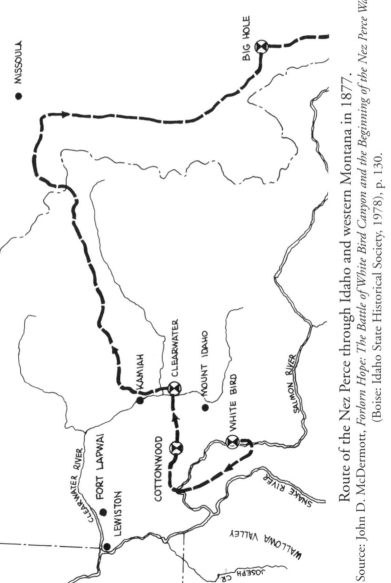

Route of the Nez Perce through Idaho and western Montana in 1877.
Source: John D. McDermott, *Forlorn Hope: The Battle of White Bird Canyon and the Beginning of the Nez Perce War* (Boise: Idaho State Historical Society, 1978), p. 130.

western Montana and encouraged them to head north through western Montana to reach safety in Canada. In one source, Camille Williams, the Nez Perce historian, indicated that Duncan's father Angus sent Duncan to the Nez Perce camp to get them to head north rather than east to Crow country. According to Williams, Angus wanted Duncan to "lead them to Canada, as Duncan knew the trail."[5] Despite any pleadings by Duncan, Chief Looking Glass and the Nez Perce hostiles continued on to Crow country.

After the Nez Perce left the Bitterroot Valley, they were engaged in a series of battles with the United States Army. Loss of Nez Perce life and property was especially severe in the Battle of the Big Hole in southwest Montana in August 1877. In late September 1877, the Nez Perce were surrounded and attacked at the Bear Paw Mountains, just forty miles from safety in Canada. Chief Joseph and most of the Nez Perce surrendered and were taken to Kansas as prisoners of war. More than 200 Nez Perce refugees from the last battle escaped and fled north over the border. The Nez Perce refugees in Canada were led by Chief White Bird, whom Duncan later interviewed for his history of the Nez Perce War.[6]

According to Duncan's February 1, 1928, letter to Mc-Whorter, the editor of the *New North-West* newspaper in Deer Lodge, James Mills, asked him to write the history:

> I was asked by Cap James Mills who was publishing the New North West in Deer Lodge he wanted to write up the cause of the war from the Indian point of view and by asking who he could get the information from Indian side. By inquiring he was told to give the job to Duncan McDonald being on the Flathead Indian reservation. This man is the writer.[7]

Duncan's father, Angus, wrote that Duncan had showed his father "the invitation to do it," and Angus gave Duncan his "views as to how it should be done but that [it] required more time and means than he had." Duncan "started to write them without my knowledge." Angus said the installments were "written originally

by Duncan and then prepared somewhat by Baird & Gregg."
Angus said he suggested Duncan delay some of the publication
for a while, because "the Country [was] now too sore about the
Nez Perces at least I think so." Some of the publication coincided
with the 1878 murder of three Philipsburg area miners by Nez
Perce warriors returning to Idaho after the war.[8]

The two white men Angus identified as helping Duncan
with the Nez Perce War history were Robert McGregor Baird
and Omar G. V. Gregg. Baird had been Duncan's prospecting
companion in 1876. He was a former school teacher in Missoula
and by 1877 was in charge of T. J. Demers' businesses at Frenchtown. In the early 1880s he was Flathead Indian Agency clerk,
and in the 1880 United States census he gave his occupation as
"bohemian." In 1884 Baird was murdered by a white man in the
British Columbia Kootenai country while taking a pack train to
the Kootenai Valley for T. J. Demers.[9]

Gregg was a Confederate Civil War veteran who worked
at various Montana newspapers in the late nineteenth century.
In 1876 and 1877, he was employed by the St. Ignatius Mission print shop publishing Indian language books. In March and
April of 1878 he wrote several letters to area newspapers complaining about the use of flogging by Flathead Reservation chiefs.
That same year, he was a justice of the peace in Missoula. At the
turn of the century, he was a forest ranger in the Flathead forest reserve.[10] Exactly what Angus meant when he wrote that the
manuscript was "prepared somewhat by Baird & Gregg" and the
extent of their editorial changes is not known.

James H. Mills, the editor of the *New North-West* newspaper in Deer Lodge between 1869 and 1891, was an exceptional
man. For a newspaperman in 1878 Montana to seek out and
support the publication of the Indian side of the 1877 Nez Perce
War was remarkable. Mills was born in Ohio in 1837. He served
in the United States Army between 1861 and 1864 and reached
the rank of a brevet lieutenant colonel. Soon after he was mus-
tered out of the army, he engaged in a mining enterprise in the
Yellowstone Valley. He and his partners gave their money to a

packer who was to purchase supplies for them in Bozeman. After the packer gambled away the supply money, the miners were broke and had to abandon their claim. Mills arrived at Virginia City with ten cents in capital. In 1866, he was offered the job as editor of the *Montana Post*, the first newspaper in Montana Territory. He continued at the *Montana Post* in Virginia City and later Helena until the newspaper ceased publication in 1869. Between 1869 and 1891, he was editor of the *New North-West* newspaper in Deer Lodge. From 1877 through 1879, he was also secretary of Montana Territory. After 1891, he held various political offices in Montana. He died in 1904.[11]

Mills announced the new series about the Nez Perce campaign in the April 19, 1878, issue of the *New North-West*. In explaining the need for the history, Mills stated, "The Red Man's side of the story has not yet been told." Mills asked Duncan to write the history because Duncan was "probably the best informed upon the subject to be written up of any one in Montana." Mills "requested that the story be told as the Nez Perces know it, regardless of the views of the whites, and hope to present an account of interest and value."[12]

The first installment of "The Nez Perces: The History of Their Troubles and the Campaign of 1877," by Duncan McDonald, "a relative of Looking Glass and White Bird," appeared in the April 26, 1878, issue. The introduction noted that, "It is a condition of the publication that the views shall be related from their standpoint, and as full particulars as possible will be given of the tribe and their great expedition."[13]

Almost as surprising at Mills' interest in publishing the Indian side of the story in 1878 was that some other Montana newspapers gave approving notices of the history. One newspaper observed that the series seems "to be a plain concise statement, and perhaps contains 'more truth than poetry,'" Another paper observed that Duncan's articles "promise to be very interesting reading." The *Benton Record* at Fort Benton, Montana, observed Duncan "no doubt will give only the Nez Perces view of the subject; but that is more likely to be a correct version of the troubles and adventures of the tribe than were the reports of the army officers who were out-generaled by Chief Joseph."[14]

On June 14, 1878, the *New North-West* announced that the publication of the Nez Perce War series was being suspended so Duncan could travel to Canada to interview the Nez Perce refugees living there. Duncan submitted a general article outlining the Indian history of white oppression and betrayal. He particularly complained about a Montana Territory law that prohibited Indians, blacks, and Chinese from testifying against white persons in court: "In a country which holds these horrible sentiments true civilization and what is worth anything of that much prostituted term, Christianity, are of non-effect." The whites had repeatedly forced land cessions on the tribes and refused to punish white criminals who murdered Indians. (Mills added a note that while the provision prohibiting Indian and other testimony against white men in court had been approved in 1864, it had been discarded when the criminal code was revised in 1872.)[15]

In middle June 1878, Duncan departed on his trip to Canada to interview White Bird in the Cypress Hills. On June 12 he "was nearly killed by a horse" and was crippled but still expected to reach White Bird's camp.[16] On June 18, 1878, Duncan passed through Helena.[17]

Before Duncan reached the Dearborn River, he met a Pend d'Oreille Indian traveling with a Nez Perce couple. They nearly encountered a Nez Perce war party that stole 140 horses on the Sun River. Duncan and his companions were captured by the Gros Ventre Indians when they reached the Milk River. Duncan protested that he was on official business for the Montana Territory Secretary, James H. Mills, and the Gros Ventre released them.[18]

Duncan made it to Canada and neared Fort Walsh, the Canadian Mounted Police post north of Havre. He met Col. Acheson Irvine, the Canadian police commander at Fort Walsh, who was also on his way to White Bird's camp. Irvine wanted to convince White Bird to meet First Lieutenant George W. Baird of the United States Army, who had traveled to Fort Walsh to negotiate with White Bird. Duncan and Irvine had met before in 1875 when Duncan was on a trading expedition to the area. When Irvine learned they were both headed for White Bird's camp and Duncan was part Nez Perce, he solicited Duncan to be his interpreter. The United States Army had received intelligence that White Bird wanted to surrender and return to the United States, but White Bird was apparently surprised at the news that a United States Army officer was at Fort Walsh to talk about surrender. When Duncan and Col. Irvine of the Canadian police located the Nez Perce camp, they headed for White Bird's lodge. The Nez Perce feared Irvine would attempt to arrest White Bird and forcibly return him to the United States. They crowded into the lodge to protect White Bird if needed. Irvine and Duncan introduced themselves but did not mention the purpose of their visit at their first meeting.

Later Irvine explained his mission was to have White Bird come to Fort Walsh and meet with Lt. Baird. Most of the Sioux and Nez Perce feared that, despite Col. Irvine's promise of safe conduct, White Bird would be arrested if he went to Fort Walsh. The negotiations were tense and some accused Duncan of being a spy for the United States government. Finally White Bird asked Duncan, "Are you telling me the truth? Do you think there is any danger going to Fort Walsh?" Duncan assured White Bird that Lt. Baird only wanted to talk to White Bird. After three days of indecision, White Bird finally agreed to accompany Irvine, Duncan, and the police to Fort Walsh.

At Fort Walsh the conference between White Bird, Lt. Baird of the United States Army, and Col. Irvine and Commissioner James Macleod of the Canadian police commenced on July 1, 1878, with Duncan serving as interpreter. White Bird stated he would only surrender if the United States government respected General Nelson Miles' 1877 promise and allowed Chief Joseph and the Nez Perce prisoners to return to Idaho.

Lt. Baird countered with an argument that if White Bird surrendered and joined Joseph in exile, it was "very likely" that the government would then allow all the Nez Perce to return to their homeland. Baird threatened White Bird, that, if White Bird did not surrender, then Joseph "will probably never be sent back." Then White Bird offered to surrender if Baird promised in front of witnesses that he and Joseph would be allowed to return to Idaho. Baird replied, "I cant promise that," and White Bird refused to leave his Canadian refuge.

When White Bird and Duncan returned to the Nez Perce camp, Duncan learned that the Indians at the camp had promised that, "If White Bird dont return, we will kill Duncan McDonald." On July 2, 1878, Duncan wrote editor Mills that White Bird had refused to surrender.[19] Duncan did, however, get his interview with White Bird about the events of the 1877 Nez Perce War.

When Duncan returned to Fort Walsh after the interview, he found Neptune Lynch selling horses. Lynch was one of the early white settlers at Horse Plains, west of the Flathead Reservation, and a legendary horse trader and trainer.[20] Duncan went home to Montana accompanied by a young Salish woman he had found living in White Bird's camp who wanted to return to the Flathead Reservation. He had planned to stop at Deer Lodge on his way back from Canada, but his horses were so worn out that he decided to return directly to Jocko.[21]

On July 26, 1878, Mills wrote in the *New North-West* that Duncan had arrived safely at Jocko Agency after a six week trip. Duncan had spent ten days interviewing White Bird: "White Bird's story was very interesting." The note promised Duncan's series of papers would "be resumed shortly...and we doubt not that [the] interested attention they have attracted will be fully maintained."[22] The next week Duncan forwarded "a very handsome and gaily decorated pipe" to Mills. It was a present to Mills from White Bird.[23]

At the same time, however, that this drama unfolded at White Bird's camp, events in Montana were threatening another war between Indians and whites. A small band of Nez Perce returning from Canada were accused of murdering five white men along the way including three white miners on Rock Creek near Philipsburg on July 12, 1878.[24]

According to a white miner who survived the killings on Rock Creek, the Nez Perce knocked on the miners' door and were welcomed into the cabin. The Indians stated they were hungry and the miners started to cook breakfast for them. Then the shooting started, and three of the miners were killed. J. H. Jones, the white survivor, stated, "The Indians when they came into the cabin laughed and talked pleasantly. Some of them could speak very good English. They asked if any of us had been fighting the Nez Perces last summer; whether our ground was paying and many other questions. They said they were good Indians and friendly. The first intimation we had of evil was when they shot Joy."[25]

D. B. Jenkins, a white correspondent from Philipsburg, threatened, "We know no friendly Indians and cannot afford to wait till we are murdered to find out when we meet one whether he is friendly or not. We do not know how to distinguish a Flathead from a Nez Perce or a Crow from a Sioux. But know how and will missionary [kill?] all that come through this valley."[26]

From Rock Creek, the band of Nez Perce hostiles fled through the Bitterroot Valley towards Idaho. In the Bitterroot they were accused of plundering the house of Joe Blodgett, a white settler married to a Salish woman.[27] The Nez Perce were pursued by a United States Army detachment from Fort Missoula led by First Lieutenant Thomas Wallace, and a party of white and Salish Indian volunteers from the Bitterroot Valley. The Salish volunteers pursuing the Nez Perce included Francois Lamoose, Narcisse, Louis Vanderburg, and Martin Charlo.[28]

The troops and white and Salish volunteers tracked the Nez Perce until the trail reached the Idaho border. At the border almost all the volunteers decided to return to their homes, and the troops continued the pursuit accompanied by two or three white civilians. Soon after the troops entered Idaho on July 21, 1878, they caught up with the Nez Perce and attacked them. Six of the Nez Perce were killed, three wounded, and the rest escaped.[29]

The murders and thefts inflamed Montana whites, and many made threats against the Salish Indians who had no part in the depredations. Duncan responded to the situation with "An Appeal to Reason: The Injustice and Folly of Threatening All Indians with Death Because Some Are Murderers."[30] Duncan emphasized his disapproval of the murders committed by the refugee Nez Perce, but he also decried those whites who threatened peaceable Indians in response. He argued,

> Their opinions, however published in a respectable journal...are capable of much greater evils than any individual action, not to mention the absurdity of urging the propriety of killing the first Frenchman met because another had murdered some one — they actually appear to approve of the principle of killing a Frenchman on account of a murder by an Italian. Do they not know that two Indian nations are as separate and distinct as any two nations of Europe? Their customs, languages, modes of living and very often their food and methods of transportation are totally dissimilar. Why a Flathead who last year proved his friendship for, or, if some prefer it, his disinclination to hostility towards the whites, would be subject to be shot by the first white man who has a safe opportunity simply because said white man does not know he is not a hostile Nez Perce passes comprehension.

He also pointed out that random murders of friendly Flathead, Pend d'Oreille, or Spokane Indians would force these tribes to fight the whites. Such an uprising would result in the death of many innocent whites and Indians.[31] Mills published an editorial with Duncan's column maintaining that the threats of Philipsburg whites to kill any Indian on sight were unfortunate but understandable. Mills argued that federal Indian policy prohibited Indians from leaving their reservations without an army escort.[32]

The debate continued and Duncan wrote a column taking issue with Mills' editorial. Duncan pointed out that the right of the Flathead Reservation tribes to hunt buffalo and other game off the reservation was guaranteed by the 1855 Hellgate Treaty. At the time the Philipsburg whites were threatening peaceful Indians, Salish Chief Arlee was returning from a buffalo hunt and could easily have traveled through the Philipsburg area. Duncan could see no reason why the peaceable Salish Indians should be threatened after they "had but lately offered to furnish scouts to warn settlers of any approach of hostiles." White murders of friendly Indians were frequent:

> With reference to your not knowing instances of Indians being killed on account of the misdeeds of their brethren, I will remark that I could cover more space of your valuable sheet than you would be willing to allow with examples thereof....Mr. J. H. Robertson of your place [Deer Lodge] could give you one very glaring case which occurred in Kootenai during his residence there.[33]

In the same issue with Duncan's reply to Mills' editorial, a white correspondent from Philipsburg wrote defending anti-Indian racism and violence: "how many [whites] can look at an Indian and tell his tribe; his face, and tell his intentions? Not one in ten thousand. No one would willingly kill a Flathead for a Nez Perces, but how is one to know?" He then went on with a racist screed that all Indians were dirty thieves: "Who ever saw a really good Indian?"[34] It was against this backdrop of racism and violence, that Duncan's history of the Nez Perce War resumed publication on October 11, 1878.

In 1878, while the Nez Perce War history was being published, Duncan continued his activities as a trader at Jocko Agency. On August 26, 1878, Flathead Agent Peter Ronan wrote the Commissioner of Indian Affairs to request a replacement check be issued for $240.00. The original check to Duncan for 6000 pounds of beef had been lost at the bank. Duncan's father, Angus, complained on November 10, 1878, that Flathead Agent Peter Ronan refused to grind wheat for Duncan at the agency gristmill for trade.[35] On October 14, 1878, Ronan wrote that there were two traders near the Jocko Agency. In addition to Duncan's store, there was also a store owned by Telesphore J. Demers, the white entrepreneur from Frenchtown who was married to a mixed blood Pend d'Oreille woman. Demers' store was managed by William H. Barron from New York, who had been a miner at Cedar Creek in 1870.[36]

Duncan took a pack train of flour to the British Columbia Kootenai River country in September 1878. When he reached Tobacco Plains, Duncan found a half dozen lodges of Nez Perce Indians led by Tuk-Alik-Shimsi, a brother of Looking Glass. Tuk-Alik-Shimsi had taken part in the July 1878 council with Lt. Baird at Fort Walsh where Duncan was interpreter.[37]

In November 1878, Duncan headed north with a load of flour he had purchased from the Eddy, Hammond Company in Missoula. On this trip he was headed for Fort Macleod in Alberta. Duncan took Kootenai Chief Eneas and an Indian named Paul as guides. They camped at the foot of a lake on the Middle Fork of the Flathead River. Duncan carved his name and the date into a large cedar tree near the camp. Soon after, the lake became known as Lake McDonald. Chief Eneas and Paul headed back to the Flathead Reservation while Duncan and the rest of his party continued with the flour. Duncan encountered about twenty lodges of Nez Perce refugees headed back to the United States, but he convinced them that it was too dangerous, and they accompanied Duncan north to Kootenai Lakes. Duncan said he appreciated the help from the Nez Perce as the combined group fought waist deep snow on the way to Kootenai Lakes. The flour was sold to Charles Conrad, the Kalispell area merchant and entrepreneur, who in 1878 had a trading post at Fort Macleod. Duncan returned to Jocko in the spring of 1879.[38]

Sometime, presumably in 1878, Duncan became involved in competing claims for a ranch at Horse Plains. The land was claimed by a Lower Pend d'Oreille woman named Elize, and had been enclosed and plowed on shares by a white man named John. After John sold his interest to another white man named James Laughlin, no record was kept of Elize's interest in the wheat crop. This led to conflict between Elize and her family and Laughlin.

Duncan became involved either as a mediator or a possible buyer of the ranch. Flathead Agent Peter Ronan investigated, but he advised Laughlin the conflict was off the reservation and therefore should be resolved in Montana Territory courts. Elize's son, Louie Cultis-toe claimed Duncan wanted the ranch for one of Duncan's wife's relatives. No record was found describing how the conflicting claims were resolved.[39]

In January 1879, a controversy broke out over Duncan's account in the *New North-West* of the Nez Perce women and children who were killed at the Battle of the Big Hole. Duncan had written that, "It was shameful the way women and children were shot down in that fight....It is a well known fact that the command wasted more powder and lead on the women and children then on the warriors. There were seventy-eight Indians, all told, killed in the Big Hole battle. Of these, only thirty were warriors. The others were women and children." Duncan charged that the soldiers had murdered forty women and children who had fled and sought shelter in a ravine to get out of the battle.[40]

In an accompanying editorial, Mills argued that some casualties of women and children were unavoidable, but Mills agreed that any deliberate targeting of women and children would be "deserving of censure." Mills wrote that the bodies of the forty women and children in the ravine after the battle had been carried from the camp by the Nez Perce. He understood the Indians had attempted to bury the bodies by caving in the bank to cover them.[41] Duncan wrote Mills a letter, that was not published, maintaining that the women and children in the ravine had been killed there, not in the camp. Mills granted that, if this were true, "we agree with Mr. McDonald that it was cruel and reprehensible in the highest degree."[42]

In early February 1879, two *New North-West* subscribers wrote the newspaper complaining that Duncan's history had failed to mention two Nez Perce-white conflicts just following the Big Hole Battle. Mills forwarded the letters to Duncan for his response.[43]

Duncan wrote on March 21, 1879, that many of the Nez Perce had not known these fights occurred. After special inquiries, Duncan wrote that just after the Big Hole Battle some Nez Perce encountered a party of white men who traded whiskey with them. When fighting broke out, the Nez Perce fired their guns into the pack train of the white men, but they did not know whether any of the white men had been killed.[44]

In Duncan's January 24, 1879, installment of the Nez Perce War history, where he condemned the United States Army for slaughtering women and children at the Big Hole Battle, the *New North-West* made a typesetting mistake. As printed, Duncan said: "The writer of these papers has had many difficulties because he does choose to believe in what the medicine men say." The next week on January 31, 1879, Mills published a correction: "In this his [Duncan's] statement was reversed. It should have read, 'The writer of these papers has had many difficulties because he does *not* choose to believe,' etc."[45]

A few weeks later, Duncan followed up with a personal letter to Mills about Indian religious beliefs which Mills published in the February 21, 1879, issue. Duncan emphasized: "I again repeat my disbelief in Indian medicine. I have said the Indians get vexed with me on account of my unbelief, and although oftentimes placed in embarrassing positions on this account, I remain to this day unconverted." Duncan related his experiences in 1871 or 1873 when he accompanied a Pend d'Oreille war party on the plains that had their horses stolen by the Blackfeet. Duncan joined the Pend d'Oreille who pursued the thieves towards the south fork of the Saskatchewan River. One morning one of the Pend d'Oreille was painted and singing his medicine song. He told Duncan and the rest of the party that unless everyone in the party painted themselves, one of the Pend d'Oreille warriors would lose his life. Duncan objected: "I told the warriors I did not believe the medicine man and would go on no wild goose chase." Finally everyone had painted themselves except Duncan and a person named Linlay. The last two holdouts were forced to join the ceremony, and, according to Duncan's account, "the scene was ludicrous in the extreme."[46]

Duncan felt the traditional medicine beliefs conflicted with the Lord's Prayer and three Hail Mary's the party repeated faithfully three times a day. On the same trip, Pend d'Oreille Chief Michelle used his traditional Indian medicine to call the buffalo for the hunters. Duncan concluded, "Yes, I am a disbeliever, and what intelligent person would not be?"[47]

About the same time as Duncan's essay on Indian medicine was published in February 1879, Duncan and Louise's first child, Mary, died of measles. No further information has been found about the death.[48]

In March 1879, Mills purchased a "handsome" engraved watch in Helena as a gift for Duncan on completion of the Nez Perce War history.[49] The last installment of Duncan's history appeared in the *New North-West* on March 28, 1879. The last paper described the recent meeting between Nez Perce Chief White Bird and the United States Army representative in July 1878 at Fort Walsh where Duncan was interpreter.[50] The finale was supposed to run on March 14, 1879, but had been delayed in the mail.[51]

Mills noted in the March 14, 1879, issue, "That the publication of these papers has been appreciated is evidenced by the constant demand for back numbers of the *New North-West* containing the history." Since many of the back issues were no longer in print, Mills suggested that "arrangements may possibly be made whereby all those desirous of getting the narrative of the Nez Perces wanderings, as told by Mr. McDonald, will be able to do so." This might have been a suggestion that the history would be published as a book. Mills did note that Duncan had promised to send future "sketches" relating to Indian customs and other topics.[52]

As part of Duncan's continuing trading enterprises, Duncan leased a pack train to two white men, E. F. Warner and George McGovern in May 1879. The Missoula County Assessor rushed down to Stevensville to catch up with the train and collect taxes

on it.[53] On July 10, 1879, Duncan paid $4.50 for a one year sub-
scription to *Harper's Weekly*.[54] This subscription illustrated the
breadth of Duncan's reading habits.

In early July 1879 a fight broke out between a party of
white men and a party of Salish Indians in Lincoln Gulch. One
white man, J. Eagleson, and an Indian, Moses, were killed in the
conflict. Flathead Indian Agent Peter Ronan and Duncan wrote
letters giving the Indian side of the events. R. Evans, the surviving white man, insisted they had not supplied any whiskey to the
Indians. According to the version told by Pend d'Oreille Chief
Michelle, however, the white men had two bottles of whiskey
and had attacked the Indian victim without provocation. Mills
published a summary of Duncan's letter, "a part of which we
think best not to publish." Duncan concluded, "Michell, the Pen
d'Oreille chief, would like to see Mr. Evans arrested and tried....
We claim protection under the flag of the United States and we
also claim our right to a hearing in this case."[55] Evans was arrested and brought to trial in Deer Lodge, but the Indian witnesses
failed to appear and the charges were dismissed.[56]

Duncan took a prospecting trip to the Kootenai mines in
September 1879 accompanied by Robert McGregor Baird. They
spent the winter in Canada. At Tobacco Plains he found the same
band of Nez Perce refugees led by Tuk-Alik-Shimsi, who had been
there in September 1878.[57] In the fall of 1879 the Nez Perce negotiated from Tobacco Plains with Flathead Agent Peter Ronan
to return to the United States. Since they feared the United States
government would send them to exile in Oklahoma with Chief
Joseph's Nez Perce, they decided to remain in Canada.[58] Duncan
observed, "These Indians are poor but not suffering from starvation. They brought us berries and cooked fish, and meat as gifts,
not expecting anything in return."[59]

While at Tobacco Plains, Duncan questioned the Nez
Perce about any white women killed in Idaho during the 1877
war. The Nez Perce said one white woman and a child were killed
accidentally when they hid in the upstairs of a house the Nez
Perce had set on fire. Another white woman and child were killed

by four drunken Nez Perce: "We could have killed many more women and citizens but our Chief Looking Glass, would not permit us."[60] Tuk-Alik-Shimsi and his Nez Perce band moved to the east side of the Continental Divide because the Kootenay Indians at Tobacco Plains tried to whip the Nez Perce who danced a traditional Indian dance with Kootenai women.[61]

According to a letter Duncan sent on October 24, 1879, Eagle-of-the-Light, the Nez Perce chief who had spent the war at the Flathead Agency, tried to get White Bird's Nez Perce band to return to the United States. Sitting Bull refused to allow anyone to take the Nez Perce from the Sioux camp.[62]

By November 21, 1879, Duncan was at Fort Macleod, and reported that the Sioux and Nez Perce refugees on the Canadian plains were very hard up for food. Other Nez Perce were at Kootenai Lakes and living on fish, but Duncan expected them to commence farming in Canada in the spring. Duncan said he knew for certain the Nez Perce had not killed any white owned cattle.[63]

Duncan wrote another letter from Canada from the Kootenai Lakes on December 13, 1879. He was with Tuk-Alik-Shimsi and ten lodges of Nez Perce Indians. Two hunters killed four mountain sheep and the next day one of the hunters, three women, an old man, and a boy started on horseback to get the meat. The party was caught in a snow storm and the women, old man, and boy could not get off the mountain. Duncan and Tuk-Alik-Shimsi accompanied a rescue party to save those stuck in the snow. Duncan carried the most seriously frozen woman off the mountain on his back.[64]

In the same month of December 1879, Duncan met a band of Mountain Stoney Indians at Kootenai Lakes. The Stoneys were starving and Duncan was able to feed them and give them one hundred pounds of flour. The Stoneys camped with Duncan and the Nez Perce. The Nez Perce were Drummers who followed the Indian prophet Smohalla. They put on a Christmas feast together with talks about their religious beliefs. Duncan sent a summary of the teachings in a report to the *New North-West*.[65]

According to another letter from Canada, Duncan was planning to travel to the plains on February 11, 1880, to interview Sitting Bull and write his life story.[66] By February 29, 1880, however, the snow was so deep that Duncan had to turn back. He had already lost four head of horses. On the plains he met two lodges of Cree Indians who were starving. During fall 1879, he had shipped some flour to Fort Macleod, but he could not get there in February 1880.[67] By March 1880, Duncan had made it to Fort Macleod. Much of the social life at the fort revolved around three to five dances a week. At one dance Duncan and his friends tried to politely ask the Indian girls to dance. They were refused. A French mixed blood told Duncan and his friends they needed to drag the girls out on the dance floor, and then they would "dance plenty."[68]

In May 1880, Duncan made an unsuccessful attempt to return to Montana from the Kootenai Lakes, but he had to retreat north because the snow was too deep.[69] It must have been nearly summer 1880 by the time Duncan returned to Jocko and ended his northern adventure.

Chapter 4

Northern Pacific Railroad Guide and Mediator
1880-1884

In the early 1880s, Duncan continued his trading business, both at his Jocko Agency store and by pack train. He also worked as a guide to Northern Pacific Railroad construction crews and officials and as a mediator to avoid friction with local tribal members. Duncan's work for the Northern Pacific Railroad was another example of his growing role as a cultural broker. His organization of a Mission Mountain climb for some of the most prominent guests attending the last spike ceremony completing the Northern Pacific Railroad was recorded in detail by a Missoula journalist.

Duncan ran a pack train to Walla Walla in the fall of 1880 to pick up a shipment of Spitzenberg apples for Christopher Higgins, the Missoula merchant. He started the pack train overland to Spokane Falls and then had a Kalispel Indian take him down river by canoe to Walla Walla. Duncan had the apples shipped to Spokane and then brought the apples up with his pack train. He paid 75 cents a pound for the apples and arrived at St. Ignatius Mission with his cargo on December 21, 1880.[1]

Mining continued to tantalize Duncan. In late May 1881, he followed an Indian to a potential copper mine fifty miles north of Flathead Lake. The prospect turned out to be worthless, and Duncan returned to the reservation. On the way back, he met a party of nine white prospectors headed for the same mine.[2]

About the same time, Duncan was enlisted as an interpreter by a *Weekly Missoulian* correspondent investigating recent conflict between Indians and white men near Missoula. One evening an inebriated Indian gentleman threw rocks through the windows of a white man's home. The white man shot the Indian twice, but the Indian escaped back to his camp. When interviewed by Duncan later, the Indian was remorseful. He had thought the house belonged to a Chinese man.[3]

Duncan sued Joseph Ashley in the Missoula court on June 21, 1881, for $401.06 plus expenses due on a promissory note. Duncan won, and the Missoula sheriff attached six horses, a wagon, and three harnesses belonging to Ashley. After the attachment, Ashey settled the claim to Duncan's satisfaction.[4] Joseph Ashley was a farmer at the foot of Flathead Lake in the 1880 census and head of a large mixed blood family.[5]

In July 1881, Duncan encountered some white men who were skeptical of the killing power of a "particularly handsome" bow and arrows owned by Eddy, Hammond & Company in Missoula. The bow had belonged to Nez Perce Chief Looking Glass. The arrows were made of hard wood. Duncan took the bow and arrows outdoors and shot one of the arrows through a one and half inch thick pine board at close range. The onlookers were suitably impressed by the bow's power.[6]

A ledger has survived describing Duncan's 1881 purchases from the Missoula Mercantile Company. His purchases on November 8, 1881, were large quantities for resale. In addition to a sack of sugar, Duncan purchased 135 pounds of coffee, 20 pounds of oatmeal, 2 caddies of tea, and one grindstone. On November 26, 1881, he purchased three axes with handles and three other ax handles.[7] In November 1881, Duncan returned to Missoula with a pack train carrying 6,000 pounds of apples.[8] A few weeks later, he received a load of apples delivered by Edward Warren. These apples had been ordered by various Missoula residents.[9]

In January 1882, Duncan wrote a short essay on the subject of the varieties of eagles. According to Duncan, the great American game or fish eagle was the best at fishing and a clean and proud bird. The American or National eagle with the white head made its living stealing fish caught by the game eagle. Duncan concluded, "We mountaineers do not approve of disclaiming the game eagle and placing the lazy white-headed eagle on American coin."[10]

Duncan began an almost two year job working as a guide and mediator for the Northern Pacific Railroad construction in February 1882.[11] That same month, Duncan and the survey crew got caught near Ravalli in a late winter blizzard that piled a foot and a half of snow on the valley bottoms. The temperature dropped so low the surveyors' instruments froze solid and no work could be done for several days. Despite the storm, an unnamed Indian left Charley Plant's ranch for the mission on foot, ignoring pleas to stay out of the weather. The next morning his body was found in a coulee near the present National Bison Range.[12] In April 1882, Duncan wrote that snow six feet deep was reported on the Clark's Fork River.[13]

In March 1882, Duncan mediated a conflict between an Indian named Dominick and a party of Northern Pacific Railroad surveyors on the reservation. Dominick objected when the surveyors came onto his farm and started cutting brush inside his field without his permission. Dominick drew a gun on the survey crew chaining a line through his field and stopped the work. The local supervisor settled the matter by paying Dominick five dollars for the damage done by the surveyors, and the work went on. Presumably Duncan interpreted during the negotiations.[14]

Duncan wrote a letter on March 12, 1882, to the *New North-West* from a railroad survey camp above Lake Pend d'Oreille. According to Duncan, when the Hudson's Bay Company arrived, the Pend d'Oreille lived on Lake Pend d'Oreille and below, and the Bitterroot Salish lived around the head of Flathead Lake in the Upper Flathead Valley. The Bitterroot Salish moved to the Bitterroot Valley when St. Mary's Mission was established.[15]

While Duncan was working for the Northern Pacific Railroad, Duncan and Louise had a son. Peter Colville McDonald was born on May 28, 1882, at Perma station.[16] Duncan and Louise sent Peter to a variety of boarding schools and the University of Montana over the years. Peter died in 1905, when only 23 years old.

During the high water in early June 1882, Duncan and two Northern Pacific Railroad officials tried to navigate by boat from near Perma to Weeksville, twenty miles below. Weeksville was between Plains and Thompson Falls. When they were still about two miles above Weeksville, their boat capsized and all the passengers were swimming in the water. Fortunately a party of Indians were passing by and fished Duncan and the two white men out of the water. The Northern Pacific officials were thankful for being rescued, and they gave the Indians an order on Eddy, Hammond & Company in Missoula to pay for replacing the clothing the Indians lost while performing the rescue.[17]

The federal government did not get around to negotiating with the Flathead Reservation tribes for the sale of the railroad right-of-way through the reservation until August 31, 1882. The government negotiator was Joseph K. McCammon, the Assistant Attorney General. Most of the tribal leaders would have preferred to see the railroad go around the reservation, but McCammon was not willing or able to consider alternative routes. McCammon was condescending and officious. Chief Arlee asked for a million dollars for the right-of-way which shocked McCammon. McCammon finally had to admit the land was worth more to the tribes than the government was willing to pay. McCammon increased his initial offer of $15,000 to $16,000. The chiefs insisted he ask the President to expand the reservation north into the Upper Flathead Valley and that the sale money be paid in cash since the government had cheated the tribes before on goods and services promised in the 1855 Hellgate Treaty. The chiefs also got McCammon to agree that the money was for the use of the right-of-way, and it was not a sale of the land by the tribes. Unfortunately, the final agreement signed on September 2, 1882, included language that the tribes sold all of their interest in the right-of-way land. Duncan did not speak during the negotiations, but most likely he was lobbying for the railroad behind the scenes. Duncan was the fiftieth to sign the agreement. He was

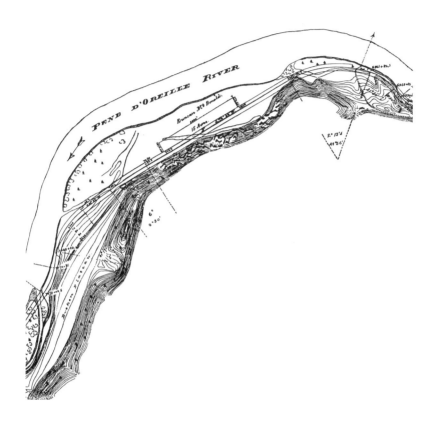

Duncan's pre-1883 ranch,
about half way between present Dixon and Perma
in Ravalli curves area,
on the south side of the Flathead River.
Source: U.S. President, "Message from the President of the United States,
Transmitting a Letter from the Secretary of the Interior....," Senate Executive
Document No. 44, 47th Cong., 2d Sess. (1883), serial 2076,
detail from map, "N.P.R.R. Final Location, Pend d'Oreille River."

also to receive $800 for 35 acres of his cultivated fields taken by the right-of-way. The congressional document approving the sale included a map of Duncan's ranch near Perma.[18]

Duncan kept up his trading business and criticism of Flathead Agency operations even while he was working for the Northern Pacific Railroad. In one business transaction in the fall of 1882, Duncan met a white man named Zeb Harris driving a load of oats on a reservation road. Duncan offered Harris $900 for the oats, four horses, wagon, and harness, and Harris accepted. Duncan took his purchase and Harris waited beside the road for the next stage.[19]

The St. Ignatius Mission account books are hard to follow, but Duncan did make large purchases of flour and other goods from the mission between 1882 and 1884. Duncan paid for most of his purchases with cash, but on April 20, 1883, he apparently traded two hogs to the mission. Most of his large purchases were of flour, butter, bacon, potatoes, ham, onions, and pork. For example, on September 5, 1882, Duncan purchased 4,400 pounds of xxx rated flour, 2,000 pounds xx flour, 650 pounds family flour, and 50 pounds Indian flour. This was in addition to 37 pounds of bacon and pork shoulder, 30 pounds of sugar, 3 large cans of yeast powder, and other items in smaller quantities. In February and March of 1884, Duncan purchased some 3,800 pounds of flour directly and by order.[20]

In June 1883, Duncan guided an unnamed writer through the reservation and pointed out Fort Connah with special pride. The writer wrote a travel log from Missoula to Spokane, but it is not known how much of the trip was accompanied by Duncan.[21]

Duncan joined with Chief Arlee of the Bitterroot Salish on the Jocko Reservation in criticizing the St. Ignatius Mission schools and Flathead Agency operations. Duncan's and Arlee's views, combined with the inspector's bigotry, were seen in Inspector S. S. Benedict's July 10, 1883, report on Flathead Agency. Benedict complained that, "Many of the leading men of the nation do not patronize the [St. Ignatius] school and have a strong prejudice against its management. Among them is Chief Arlee, head chief of the Flatheads. Although a Catholic by profession, he says he wants his people to be taught something besides how to pray." Benedict suggested that government aid for the schools be limited, because with its farm, shops, and cattle herds, "The Mission as managed is a money making institution." Benedict's personal views about the Roman Catholic Church seem to have been bigoted: "The quarters of the priests [at St. Ignatius] were dirty and ill kept as bachelors quarters always are...it seemed a relief to leave the place. The surrounding atmosphere seemed as mouldy as a cloister of fifteenth century."[22] Reflecting Duncan's personal interests, Benedict suggested that annuity goods provided for the Flathead be reduced and the money be used to hire more employees. Then Agent Peter Ronan would not need to require Indians to help when the agency sawmill was cutting their lumber or the agency gristmill was grinding their flour.[23]

On November 24, 1883, Flathead Agent Peter Ronan wrote the Commissioner of Indian Affairs, that Arlee was the only chief who refused to patronize the St. Ignatius schools. Arlee had had one son at the school, but Arlee objected when the boy was required to work with the other students on the school farm. Ronan agreed with the recommendation to hire more employees to operate the sawmill and gristmill. In a later letter, on December 26, 1883, Ronan explained his reason for not wanting to use the agency gristmill to grind the wheat Duncan purchased through his store. Ronan complained that Duncan "desired to be enabled to induce Indians to sell him all their wheat (which he could easily do by advancing goods before the Crops were harvested) & then have the whole ground for himself personally; where he would be in a position to sell it back to the growers in Flour; thus monopolizing the benefits of the mill and employés." Ronan also claimed that during one year the agency sawmill had sawed 60,000 feet of lumber for Duncan, some of which he sold.[24]

Possibly the most interesting and entertaining part of Duncan's work for the Northern Pacific Railroad was in September

Peter Ronan,
Flathead Indian Agent, 1877-1893.
Source: Montana Historical Society Photograph Archives,
Helena, MMM 900-004.

1883, when he treated prominent guests returning from the last spike ceremony completing the railroad to a tour of the Lower Flathead Valley. Henry Villard, the President of the Northern Pacific Railroad, had Duncan construct a wagon road to Mc-Donald Peak in the Mission Mountains before the dignitaries arrived. Duncan and Flathead Indian Agent Peter Ronan met the train at Ravalli Station. The most adventurous of the guests were to take wagons to McDonald Peak. The less ambitious were set to travel by wagon to St. Ignatius Mission and McDonald Lake above Post Creek. The least ambitious remained with the train at Ravalli. All were told to return to Ravalli by 4 p.m. in the afternoon. Duncan's younger brother Angus guided the Mc-Donald Peak party, and Duncan set off with the group touring McDonald Lake.[25]

Duncan described his experiences with the McDonald Lake branch of the tour to Arthur L. Stone, a Missoula journalist:

So I told Angus, my brother, to take the ones who were going to climb the mountain and get started with them right away as they would have to move fast to get back on time, Angus took them after a short wait and I had to stay for the old ones, the fat ones and the English lords to get ready. There were provisions enough packed, to take the expedition to the pole, though they were not just of the sort that an Arctic expedition would take. Champagne and fried chicken were the chief provisions and the room which was left was filled in with bread and the rest of the accompaniments.

We finally got them all loaded. As guide, I had to ride ahead and the long line of carts, wagons and buggies followed. You can imagine how many it took to carry almost three hundred of them, with the drivers and the lunch. The wagon right behind me had a driver and three passengers. Right behind that drove Major Ronan in a cart with one passenger. I don't remember who it was that the major had, but in the wagon right behind me there was a little, slim New York man sitting beside the driver and on the back seat were Senator [George F.] Edmunds of Vermont and Lord Norwood of England. I shall never forget that wagon-load; it made me more trouble than all the rest of my experiences that day.

As we went up the hill, leaving Ravalli, the little man on the front seat called out to me to get out of the way as I was making too much dust. I knew I wasn't making dust enough to annoy anybody who was decently civil and I kept right on. He kept calling to me, though, and I got tired of hearing him. So I rode ahead, faster, and got out of the way. I could even then hear him saying something, but I had got far enough out of the way so that I couldn't tell what it was he was saying and I didn't care.

They made a great picture, those fellows in that wagon. The little, mean chap on the front seat leaned forward and away from the driver as far as he could, all curled up and squinting ahead at me. He would have like to shoot me, by the way he looked. On the back seat Edmunds leaned back comfortably and seemed to take a good deal of interest in the country. Lord Norwood, the representative of British nobility, was a weak little fellow. He hadn't strength enough to hold himself on the seat. Every jolt of the wagon sent him bobbing one way or the other; he flopped about all the way over the hill but he made no murmur. The little lad on the front seat did all the murmuring for the crowd. The Englishman tried to be good natured about it but it was hard work for him to smile.

Well, I kept so far ahead that I couldn't hear his growling and I don't know whether it was far enough or not to keep my dust from bothering the lad on the front seat. I'm sure I didn't care whether it bothered him or not. We went over the hill and down the road to the mission; there was plenty of admiration for the scenery and the kicker didn't have so much to say after we got out of the draw into the road down to the valley. Things were going first rate, when a accident happened to that front wagon.

Getting down into the valley toward the mission, the road crossed some low, wet places. Cattle had been wallowing in some of these sloughs and had made them rather miry and that front wagon drove through one which was particularly soft. The team gave a jump to pull the wagon through the mire and the sudden yank threw the back seat with its two occupants right over backward into the soft mud.

I heard a yell and turned back. It was the funniest sight I every looked at. The seat had dropped so that its back was in the mud and the men had retained their positions on the seat. This left them with their feet in the air and their heads and backs in the mud, into which they were sinking without any more effort to get out than a mired mule would make. They were just settling down into the soft mud and their friend from the front seat was doing a dance around them, shouting that they would be drowned, calling for help and accusing me of having arranged the spill on purpose.

Major Ronan, who was driving right behind the unfortunate rig, just turned his cart so as to avoid the mudhole and the other rigs behind followed him so there were no further accidents and the long procession passed the men in the mud, some of the travelers being amused and some of them being alarmed, but none offering to help them out.

I got to the scene of the trouble and as quickly as I could helped Lord Norwood and Senator Edmunds to their feet on solid ground. They were fairly plastered with soft mud. I got some grass and curried them down, getting all of the mud off that I could, but they were rather streaked even when I had done my best. And all the time that mean little fellow from New York was jumping and

accusing me of doing it all on purpose. He said I had arranged it with the driver and he talked to me as he were a
slavedriver and I, his slave. But I kept on wiping the mud
from the unfortunates and wishing all the time that it
had been the front seat that had upset. If that mean little
cuss had been the one in the mud, he would have gone
a whole lot deeper before I pulled him out. I tried to tell
him that it was the fault of the men on the seat that they
had not got out more quickly.

Well, I got them loaded into the wagon again, with
the seat tied down, and we went on to the mission, where
the rest of the party had landed ahead of us. It was all so
new to them that these easterners had scattered all over
the place. They were examining the beadwork on the Indians' clothes; they were guessing as to whether certain
Indians were men or women and making bets on it; they
were chasing butterflies; some were chasing the naked Indian babies that were toddling about the grounds; others
were investigating the old church and some were looking
at the schools. They were everywhere and I had to read
the riot act to get them together.

I got a few of them together and told them that
my instructions were to get them back to their train at 4
o'clock in the afternoon and if they wanted to see Lake
McDonald they would have to get together in a hurry or
we would turn back right there. There was a scurrying
and the roundup was made. We got the line formed and
we moved on toward Post creek.

We got to the lake all right. The visitors were well
pleased with a small look at the scenery and then demanded lunch. Out of the wagons came the greatest
lunch that was ever spread in the Mission valley; there
was an ocean of champagne and there was fried chicken
and cake and fruit in great quantities. It was a champagne crowd, all right, and when they had taken one dip
into the wine, the scenery looked better to them than it

had before. They scattered along the shore of the lake and admired the scenery as they ate their lunch. They were hungry and they showed it.

But there was not one of them who thought that I might be hungry. There was never an invitation to me to have a bite. And I was getting angry the longer I watched them eat. Lord Norwood had recovered from his scare and was doing more eating than I ever saw a weak man do before. He was still muddy, but he was happy and didn't seem to remember his troubles at all. I lost sight of the mean little fellow of the front seat and I didn't care if I never found him.

But I finally saw Edmunds detach himself from his companions and with an old chum who had been in another wagon, move from the crowd a bit behind a bunch of bushes. I followed them and got up to them in time to hear Edmunds say to his friends: "This is the greatest trip I have ever had. I never saw such wonderful scenery as this and I never in my life saw anything half as funny as our spill in the mud. I haven't dared laugh before for fear of hurting the feelings of somebody. But I have got to laugh now."

I let him laugh some and then I stepped up to him. "Mr. Edmunds," I said, "has it occurred to you that I might like something to eat. If somebody doesn't get me some lunch right away, I am going back to the mission to get some, and I shall not come back here again. I'll just leave you to find your way back to the train."

Well, I think Edmunds was truly sorry that I had been overlooked. Of course my threat about leaving them didn't amount to anything; they couldn't miss the way back to Ravalli; all they would have had to do was to follow their own tracks, but they didn't think of that. They were scared as well as sorry and they hustled when Edmunds told them the conditions.

You should have seen the lunch that I got then. There was everything that anybody could want and there was enough of it for a dozen men. I ate till my hunger was satisfied and then I couldn't do anything more to trouble them or to entertain them. They looked at the scenery and admired the light on the peaks and marveled at the glaciers till I told them it was time to go back to the train.

The return trip was made without incident and it was a tired crowd that got back to Ravalli, just in time. When I saw the way those fat old fellows went for the fried chicken and champagne, I understood why it was that they didn't feel equal to the longer trip up the mountain. The ride they had was all they could stand; they were all in when we got back to the train and there was another raid on the commissary right away. Angus got back with his smaller party from the climb up the mountain and we turned over to Mr. [Henry] Villard all of his guests, uninjured except for the clothes of Senator Edmunds and Lord Norwood. And they were not troubled about that. The injured feelings of the mean little fellow on the front seat were slower in healing than were the scattered wits of the two men who had fallen out of the wagon.

We turned away from the train after we had received the thanks of Mr. Villard and pretty soon the excursionists left for the west, to see new wonders and more scenery. That was one of the queerest experiences I have ever had in connection with visitors at the reservation and I have met a good many since then.[26]

In partial reward for Duncan's patience and assistance during the Northern Pacific Railroad construction, Duncan received a lifetime pass to travel on the railroad.[27] Soon after the railroad construction was completed, Duncan took the train to Portland, Oregon, and had his first urban experience. He toured the city but was not impressed: "I saw the ships, and the streets, and the big, fine houses,...but I did not care a copper for them all. I would rather get on my pony any day and go to the mountains to hunt than to see the biggest city in the world."[28]

Duncan also continued to join with Chief Arlee in criticizing Flathead Indian Agency operations. In November 1883, Duncan and Arlee voiced their complaints to Inspector C. H. Howard. Most of the complaints involved cattle herds on the reservation allegedly owned by white men including Agent Ronan, the excessive number of railroad employees located on the reservation, the lack of a government school at the agency, the St. Ignatius Mission practice of forgiving sins in the confessional, that Ronan would not grind wheat for Duncan at the agency gristmill, and that Duncan should not have to give a bond to trade on the reservation. Howard did note that Peter Irvine, who was said to have driven the cattle Ronan misappropriated, flatly denied the charges against Ronan.[29] On January 15, 1884, Ronan replied that the cattle herds on the reservation claimed to be owned by white men, were owned by Indian relatives of the white men. Ronan also produced statements by Dandy Jim and Thomas McDonald, Duncan's brother, denying the charges that Ronan had misallocated any cattle for his personal benefit.[30]

Duncan supplied a picnic party of white people traveling to St. Ignatius Mission in May 1884 with saddle horses and other accommodations. *The Weekly Missoulian* noted the gentlemen on the trip were "loud in their praises of the attentions of Duncan McDonald, who made the necessary preparations for the ride and took care of the party on their return, while waiting for the train."[31] According to one source, Duncan was negotiating with Samuel Walking Coyote in 1884 to buy his herd of buffalo. The buffalo were purchased by Charles Allard and Michel Pablo instead.[32] In July 1884, Duncan went to Missoula to take in the "horse opera." Presumably this meant he attended Cole's circus that was then performing in Missoula.[33]

Duncan wrote the *New North-West* in October 1884 to correct a statement by W. J. McCormick about the origin of the name "Missoula." According to Duncan, the name was derived from In-may-soo-let-tqui, the Salish name for the portion of the

Clark's Fork River below the mouth of the Bitterroot River. He also gave the Indian names for the Bitterroot River and Rattle-snake Creek.[34]

Chapter 5

Hotelier
and Entrepreneur
1885-1891

Duncan's influence and reputation continued to grow between 1885 and 1891 as he operated a hotel and a range of other businesses at Ravalli station on the Northern Pacific Railroad. Ravalli was the station where passengers for the Upper Flathead Valley disembarked from the Northern Pacific and took the stagecoach north. During the construction of the Great Northern Railroad in 1891, an especially large volume of passengers and freight shipments passed through Ravalli and patronized Duncan's businesses. Fortunately some of the guests at Duncan's hotel left descriptions of their visits. Many of Duncan's hotel reviews were not positive. In March 1904, when Duncan was negotiating the possible sale of the Ravalli hotel building to the government for use as an Indian school, he provided a description of the building. The overall dimensions were 40 feet six inches by 28 feet six inches with three stories. The first floor had four rooms with an eleven foot high ceiling. The second floor had four rooms with a nine foot ceiling. The third floor was open in one big hall with an 8 foot six inch high ceiling. Duncan noted that the third floor could be divided into six rooms.[1]

The first account of Duncan's new store at Ravalli was in the December 25, 1885, *Weekly Missoulian*. Duncan had left a clerk in charge of the store and traveled to Missoula. The evening after he left Ravalli, a drunken Indian threatened the clerk who refused to give the Indian something he wanted. The disappointed customer pulled out a knife and menaced the clerk. Two sober Indian customers escorted the inebriated gentleman out of the store. Duncan proceeded to the Missoula Mercantile Company, where he purchased a Winchester gun, a revolver, and a hundred rounds of ammunition. He took the arms back to Ravalli in case of future trouble.[2]

Duncan hired a white man named C. A. Stillinger as his clerk at the Ravalli store. Originally from Kentucky, Stillinger was discharged from the U.S. Army in 1885. Shortly after his discharge, Stillinger took a job as clerk for Duncan at $35 a month. He worked for Duncan as a clerk/manager until 1892 when he bought out Duncan's Ravalli businesses and Charles Allard's Ravalli-Kalispell stage line. Stillinger was also part owner of the first steamboat on Flathead Lake. Duncan relied on Stillinger to operate the businesses, which left Duncan free to pursue other interests. Stillinger's management skills probably played a critical role in the financial success of Duncan's many enterprises at Ravalli.[3]

Flathead Agent Peter Ronan reported to the Commissioner of Indian Affairs on October 23, 1886, about reservation traders, including Duncan. Ronan described Duncan as "an educated, sober and industrious man" and said Duncan's gross receipts were $13,000 per year.[4] On December 1, 1886, Duncan's and T. J. Demers' bonds as traders needed to be approved by the judge of the U.S. District Court. Ronan promised to send them to Washington, D.C., as soon as possible.[5] Later that month, on December 14, 1886, Ronan received approval from the Commissioner of Indian Affairs to purchase 14 milk cows and calves from Duncan.[6]

Duncan announced on January 18, 1887, that a new company had been organized to run the steamboat named Selish on Flathead Lake. The new boat was supposed to go ten miles an hour when fully loaded and offer the latest in life preservers. Duncan described the new boat as "an open-hold stern-wheeler some forty feet in length with canvass corner [cover?] and sides. The propelling engine is fourteen horse power." According to one newspaper account, Duncan was not listed as part owner of the boat, but C. A. Stillinger, his manager and clerk, was. Another

FOR FLATHEAD !

Stage Leaves Ravalli,

On the N. P. R. R., every

Monday, Wednesday and Friday Morning

For Flathead Lake.

Returns on Tuesdays, Thursdays and Saturdays.

DUNCAN M'DONALD, Manager.

Source: *Missoula County Times*, May 4, 1887, page 2, col. 3.

account, in a Butte newspaper, suggested Duncan was a part owner of the boat. Duncan was to run a four horse covered stage from Ravalli to connect with the boat at the foot of Flathead Lake. He also promised good freight teams to haul freight north as fast as it came in. The freight arriving at Ravalli during the summer of 1886 had sat around the station for up to a month.[7]

In an advertisement in the May 4, 1887, *Missoula County Times*, Duncan announced his stages left Ravalli on Monday, Wednesday, and Friday mornings for Flathead Lake and returned to Ravalli, on Tuesday, Thursday, and Saturday. Duncan said the traffic on the stage was "rapidly increasing" and he often had to add another coach to handle the demand, especially on Mondays. A new and larger steamboat for Flathead Lake had arrived at Ravalli a few days before, and Duncan was part owner.[8] Duncan's stage company was named the Selish Stage Company.[9] In June 1887, Duncan began work on a large hotel at Ravalli to handle the increasing traffic to Flathead Lake. Duncan also made arrangements to guide a small party climbing McDonald Peak in the Mission Mountains in July 1887. Duncan planned to use the trail he had constructed to the peak in 1883 for the guests from the Northern Pacific Railroad last spike ceremony.[10]

Duncan wrote in September 1887 assuring readers that, despite rumors to the contrary, the steamer Pocahontas was repaired and running in good order on Flathead Lake. According to an April 1888 note in the *New North-West* newspaper, Duncan owned the Pocahontas. During the winter of 1887-1888, the boat was enlarged with twenty more feet in length and two feet more in width.[11] In February 1888 Duncan argued that the logical route for a railroad north from the Northern Pacific Railroad started at Ravalli and headed north through the Flathead Valley. Duncan and his friend, Judge Frank Woody, were jousting about whether the north-south railroad should start from Ravalli or Missoula.[12] Duncan and Charles Allard announced on March 7, 1888, that they had jointly formed a new company, the Selish Express Company. The company would transport passengers and freight between Ravalli and the foot of Flathead Lake.[13] A March

Duncan McDonald's hotel at Ravalli.
Source: Toole Archives, Mansfield Library,
University of Montana, Missoula, photograph 77-280.

16, 1888, advertisement for the stage line declared it ran twice a week from Ravalli to Ashley above Flathead Lake.[14]

In June 1888 a Methodist minister, E. J. Stanley, made a trip to Flathead Lake. At Ravalli he found Duncan's hotel, store, and stage line. Stanley wrote that Duncan had acquired many horses and cattle that grazed on the open range on the reservation. A new and fine hotel was still under construction with log walls, including some logs forty inches in diameter. Stanley held a Methodist service in the hotel dining room before taking the stage north to Flathead Lake.[15]

In about 1888 a white woman named Catherine Walsh was returning from Butte to Columbia Falls. She got off the train at Ravalli after dark. Carrying her baby and a small satchel, she walked around trying to find the hotel. An Indian man followed her. She was deathly afraid of Indians. After getting directions from some Chinese men playing cards, she arrived at the hotel. The Indian was still following her. The next morning when she left her room in the hotel, she saw the same Indian come out of the room next to hers. She went to Duncan and asked for protection. Duncan explained that the train had been late the night before, and he did not want to stay up, so he asked the Indian to watch for her and make sure she was safe.[16]

As a child Oliver Vose arrived with his family at Ravalli on March 8, 1889, and stayed at Duncan's hotel. It was cold and there was no heat in the hotel. Oliver's two year old sister complained loudly. The Voses were able to get into Duncan's private living room to warm up, but the Voses felt Duncan and his family acted as if they did not want them there.[17]

In his diary for May 7, 1889, Father Jerome D'Aste, S.J., wrote that he paid Duncan $16 for 8 sashes which Duncan claimed the mission still owed. Duncan paid the mission $47.85 for a bill owed by Duncan's stage company.[18]

Duncan and Charles Allard announced on May 31, 1889, they were dissolving their partnership in the Selish Stage Company. The company was to continue with Allard as the sole owner.[19] In June 1889, Duncan was in eastern Montana on business, but the sources do not say what business he was pursuing.[20] Duncan was visited by an uncle, John McDonald, from Middleton, Connecticut, in late June 1889. John arrived at Ravalli by train late in the evening and headed for the hotel, because he did not want to disturb Duncan and his family at that hour. To John's surprise, Duncan owned the hotel at Ravalli. John had to wait several days to meet Duncan, because Duncan was away selling horses.[21] Father D'Aste stayed at Duncan's hotel on January 7, 1890. It was winter, but the hotel had no heat, and D'Aste was unhappy about having a "room without fire!"[22]

After a May 1890 trip through Ravalli, a *Helena Journal* correspondent commented on the service and pricing at Duncan's resturant at Ravalli. Duncan did not offer diners a menu of choices but limited patrons to a single bill of fare. For this simple, no-choice meal, Duncan charged the same price as the best first class eating establishments in Helena and Butte.[23] Duncan announced the completion of a new blacksmith shop at Ravalli in June 1890.[24]

David R. McGinnis stopped at Duncan's hotel on August 9, 1890, on his way to the Upper Flathead Valley. Duncan regaled the visitors with stories of Salish life before the white man arrived. The tales continued until late in the night:

> McDonald told how in the early days of yore the Flatheads had the valley, both north and south of the lake, for their chosen home and how idyllic the life was then. Game, both large and small, elk, deer, bear, with sheep and goats high up in the mountains, with all kind of winged fowl, and the streams teeming with fish. Food was abundant, and life was idyllic in the highest degree. The Flatheads moved from time to time to various parts of both the north and south valley, according to the season, and happiness and plenty was their life.

The next morning Duncan failed to waken McGinnis and his fellow traveler in time to catch the stage to the foot of Flathead Lake. Duncan helped McGinnis hire a neighboring mixed blood with a horse and buggy to rush McGinnis to Charles Allard's ranch where the stage stopped for lunch. McGinnis arrived at Allard's in time to eat and then take the stage north.[25]

On August 28, 1890, C. A. Stillinger, who managed Duncan's store at Ravalli, was in Missoula purchasing goods for the store.[26] On December 6, 1890, another white employee of Duncan, L. S. Jones, visited Missoula and commented on the large volume of traffic between Ravalli and the foot of Flathead Lake.[27]

An unnamed correspondent for the *Northwest Illustrated Monthly Magazine* in St. Paul, Minnesota, described an early March 1891 visit to Ravalli. According to this account, at Ravalli:

> you can witness the somewhat phenomenal feat of an ordinary-looking frame house with a capacity for accommodating ten or a dozen people being made to accommodate from forty to fifty persons, and some nights even more, for which each person is charged the modest sum of one dollar. If the train is on time, you will have about three hours in which to secure the alleged night's rest for which you have paid so dearly, for, at 1 o'clock you are called and informed that the stage will leave for the foot of the lake as soon as you have finished your midnight meal, called breakfast. This you take in a one-story log structure where several almond-eyed celestials [Chinese] serve you illy or well, according to what use you make of the coin of the realm, in addition to the regular charge for what you eat.

While the writer was at Duncan's hotel, two white women from Helena with babies under six months old were given no special consideration.[28]

Samuel William Carvoso Whipps stayed at Duncan's hotel on March 17, 1891. Whipps described the hotel as "a small store-like building with a few rooms on the second floor." He wanted a room for himself, but Duncan said that would depend on how many guests came off the train. As it turned out, Whipps was the only guest that night, and he got his own room. Whipps sat up late in the night listening to Duncan's reminiscences and stories. Whipps had a bull dog with him despite a sign saying no dogs were allowed. When an unnamed mixed blood pointed to the sign, Whipps said the mixed blood could put the dog out if he wanted. The dog stayed with Whipps in his room for the night.[29]

The construction of the Great Northern Railroad through the Upper Flathead Valley swelled the volume of freight and traffic through Ravalli. On March 25, 1891, Duncan was in Missoula purchasing household goods for his business. Duncan said he had to greatly expand the accommodations due to the amount of traffic.[30]

On May 12, 1891, a correspondent from Helena wrote that Duncan's two-story log cabin hotel was "nicely furnished." When the number of lodgers was large, some had to sleep in the hay shed or some small cabins. Duncan and his wife slept in a tepee. Duncan took in $40 to $50 a night and that was increasing. Sleeping was one dollar and meals were fifty cents. Duncan employed a half dozen Chinese men in the restaurant which served from 350 to 500 meals a day. Freight for the Upper Flathead Valley was backed way up despite having freighters with 750 head of horses working on it.[31] A travelog in the same Helena newspaper on May 24, 1891, described the lodgers being sent to bed at night by Duncan. Breakfast was served in an adjoining log cabin with Chinese waiters rushing to offer coffee, tea, and pancakes. The diners, however, rushed through the meal to try and get the best seat on the top of the stagecoach with the driver.[32]

The summer of 1891, a Kalispell newspaper described Duncan's growing enterprise. There were two blacksmiths, one helper at the forge, and a wagon-maker to make repairs. Bathing facilities for the travelers were under construction.[33]

Duncan did not want any competition at Ravalli and on June 8, 1891, complained to Agent Ronan that the section house at Ravalli, maintained for accommodation of railroad employees, was serving meals to travelers. The section house operator was charging less for meals than Duncan was. The section house

Ravalli, Mont.

DUNCAN McDONALD,

——DEALER IN-——

GENERAL MERCHANDISE.

RAVALLI, - MONTANA.

On Line of Northern Pacific Railroad.   Outfitting point for the Flathead and Kootenai country.   It is the Shortest and Most Feasible Route.   Plenty of Grass and Water, and Good Roads.

Large Stock of everything in the Outfitting and Supply and Outfitting Line, at Lowest Market Prices.

HAY AND GRAIN IN ANY QUANTITY.

DUNCAN McDONALD, Ravalli, Montana.

Source: *Missoula Weekly Gazette*, Nov. 4, 1891, page 3, col. 5-6

was on railroad right-of-way. Ronan asked the Commissioner of Indian Affairs for instructions. On June 26, 1891, the Commissioner decided the government could not protect Duncan from competition. On July 14, 1891, Ronan reported that the Missoula Superintendent of the Northern Pacific Railroad negotiated a truce between Duncan and the competing restaurant. The section house restaurant would continue to serve meals to the traveling public, but agreed to not use runners to advertise for business.[34]

A correspondent for the *Missoula Gazette* during the summer of 1891 described Duncan as "a very wealthy man and his fortune is rapidly increasing." Duncan had recently added a large eating house, stables, and blacksmith and wagon shops at Ravalli. He also had a large ranch a few miles down the valley where he raised good crops of hay and grain.[35]

Miss Leila Sawhill, a young white woman from Ohio, traveled through Ravalli on October 7, 1891. Duncan had a wagon at the Ravalli railroad station to convey passengers to his hotel. She reported that she "got a pretty good sleep" at the hotel. Breakfast was at 5:30 in the morning and consisted of "burnt coffee, oat meal mush, fried potatoes, tough steak and hot cakes" served by Chinese waiters.[36]

The *Missoula Weekly Gazette* on November 4, 1891, had a large display advertisement for Duncan McDonald, dealer in general merchandise in Ravalli, Montana. He offered a "Large Stock of everything in the Outfitting and Supply and Outfitting Line at Lowest Market Prices. Hay and Grain in any Quantity."[37]

Mary Finley Niles waited tables for Duncan at his restaurant in about 1891 when she left school at the Sisters in St. Ignatius. Duncan's wife was her godmother and Mary lived with Duncan's family in their huge log house at Ravalli. She remembered playfully threatening to cut the queue of the Chinese cook.[38]

On January 5, 1892, C. A. Stillinger and Arthur Larrivee announced their purchase of Charles Allard's stage line and Duncan's Ravalli businesses, except the farm. Larrivee was a

mixed blood nephew of Charles Allard. Stillinger was identified
as the general manager of the new business partnership, so
evidently he continued in charge of the day-to-day operation of
the enterprises.[39]

* * * * * * * * * *

But Duncan found time between 1885 and 1891 to continue other activities in addition to operating his hotel and travel
businesses at Ravalli. He continued to prospect for minerals and
critique Flathead Agency affairs. Duncan also played his role a
cultural broker, mediating between the Indian and white communities. In 1889 and 1890 he played an important role in
avoiding violence between the communities while the Missoula
County Sheriff tracked down and arrested several Indians accused of murdering white people.

In March 1885, Duncan and his father visited Missoula
and remarked on the prevalence of sickness among the reservation Indians and the unusual number of deaths resulting.[40] That
summer Duncan was nominated by Agent Peter Ronan as a private in the first government controlled Indian police force on the
reservation. His pay was $8 a month.[41] No details have survived
about his tenure as a policeman, and by July 1, 1886, Duncan
was no longer a member of the force.[42]

Duncan wrote a letter to the *New North-West* on July 1,
1885, to clear up some misleading newspaper reports about Big
Bear, a Canadian Cree chief. In the summer of 1878, Duncan
had seen Big Bear in Sitting Bull's camp on the Saskatchewan
River when Duncan had gone to interview White Bird, the refu-
gee Nez Perce Chief. Big Bear and the Cree got caught up in the
Reil Rebellion of 1885 pitting the Metis and Northern Plains
Indians against the Canadian government in a dispute over land
rights. Duncan assured Montanans that Big Bear was a full blood
Indian.[43]

Gold prospects continued to entice Duncan and his white
friends. On November 6, 1885, a correspondent at Thompson
Falls reported that Duncan and other miners were working a
quartz mine in the area.[44]

On December 17, 1885, and January 7, 1886, an anonymous writer from Missoula made charges of corruption against Indian Agent Peter Ronan. The letters were signed "Citizen of Missoula" and "Missoula Democrat." They asked the Commissioner of Indian Affairs to consult Duncan about the alleged theft of annuities and government property at Flathead Agency. The letters were filed at the Indian Office without further consideration.[45]

In the spring of 1886, Duncan was part of a prospecting party digging for gold near Sand Point, Idaho. Other members of the party included T. J. Demers, the Frenchtown businessman, and F. H. Woody, a Missoula lawyer and judge. The Lower Pend d'Oreille Indians under Chief Victor lived in the area and had not signed a treaty with the United States government surrendering their land for white settlement. The Pend d'Oreille in the area of Duncan's mining prospect insisted that the miners stop their tunneling and leave. They feared that if gold were found, the resulting rush of white men could overrun the tribe. The miners abandoned their claim and returned to Missoula. Duncan interpreted for the miners and concluded:

> The Indians thought the party of prospectors were very rude to invade their [camas and gathering] ground and commence digging for gold without as much as asking permission. They had no guns and made no open resistance, but told the party to quit prospecting....
>
> Mr. McDonald thinks that when all the facts are considered the Kalispels acted with moderation, candor and discretion.[46]

Indian Inspector Geo. B. Pearsons submitted a report to the Secretary of the Interior on November 11, 1886, that reflected many of Duncan's and Chief Arlee's complaints about Flathead Agency operations. Pearsons did not identify the source of most of his criticisms, so it is not possible to tell which ones were Duncan's. Pearsons found Ronan to be "kind perhaps to his Indians," but concluded that Ronan did not assist the Indians as he should. He complained that Ronan personally drank liquor, and he felt

Ronan should move more aggressively to eliminate Indian access to alcohol. Another recommendation was that the Indian police be armed and have a white man or a mixed blood as chief. He also criticized the St. Ignatius Mission schools as ineffective. Pearsons conveyed Duncan's and Father Leopold Van Gorp's opinion that far less grain was raised by tribal farmers than Ronan claimed. The inspector recommended that Henry A. Lambert, the long-time Flathead Agency farmer, be discharged and an Indian be put in the position. Chief Arlee complained that Indians who rode the trains for free were forced to ride on the platforms of the cars and were abused by railroad employees.[47] Ronan responded on December 2, 1886, to Pearsons' recommendation that Lambert be dismissed. According to Ronan, Lambert performed many of the duties of agency clerk as well as agency farmer. Ronan commended Lambert's "energy and intelligence" and wanted him kept on the Flathead Agency payroll.[48]

According to a story Duncan related later to Louisa Mc-Dermott, a teacher at the Jocko Agency government school, the winter of 1886-1887 was long and severe. Many of the Indian horses and cattle were dying from cold and hunger. A medicine man prayed for a Chinook and offered to give a horse if he failed. The Chinook did not come and the medicine man forfeited his best horse. Then the medicine man put his ear to the ground to listen for the Chinook wind. He said he heard the wind coming, and, if he was wrong, they could tie him to a rock and throw him into the river. The Chinook came in less than a day, and the melting snow flooded everything.[49]

About this time, Duncan told the story of a herd of large black horses on Wild Horse Island in Flathead Lake. In the late 1830s a Blackfeet war party tried to capture the horses on the island. Most of the wild horses were chased into the lake and escaped on the mainland. The large black wild horses and their descendants survived in the lake area until the early 1870s.[50]

Archie McDonald, Duncan's younger brother, died on September 5, 1888, in a tragic accident at the foot of Flathead Lake, where Polson is now located. Archie fell overboard and drowned as the boat was coming in to dock. One of Archie's brothers — possibly Duncan — witnessed the accident but was unable to help.[51]

Duncan took time out from running the hotel to prospect for copper in the Blackfoot Mountains in Deer Lodge County in the fall of 1888. In November he stopped in Deer Lodge on his way to Butte to consult his partners in the mine.[52] According to one newspaper account, some unnamed Flathead Indians had known for years of a rich mineral deposit on the north fork of the Blackfoot River. Duncan had recently persuaded them to guide him to the location.[53]

Duncan suffered another tragic personal loss on February 1, 1889, when his father, Angus, died at the family home on Post Creek. Angus had requested to be buried in the Indian grave-yard at Fort Connah next to his old friend, Pend d'Oreille Chief Sil-lip-stoo. The family honored his wish.[54] In February 1890, Duncan filed in the Missoula District Court to administer Angus' estate.[55] The cattle, the main asset in the estate, were divided up among the children. Duncan got 233 head as his share.[56]

In March 1889, Missoula County paid Duncan $1.50 each for three different interpreting sessions. Presumably this was for interpreting at court sessions.[57]

Duncan got involved in raising money for horse races at the 1889 Missoula County Fair. In May 1889 he was asked to contribute to the horse racing fund, and he agreed if he could race some of his colts from his stage line. On May 30, 1889, Duncan wrote that he had recruited two other contributors for $100 each. They wanted to race cayuses against the pedigree horses in Missoula.[58]

In 1889, Lawrence Finley, a mixed blood, accused two Pend d'Oreilles, Pierre Paul and Lalasee, of murdering two white men in 1888. The Missoula County Sheriff and a trigger-happy white posse invaded the reservation to arrest the two men. The posse failed to capture the two fugitives, but it did manage to kill an innocent Indian in the process. The posse did not know the Indian, but they approached him with weapons drawn and then

shot him because he ran. Agent Ronan requested troops from
Fort Missoula to keep the situation from escalating. Most tribal
members did not object to punishing Indians who killed white
men, but they thought white men who killed Indians should
also be punished.[59] In an interview on August 21, 1889, Duncan
blamed most of the trouble on whiskey: "He thinks every Indian
on the reservation should be punished under the law, and thinks
that [is] the only way to stop the frequent outbreaks."[60]

Duncan continued his farming activites, and in the fall of
1889, one of his piglets was born with five feet. According to the
newspaper report, the animal was perfectly healthy.[61]

Between January 15, 1890, and February 10, 1890, Duncan was seriously ill in Missoula with influenza. At first he stayed
at the Florence Hotel, but on January 20, 1890, he was trans-
ferred to St. Patrick's Hospital.[62] In one account Duncan was
given "but little hope of recover[y]."[63] But a few days later he was
"fast improving."[64] While he was sick, he was visited by a Miss
McDonald of Ravalli and Charles Allard.[65] By February 1890, he
had entirely recovered.[66]

William Finley, a mixed blood, was killed in the Upper
Flathead Valley in early July 1890 as he tried to mediate a scuffle
between two Indian men who were drinking. Antoine had pulled
a gun on Grotia when Grotia reacted violently to efforts to re-
strain him. In the struggle Antoine shot and killed Finley. The
newspaper coverage noted that Antoine previously had a run-in
with Duncan, and Duncan had shot him. The report did not say
when Duncan's shooting occurred.[67]

William Houston was elected sheriff of Missoula County
in the fall of 1889 based largely on promises to aggressively pursue Indians accused of murdering white men. In a series of cases,
however, he made little effort to punish white men who killed
Indians. In the summer of 1890, Houston and a white posse
held Kootenai Chief Eneas and later Pend d'Oreille Chief Michelle hostage to force the Indians to help capture Indian murder
suspects.

In August 1890, Houston and his posse held Chief Michelle hostage at Duncan's hotel in Ravalli. About forty Pend d'Oreille warriors arrived at Ravalli to free Michelle. According to newspaper reports, Houston had gone to Missoula but sent a telegram to Ravalli advising Michelle's guards to fight if any Indian tried to free the chief. Duncan showed the telegram to Michelle, who advised the Pend d'Oreille to avoid hostilities. The rescuers left and Michelle remained at the hotel. Afterwards, the Indian police and the white posse pursued and captured Pierre Paul, one of the accused Indian murderers. Local newspapers gave most of the credit to the white posse, but, in Agent Ronan's account, the capture was made by the Indian police accompanied by the white posse. One white witness to the events later claimed that the telegram threatening the use of force to keep Michelle prisoner had been a fake.[68]

One accused Indian murderer, Lalasee, surrendered personally to Duncan, who escorted him to jail in Missoula. Before the surrender, on August 19, 1890, Lalasee, his wife, brother, and friends went to St. Ignatius Mission to confession. According to one source, Lalasee's wife was a niece of Duncan's wife. After some confusion, Duncan met up with Lalasee at Ravalli. The evening of August 20, 1890, Duncan and Lalasee headed for Missoula, avoiding the main road to keep Lalasee safe. When they arrived at Evaro Station, however, their horses were worn out, so they took the train the rest of the way to Missoula. They arrived late in the evening and had to search for the jail keeper before Lalasee could be locked up. There was a reward for Lalasee's capture and at first Duncan considered claiming it and giving it to Lalasee's children. Years later Duncan complained that many tribal members accused him of turning Lalasee in for the reward money. In 1895 when the reward was finally paid, Duncan declined any part of the money.[69]

In an interview with the *Missoula Weekly Gazette*, Duncan explained that Lalasee had murdered the two white men on the Jocko River because other white men had recently killed his brother. Before his brother was killed, Lalasee had been law abiding with a family and little children he loved dearly. Duncan pointed out a young mixed blood, Antoine Morigeau, as the man who got the drop on Pierre Paul and forced Paul to surrender. The only remaining Indian accused of murder on the loose was Antoine, who headed for Canada.[70]

Later in the fall of 1890, Duncan passed through Missoula to take his son, Peter Colville, to Helena to have his eyes treated. Peter had "something like a pimple" growing in one eye. On October 30, 1890, Duncan and his son stopped in Missoula on their return trip to Ravalli.[71]

In early June 1891, Duncan and Missoula County Deputy Sheriff and Kootenai Indian farmer, Robert Irvine, escorted Charles Redhorn to the Missoula County jail. Redhorn was accused of murdering a Kootenai Indian named Patrick at Dayton Creek in an dispute over a woman.[72] Irvine was a mixed blood of white and Snake descent who spoke Kootenai and operated a cattle ranch on Crow Creek in the Mission Valley. Irvine had purchased $115 worth of fruit trees in 1887 and in 1891 sold his herd of 250 cattle to Alex Dow, a trader at Arlee. Irvine also spoke Nez Perce and in 1877 served as interpreter during the Nez Perce War. In 1890, Agent Peter Ronan appointed him Kootenai farmer and in 1891, with Irvine's help, the Kootenai had done well raising wheat at Elmo. He died at Crow Creek on February 10, 1900.[73]

Duncan took part in a buffalo roundup on the Flathead Reservation in late August 1891. Duncan was part of a crew of twenty-five Indians who pursued Charles Allard's herd of 63 buffalo. Duncan led the chase of an old bull they were trying to capture, but the bull died after being lassoed. Duncan lamented the death with memories of the days before the white people arrived:

"This makes me long for my breech-clout and blanket once more," said Duncan McDonald to me, as his bright eye scanned the recollection of departed days and the memory of the long ago past came flooding back upon him.

"In those days we were happy," he resumed. "We realized the charm of living in nature's boundless solitudes away from the restraints, the worries, and the conventionalities of a corroding civilization, amidst the surroundings that contributed to build up a healthy physical frame and a happy heart. Is it any wonder that I grow sad when I think of the days that are gone? I have stood under the peak of yonder mountain and looked out upon these prairies when 10,000 of these noble beasts were feeding peacefully hereon. I had a good gun and plenty to eat and my liberty then. Now I look upon the same landscape but a changed scene, not even a coyotte [sic] greets my eye to relieve the desolateness of the plain. We are all struggling after the almighty dollar, and our methods are surely not less savage than those we once employed to gain our livelihood upon these hills and plains. I must confess there are times in my life when I question the civilizing influences of civilization."[74]

On September 7, 1891, Duncan got into an argument with Joe Solomon in front of the Missoula Hotel. During the course of the dispute over an old $50 unpaid bill, Duncan slugged Solomon, and Solomon got a bloody nose. Duncan was arrested and taken to jail. He was immediately bailed out by his friends. The next day, Duncan pled guilty to assault in Justice Court and was fined one dollar and costs, which he quickly paid.[75]

Duncan was struck down with typhoid fever and hospitalized in October and November 1891. He first came down with a fever on October 9, and was admitted to the St. Patrick's Hospital before October 14, 1891.[76] By October 30, 1891, Duncan was reported to be rapidly convalescing under the care of Dr. W. Buchanan Parsons, a prominent Missoula physician. Duncan was out of the hospital on November 11, 1891, and returned home to Ravalli soon after.[77] A month later on December 24, 1891, Duncan purchased two bear cubs in Missoula. He planned to raise them in Ravalli.[78]

Chapter 6

Agency Critic
and Orchardist
1892-1901

After selling his hotel and other businesses at Ravalli, Duncan concentrated on building up his apple orchard and cattle herds. He continued to criticize government policy on the reservation and took part in an especially hostile 1895 confrontation between tribal leaders and Agent Joseph Carter. The historical documents that have survived do not give a complete account of Duncan's concerns and ideas about Flathead Reservation management. The sources do, however, clearly indicate Duncan was never afraid to voice his opinions or to work for what he saw as the best interests of the tribe.

On February 18, 1892, Agent Peter Ronan responded to a criticism of an unnamed Indian judge — possibly Baptiste Kakashe of St. Ignatius — by a United States Indian Inspector. The judge had gotten drunk one Fourth of July but then earnestly promised Ronan it would not happen again. Ronan charged that the complaint had been initiated by a mixed blood "who is wealthy and always has a grievance if things are not conducted... to suit his particular views." Ronan had decided not to fire the judge over the drinking incident and the Commissioner of Indian Affairs agreed.[1]

Duncan, Indian Judge Joseph Cathoulihou, and other tribal members worked to get justice for the early July 1892 murder of Felix Burns by a white man in Idaho. Burns was a well-to-do tribal member who had celebrated the Fourth of July drinking whiskey with a white man named Robert Philips. Burns disappeared after going off with Philips. Duncan joined a party of

tribal members searching for Burns. After Burns' body was discovered, Duncan and the Indians had a warrant sworn out for
the arrest of Philips. When the Idaho court postponed the murder trial, Ronan insisted Philips post a heavy bond to appear at
a later date. Unfortunately, no information has been found to
indicate how the trial turned out.[2]

A few weeks later, on August 23, 1892, Duncan left Missoula on a tour of the Clark's Fork, the head of Thompson River,
and Horse Plains, which was planned to take three weeks. Presumably the trip was a prospecting trip.[3] By September 6, 1892,
however, Duncan was back in Missoula attending the Missoula
County Republican convention.[4] In April 1893, Duncan spent
several weeks at Boulder Hot Springs.[5]

Duncan's half brother, Angus P. McDonald, was tried in
late June 1893 for the May 23, 1893, murder of John Stevens.
Duncan and other family members attended the trial in Missoula to support Angus P. Angus P. and Stevens had been drinking
whiskey while traveling on the road from Horse Plains to the
reservation. At one point, the two men dismounted, took a few
more drinks, and Angus P. blacked out. Angus P. came to later
with one arm around Stevens' dead body. Stevens had died of
a fractured skull, but Angus P. denied any memory of Stevens'
death. The jury acquitted Angus P. of the murder charge.[6]

In mid-July 1893, the Flathead Agency police were search-
ing for Tsil Peh who was accused of stealing a horse in Arlee.
Duncan spotted Tsil Peh at the Ravalli railroad station and called
Oliver Gebeau, an Indian policeman. Gebeau arrested Tsil Peh,
but the accused man escaped custody on the way to the Jocko
Agency. Tsil Peh was recaptured in 1894 and tried in the United
States courts for the theft.[7]

On July 14, 1893, the Commissioner of Indian Affairs
wrote Agent Ronan asking if the McDonalds wanted allotments
on the Nez Perce Reservation. Ronan replied that he doubted
they wanted to leave the Flathead Reservation, but he would confer with Duncan when Duncan returned to the reservation from
a trip. No further report on the matter was found, but Duncan

and his family obviously preferred to remain on Flathead where they had deep personal roots and investments.[8]

Granville Stuart was assistant Montana state land agent in 1893. In September 1893, he made a trip to examine the country between the Big Blackfoot River and Flathead Lake to select land for the state of Montana. During the trip, Stuart's traveling companion suffered a broken arm. Stuart finally got the patient to Kalispell where he boarded a train to Helena for medical attention. Stuart then took the horses and camp equipment south to the foot of Flathead Lake, where he met his wife. The Stuarts stopped at Ravalli on their way to Missoula. Duncan provided them with supper and lodging in his home because there was "no comfortable hotel at Ravalli."[9]

About the same time, on September 5, 1893, a thief stole a horse from Duncan's stable, a rifle, several pairs of blankets, and a saddle. The thief was sighted at the foot of Flathead Lake headed for Kalispell.[10]

In the 1890s, Duncan was one of the most vocal tribal members complaining about two problems with the Flathead Reservation boundary as surveyed by the government. The surveyors had cut valuable land off the reservation along the northern and southwestern boundaries. The 1855 Hellgate Treaty located the northern boundary of the Flathead Reservation "half way in latitude between the northern and southern extremities of the Flathead Lake." During the annual spring runoff, however, the lake flooded wetlands to the north, causing the halfway point to move with the seasons. The Kootenai located the northern boundary on a small range of hills just north of the surveyed boundary. An 1872 survey of the southern boundary of the public land in the Flathead Valley and, finally, an 1887 survey of the reservation boundary by U.S. Deputy Surveyor Edmund Harrison placed the boundary south of the natural boundary observed by the Kootenai. In 1965, the U.S. Court of Claims determined that the 1887 boundary survey had been in error and should have been 820 feet further north. As a result of the mistake, over 4,200 acres of land and water were excluded from the reservation. Since the northern boundary of the reservation was not fenced, the lack of a natural barrier to keep neighboring cattle out led to years of conflict. The survey cut the Kootenai village off from a meadow which they had long used for grazing and hay. Agent Ronan encouraged the Kootenai to establish farms on the meadow and filed off-reservation allotments on the land. The allotments were almost immediately legally and physically contested by white settlers moving into the area, and, after Ronan's death, no one pressured the federal government to protect the Kootenai farmers.[11]

The southwest boundary line of the reservation was to run through the junction of the Clark's Fork and Lower Flathead Rivers. The government survey, however, ran above the junction and cut off some valuable farm and timber land from the reservation. In 1965, the U.S. Court of Claims ruled that the survey had cut off 11,900 acres that should have been on the reservation.[12] In 1893, Duncan played a role in trying to convince some of the white settlers on the southwest corner land to move, but no details have survived. Duncan did deliver a letter from the Flathead Agency to the white farmers asking them to not harass the Indian farmers located on the contested land.[13]

In an ironic adjunct to Duncan's years as critic of Flathead Agency operations, in September 1893 his many friends in Missoula advanced him for the position as agent. Longtime agent Peter Ronan had died on August 20, 1893. According to an article in the *Evening Missoulian*, "Mr. McDonald would make a capable officer, his knowledge of the tribes and affairs of the government in connection therewith would make his services almost indispensible [sic], and his honesty and uprighteousness would insure to the government an excellent administration of this branch of the nation's affairs."[14] The agent position went to Joseph Carter, Ronan's clerk and son-in-law, instead.

Duncan answered an 1893 inquiry from W. F. Wheeler, the Montana state librarian, about the Nez Perce son of William Clark of the Lewis and Clark expedition. Wheeler was following up on an information request from Dr. Elliott Coues who

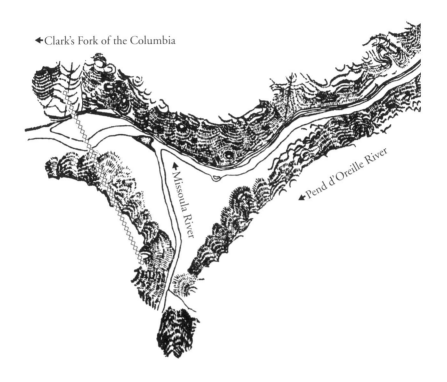

Clark's Fork of the Columbia

Missoula River

Pend d'Oreille River

Southwest corner of Flathead Reservation.
Line of white diamonds is western boundary
according to tribal chiefs in 1881.
(Called Pend d'Oreille and Missoula River in this 1881 map.)
Source: Redrawn from "Plan Showing the Line of the Western Boundary
of the Flathead Indian Reservation," enclosure with Peter Ronan to
Commissioner of Indian Affairs, March 10, 1891, LR 9,930, RG 75,
National Archives, Washington, D.C.. Caption on negative copy in the
National Archives is "Western Boundary of Flathead Indian Reservation As
established by Maj. Peter Ronan and I. S. P. Weeks from Landmarks pointed
out by Indians in Dec. 1881."

was editing the Lewis and Clark journals for publication later that year. Duncan related that Clark's Nez Perce son had been captured at the Bear Paw Battle and then died while a prisoner of war in the Indian Territory.[15]

In January and February 1894, Duncan called tribal meetings at St. Ignatius on the boundary matters. The Indians at the meeting signed two petitions to the Commissioner of Indian Affairs. The first petition, January 31, 1894, asked for the removal of Alex Dow as a licensed trader on the reservation. The second one, February 1, 1894, asked the Commissioner of Indian Affairs "to send other surveyors and survey the lines over again and according to the treaty specifications. As the former surveys has been done without our Knowledge." Duncan signed the second petition, but not the first. Agent Joseph Carter forwarded the petitions to Washington, D.C., but complained: "The council was called ie: (beef furnished), by a meddlesome halfbreed, an 'extrader' who desires to shine as a man of influence and who properly belongs upon the Nez Perces reservation. In past years he has caused considerable trouble to the former Agent. The objection to the trader Alex Dow is very vague, at present I would not recommend his removal."[16]

Carter wrote regarding the boundary survey problems: "I would scarcely recommend reopening the matter. The Indians while claiming more, had acquiesced to the line as surveyed until the matter was agitated by this halfbreed. Allotments to all Indians claiming land outside of the boundary survey, had been under way and the Indians apparently satisfied, but now persuaded that their petition will cause a new survey to be made and gain them the lands they claim, the Indians now refuse to take the allotments" along the southwest boundary.[17] On February 21, 1894, the Commissioner of Indian Affairs declined to resurvey the boundaries.[18] Duncan would bring up the problem many times again over the years before the case came before the U.S. Court of Claims in the twentieth century.

The spring runoff in western Montana in June 1894 reached record heights. The flood washed out the Northern Pacific Railroad tracks and the telegraph in multiple points along the Jocko, Flathead, and Clarks Fork Rivers.[19] According to an *Anaconda Standard* report, Duncan's entire ranch was underwater at the height of the flood. Only a small part of his grain crop was saved.[20]

Duncan and his son, Peter Colville, were in Spokane in August 1894 to get Peter's eyes treated. While in Spokane, Duncan was interviewed about his views on the "progress" Indians had made since the white man arrived:

"Yes, we're civilized now," said Mr. McDonald to a [Spokane] Chronicle reporter. "But I wish you could take your civilization and give up [us] the old days back again. Life was worth living then, every minute in the day — something to give excitement and keep one's blood bounding from morning till night. Give us back our buffalo and bears and deers and herds of horses and take your brass bands and electric lights back across the Mississippi again and you'll get our thanks.

"Improving the Indian's morality? Our people were honest in those days. You wouldn't find a faithless wife among the Indians then. One could leave things lying anywhere in camp and never worry about them. If anything was found it was taken to the chief and he returned it to the owner. Quarrels in the tribe were almost unknown, and as for cheating a tribesman, that was an infamy. Why, even the wars between tribes didn't really amount to much. Lots of times they would run along for months without anybody being hurt in them.

"And what have the white men done for the Indian? Taught him all kinds of meanness, made him as selfish and greedy as they are themselves, shut him upon little reservations and killed off all the big game. Why, they won't let us develop the wealth of the land we still hold. We must not even open the mines or cut the timber from the reservation. And then they tell us the Indians are lazy! Its like putting brains into a man's head and telling him not to think."[21]

A bill was introduced in the 1895 session of the Montana Legislature to appropriate $1,000 to pay the advertised reward for the 1890 capture of Pierre Paul and Lalasee. In its original form, the money was to be paid to three white men and Duncan. Duncan, however, refused to sign the affidavits that would have allowed him to collect the reward. Lalasee had surrendered to Duncan, who escorted him to the Missoula County jail in Missoula. Pierre Paul had been captured by Pierre Cattullayeah, the chief of the Indian police, and Antoine Morrigeau. After Cattullayeah and Morrigeau had disarmed and bound Pierre Paul, they turned him over to the white posse. The bulk of the reward money was to go to three white men who were members of the posse. The bitter feeling on the reservation against the white posse that invaded the reservation to arrest Pierre Paul caused Duncan to refuse the reward. In 1889 the posse had murdered an innocent Indian in a failed attempt to capture Pierre Paul.[22] In 1896, when the reward was finally paid, the money was split between four white men and Pierre Cattullayeah.[23]

Horse racing continued to interest Duncan in 1895. In the spring of that year, he arranged to breed Telegraph, his fast running mare, to a thoroughbred runner named St. Croix, owned by the Higgins brothers of Missoula.[24]

Duncan played an important role in a spring 1895 conflict between Flathead Agent Joseph T. Carter and several traditional Salish leaders in the Jocko Valley. Duncan hired a white lawyer in Missoula to defend three Indian leaders opposed to Carter's actions. Agent Carter's handling of these events was one of Duncan's major complaints against Carter when Duncan filed written charges in 1896. His 1896 letter was also the most complete description of the original conflict that has survived.

The incidents began with an early March 1895 evening pre-Lenten dance held by tribal members of the Salish and Pend d'Oreille tribes in the Jocko Valley. Since it was a traditional Indian dance with Indian music and not a fiddle dance as conducted by the whites and mixed bloods, it was illegal under the agency code of Indian offenses. Agent Joseph T. Carter sent a party of agency Indian police to the gathering to order it dispersed. A former Indian judge, Louison, was at the dance and spoke to encourage the Indians to cease dancing and go home to prepare for Lent the next day. Louison had been one of the original tribal judges in 1885 and had held that office until 1892 when Agent Peter Ronan dismissed him as a result of the "dancing craze" of 1890-1891.[25]

Louison was later arrested by the Indian police under orders of Agent Carter and charged with having encouraged the dancers to keep on dancing despite Carter's order to cease. Louison was locked up in the tribal jail at the Jocko Agency. According to Duncan's account, Louison's arrest resulted from a mistranslation of Louison's remarks which made them appear seditious. Carter wrote the Commissioner of Indian Affairs on March 4, 1895, requesting authority to remove Louison from the Flathead Reservation because his father was Nez Perce. Carter charged that Louison was "non-progressive" and encouraged traditional Indian customs and ceremonies.[26]

While Louison was being held in the agency jail, a crowd of Indian men attempted to break him out. Carter rounded up enough supporters, Indian and white, to stop the attempted release and arrest the three leaders. One source gave the names of the three as Nicholas, Voissant, and Pierrilot; another identified them as Swasah, Nicolla, and Louis Coull-Coullee. Carter's group loaded up the three prisoners and attempted to drive them to confinement in the Missoula County jail. Before they were out of the valley, however, Chief Charlo asked a group of his followers to prevent the removal of the three prisoners to Missoula. An opposition group, led by Big Pierre, confronted Carter and the Indian police escorting the prisoners. Carter bluffed his way through this obstruction by claiming that U.S. Army troops were on their way to enforce his order. Carter delivered the three prisoners to the county jail.[27]

Top:
Judge Louison,
Salish/Nez Perce.

Bottom:
Chief Charlo,
Salish

Sources: National
Anthropological Archives,
Smithsonian Institution,
Washington, D.C., negative
03545500, photograph
by F. A. Rinehart; and
Montana Historical Society
Photograph Archives,
Helena, detail of 954-526,
photograph by John K.
Hillers, Bureau of American
Ethnology, Washington,
D.C., 1884.

When the three men were imprisoned at the jail, the U.S. Attorney for Montana was supposed to file charges against them. After about a week, Duncan hired an attorney, Joseph K. Wood, who filed for a writ of habeas corpus to get the prisoners released. P. H. Leslie, the U.S. Attorney, was not able to be in Missoula on March 13, 1895, when the hearing was held, and Judge Frank Woody ordered them released.[28] A Deputy United States Marshall was sent from Helena to arrest the three prisoners again. Since he did not know the prisoners personally, he passed them on the Missoula railroad station platform on his way to the agency.[29] Carter's account claimed that the agency Indian police assisted the Deputy United States Marshall in making the re-arrests. By March 22, 1895, Big Pierre and the other three accused were back in custody and brought before the United States Commissioner in Missoula. Big Pierre, Swasah, and Nicolla were bound over to the United States Grand Jury and Louis Coull-Coullee was discharged, apparently because he had been arrested by mistake.[30]

The three remaining prisoners were taken before the U.S. Grand Jury in Helena in early May 1895 where they were indicted. U.S. Attorney Leslie, however, could not find any specific law which they had broken and so could not draw up the charges. Agent Carter appealed to the Indian Office in Washington, D.C., for legal help but does not seem to have received a reply. Acting in spite, Carter renewed his appeal to have Louison allotted on the Nez Perce Reservation and forced to move to that reservation.[31] One newspaper account reported that in May 1895, Carter arrested Duncan and Chief Charlo. They were not jailed but ordered to not leave the reservation.[32] Finally in middle May 1895, the charges against Swasah and Nicolla were dismissed and they were released in Helena to make their own way back to the reservation. Big Pierre was indicted but not tried due to scheduling problems. He was sent back to the reservation and apparently returned to the agency jail.[33]

In the midst of the legal conflict over Carter's intervention in the pre-Lenten dance in the Jocko Valley, Duncan made a trip to the Bitterroot Valley. At the end of April 1893, Duncan visited the Bitterroot Valley fruit growers to study their methods. He wanted to learn new techniques he could use in his orchard on the reservation.[34]

Agent Carter was both delighted and apoplectic in early August 1895 when the Montana U.S. District Attorney notified him that Duncan had been appointed as a commissioner for the U.S. court by Judge Hiram Knowles. The commissioner for the U.S. court was the first official to hear cases in the federal court system. He was the person who decided if cases should be referred to the U.S. Grand Jury or dismissed. Carter thought that if Duncan accepted and qualified for the position, he would automatically become a U.S. citizen. As a citizen, Duncan could then be ordered off the reservation. If the position would not make it possible to remove Duncan from the reservation, then Carter wanted the appointment revoked. Carter reasoned, "to appoint an Indian who from some motive does his utmost to annoy and interfere with the government of this reserve seems at least unwise...Imbued as he is with Indian prejudices, justice could not be expected of him."[35]

The Commissioner of Indian Affairs replied that the appointment would not make Duncan a citizen. The Commissioner could not see how a non-citizen could be appointed to the position, but left that decision to the court. If Carter felt that Duncan was not a fit man for the position, he was told to send his information to the court.[36] No further reference to the appointment has been found in the surviving documents.

Duncan's apple orchard produced an "abundant crop" in 1895. On September 9, 1895, he brought samples with him to Missoula.[37] On the same trip to Missoula, Duncan paid for a one year subscription to the *Evening Republican* newspaper.[38] During late 1895 and early 1896, Duncan traveled to Portland and San Francisco. According to a note in the newspaper on his return to Missoula, Duncan was "considerably improved in health."[39]

Duncan was a witness in the 1896 trial of F. M. Cory for impersonating a federal officer. In mid-August 1895, a F. M.

Duncan McDonald's hotel and orchard, Ravalli, Montana.

Source: Toole Archives, Mansfield Library, University of Montana, Missoula, Montana Photographs by Subject MS 562, folder 13/4.

Cory [or Corey] presented himself at the Jocko Agency as a Secret Agent of the U.S. Treasury Department. Cory presented only a general letter of recommendation from John Lane, a legitimate special agent for the Department of the Interior.[40] During the four months or so that Carter accepted Cory as a government agent, Cory pressed a vigorous campaign against white trespassers on the reservation. In October 1895, Cory was directing a roundup of horses on the reservation range. According to the newspaper report, 2,000 of the estimated 15,000 horses running on the reservation were owned by Nez Perce Indians from the Umatilla Reservation or other owners who were not entitled to graze on the Flathead Reservation. Carter and Cory were attempting to drive out the foreign horses to make more room for tribal member horses and cattle.[41] Two of the Nez Perce horse owners traveled to Missoula and hired Joseph Dixon as their attorney. They offered to pay for grazing until spring 1896, the soonest they could safely drive their stock to the Umatilla Reservation.[42] In late December 1895, Carter published a long list of brands and descriptions of stray horses being held for pickup by off-reservation owners.[43]

During January 1896, F. M. Cory was exposed as an impostor and not a federal government agent. The documents suggest he turned all or almost all of the fine money and other funds he had collected over to Agent Carter, so financial greed did not seem to have been his goal. Apparently Cory never did explain his motivation, but he was arrested and charged with impersonating a federal official. One consequence of the deception was that some of the trespassers he fined sued to get their money back. They did not claim to be innocent of cattle trespass, but they wanted their money back anyway.[44] In June 1896 Cory was convicted and sentenced to nine months in jail in Helena.[45]

On February 12, 1896, Duncan wrote a long letter to a Missoula law office, Binford Stiff & Hershey, complaining about Carter's handling of the Flathead Agency. The Missoula lawyers sent the letter to Montana Senator T. H. Carter, who forwarded it to the Commissioner of Indian Affairs. Duncan wrote that

Agent Carter had thwarted all their previous attempts to complain. When they protested to the agent, he refused to forward the complaints to the Commissioner. Three times, when they remonstrated to the military officers at Fort Missoula, they were told to submit their grievances through the agent. When they tried to reach the U.S. Grand Jury in Helena, Carter had them arrested for the attempt.[46]

Duncan complained about Carter's 1895 arrest of Louison and the legal conflict that grew out of it. He also objected to the activities of F. M. Cory in 1895 and 1896 impersonating a federal officer. The letter included charges that Carter had torn down the fences of Duncan and an Indian named Paul Andre to create the right-of-way for a new road. Finally Carter had refused to listen to charges that Vince Ronan, the agency clerk, and Pierre Pims, the captain of the agency police, had tried to seduce Indian women. Duncan requested that tribal members vote once a year on July 1 to decide who should be judges on the agency court. The letter was filed at the Indian Office with no reply.[47]

A month later, on March 14, 1896, C. A. Stillinger, Duncan's former clerk, asked authorization to rent Duncan's ranch. The Commissioner of Indian Affairs, however, decided that tribal members could not lease their land until after allotments were made on the reservation.[48] Later that year, Duncan's younger sister, Annie Cole, died in December 1896. Her funeral was held at Duncan's house at Ravalli, and she was buried at Fort Connah.[49]

In July 1897, Duncan was one of 46 tribal members who signed or made their mark on a petition to the Secretary of the Interior protesting the possible reappointment of Flathead Agent Joseph Carter. The petition also requested an inspector be sent to the agency to "make a thorough investigation into the affairs and management of this Agency."[50]

Peter Colville McDonald had been attending the Bishop Scott School in Portland, Oregon, in 1897. In October 1897, Peter enrolled at the University of Montana in Missoula.[51] A month later, on November 18, 1897, Duncan presented the university with a pair of moose antlers and the scalp for mounting.[52]

Duncan's interest in gold mining continued, and, in March 1898, he was preparing to guide a party to the Klondike gold fields. He planned to guide about forty people to Alaska overland by way of Edmonton, Alberta. The party would take 100 head of pack horses, a few beef cattle, and a lot of hogs and sheep.[53] No record was found indicating how the trip worked out, but Duncan was back in Missoula in June 1898.

On June 10, 1898, Duncan was in Missoula and made comments that appeared to support the efforts of Missoula County to tax cattle on the reservation owned by mixed bloods and Indian women married to white men. This was the same time when the new Flathead Agent, W. H. Smead, was fighting Missoula County's efforts to tax cattle on the reservation owned by tribal members.[54] Contradicting the above sources, a July 26, 1898, article in the *Anaconda Standard* claimed Duncan arrived in Missoula for the first time in several months. This report said Duncan had just returned from an extended visit to Washington State.[55] Duncan was in Missoula shopping for yearling cattle in September 1898.[56] A little later that fall, Duncan entered some "splendid specimens of apples" in the Western Montana Fair in Missoula.[57]

Judge Frank Woody was researching the origins of the name Lo Lo in February and March 1899 for the Northern Pacific Railroad historical department. Duncan, and most of the other sources Woody consulted, agreed that Lo Lo was the Salish language rendition of the Christian name Lawrence.[58]

Peter Colville McDonald left Flathead for the Fort Shaw Indian School in central Montana in March 1899. At that point he was 16 years old, 5 feet 8.5 inches tall, and weighed 130 pounds.[59] A few days later, Peter's mother, Louise, complained that, before leaving for Fort Shaw, one of the agency policemen was gambling with Peter and won money from him.[60] On July 1, 1899, Agent Smead telegraphed permission to Fort Shaw for Peter to come home for the summer.[61]

Duncan joined Missoulians Daniel Heyfron, George C. Higgins, and Will Cave in September 1899 on a hunting and fishing trip to the Bitterroot Valley.[62] A month later in October 1899, Duncan was summoned to Helena as a witness in the federal suits against Missoula County over taxing mixed blood tribal members.[63]

Duncan met Louisa McDermott, the teacher at the new government school at the Jocko Agency, during the fall of 1899. McDermott described Duncan as "a civilized man, well educated and of fine mentality. He is a prosperous farmer, has a comfortable home and a fine fruit farm. Duncan is a Catholic, but he doesn't bother the church often."[64]

An Indian named Lolo was sent to the Montana Penitentiary in December 1899 for the murder of another Indian named Ambrose. Duncan wrote a letter to the Missoula County Attorney about the two men. Ambrose and Lolo had been fighting over a woman when the murder occurred. Ambrose was the son of Chief Ambrose of the Bitterroot Salish. Unlike his father, who was a respected leader, the younger Ambrose was a "bad" man who chased married women. In 1882, when Assistant Attorney General Joseph McCammon had come to the reservation to negotiate for the Northern Pacific Railroad right-of-way, Ambrose attempted to assault A. B. Hammond, who was helping with the negotiations. Duncan felt both men were "first-class drunkards and gamblers."[65]

Duncan considered joining the Flathead Agency police force in January 1900, but did not want to have to work at the Jocko Agency. Agent Smead was willing to put Duncan on the force to keep a watch out for the whiskey trade going through the Ravalli railroad station. Duncan would have only had to go to the agency to be sworn in. Apparently Duncan changed his mind and decided not to join, as he did not appear in the 1900 rosters of agency police at the National Archives.[66]

Duncan received a letter on March 3, 1900, from Susan Ogden, his niece, who was attending Fort Shaw Indian School with his son, Peter Colville. Ogden was concerned about Peter's conduct at the school. Duncan wrote Agent Smead and asked him to quietly investigate the matter: "As you know my greed is

to have my son educated to be a man." Smead wrote to the superintendent at the school who replied that it was "nothing serious...
The origin of the trouble was a 'Breed' that was acquainted with
the Flathead boys, on passing through supplied some of them
with whiskey and Peter was in the crowd." Duncan noted that
Peter had attended military school and Ogden the Sisters of Providence girls school at St. Ignatius, so it was normal that Peter was
not overly religious and Ogden was worried about Peter's soul.[67]

Duncan was taking two railroad carloads of horses to a
sale in St. Paul, Minnesota, on April 18, 1900.[68] According to
Duncan's June 22, 1900, testimony before a U.S. Indian Inspector, he netted $3.13 each for the horses in that shipment.[69] On
the way back from St. Paul, Duncan stopped at Fort Shaw to
visit his son. He met his wife Louise at the school, and they both
attended an entertainment put on by the students. According to
Susie Ogden, Duncan "expressed himself quite satisfied with our
performances."[70] Duncan stopped at Helena for a short visit on
his return trip to the reservation. While at Helena, he reminis-
cenced about how much the Helena Valley had changed since he
first visited it as a child with his father in 1858.[71] On June 12,
1900, Agent Smead wrote to the Fort Shaw school requesting
that Peter and two other students related to Duncan be allowed
to return to Flathead for the summer vacation.[72]

Arthur L. Stone, the editor of the *Missoulian*, described an
undated summer meeting with Duncan in Ravalli. Stone did not
give the year of the meeting, but it would have been about 1900.
Stone was at Ravalli waiting for a much delayed train when Duncan came by and started telling traditional Salish coyote stories.
One of the stories Duncan related was that of the dragon of the
Salish. The dragon in the Jocko Valley was holding the animals
captive, and Coyote killed the dragon and freed the animals. The
remains of the dragon can be seen in the landscape of the Jocko
Valley today.[73]

Over the years, Duncan repeatedly advanced the claim of
Anthony Finley, a Flathead Reservation mixed blood, as the first
man to discover gold in what became Montana. In July 1900,

Duncan introduced Finley's widow who was visiting Missoula and retold the story of Finley's gold discovery. Duncan was countering the claims of several white men for the honor.[74]

On July 23, 1900, Duncan testified before Cyrus S. Beede, a U.S. Indian Inspector, about his language skills in a legal conflict over a contract to sell horses. Flathead Agent W. H. Smead was trying to develop a market for selling some of the thousands of small Indian cayuses that were crowding the Flathead Reservation range. He was particularly interested in reducing the large herds of horses on the reservation that were owned by Indians from the Umatilla and Nez Perce Reservations. Allicott, Johnson, and Kiola were three Nez Perce and Umatilla Indians who together had about 3,000 horses grazing on the open range on Flathead. On March 16, 1900, Allicott signed a contract with W. W. White, an agent for Arlee trader Alex Dow, to sell all of his 3,000 horses except 30 head. Duncan interpreted the contract for Allicott. Agent Smead claimed in a June 7, 1900, report to the Commissioner of Indian Affairs that he had requested that Duncan interpret the contract for Allicott as a special precaution. During White's testimony, however, White said Allicott had requested that Duncan interpret. After Dow had received 1,450 head of horses from Allicott, Allicott refused to deliver the remaining horses provided for in the contract. Dow resold some of the 1,450 horses in eastern markets and kept the others for slaughter for their hides and used the meat to feed hogs.[75]

Duncan played down his language skills in his testimony about the contract:

[Inspector:] Did Allicott understand this contract? [Duncan:] I suppose he did. It was interpreted to him in four different languages. In Flathead, Nez Perce, English, and in Indian signs. He can talk the Flathead language in my opinion better than I can Nez Perce. He understands a few words of the English language....

[Wm. Parsons, attorney for Allicott:] Do you speak the Nez Perce language acurately [sic]? [Duncan:] No sir. [Parsons:] About how many Nez Pe[r]ce words do you know? [Duncan:] I couldent tell you sir. Not as many as I do of Flathead.

[Parsons:] Was the reason you do not know Nez Pe[r]ce accurately the reason you used the other languages? [Duncan:] Every few words I spliced in with Flathead because he understood Flathead better than I did Nez Perce. I kept asking him if he understood and he said yes.

Duncan's testimony was vague, but it may have meant that, while he could communicate in Salish and Nez Perce, his command of these languages was limited.[76]

The Commissioner of Indian Affairs decided that, since the Indians owning these horses had no rights on the reservation, the contract for sale should be enforced. On April 29, 1901, Smead wrote to agent Charles Wilkins at Umatilla that, if the owners of the horses still refused to sell their horses on Flathead, the horses would be driven off the reservation. According to Smead, the Flathead Reservation Indians met in a council and agreed to forcing the removal of the horses belonging to Indians enrolled on the Umatilla and Nez Perce Reservations.[77]

A few months after the investigation into Allicott's horse contract, in a short note in the *Plainsman* newspaper on August 10, 1900, Duncan indicated he had hired a white man named Mr. Brown to run his apple orchard or fruit farm. According to this note, Duncan expected to ship 1,500 boxes of apples in 1900. Two months later on October 19, 1900, a note in the *Kalispell Bee* newspaper claimed Duncan had shipped 3,000 boxes of apples to eastern markets in 1900.[78]

Duncan complained on August 18, 1900, about a suggestion by Professor Morton J. Elrod of the University of Montana to change the name of Lake McDonald on the reservation. Elrod wanted to change the name of the Lake McDonald in the Mission Mountains to Post Lake so it would not be confused with the Lake McDonald in what was to become Glacier National Park. Duncan responded that the Lake McDonald on the reservation had the better claim to the name because the Lake McDonald in

Glacier did not get that name until after Duncan and a trading party camped there in 1878. While there, Duncan carved his name on a tree near the lake which presumably gave that lake the McDonald name. Duncan also argued that Jocko River was misnamed along with other reservation features.[79]

During the winter of 1900-1901, three government commissioners, called the Crow, Flathead, Etc. Commission, tried to convince the Flathead Reservation tribes to sell the northern part of the reservation. They convened several general councils, but they met determined opposition to any land sales. Salish Chief Charlo was particularly opposed. Charlo declared, "You all know that I won't sell a foot of land." Kootenai Chief Isaac elaborated: "You told me I was poor and needed money, but I am not poor. What is valuable to a person is land, the earth, water, trees, &c., and all these belong to us. Don't think I am poor....We haven't any more land than we need, so you had better buy from somebody else." Duncan made a few comments at a January 3-4, 1901, council at A. L. Demers' store in St. Ignatius. Duncan tried to clarify some points and also sought to explain to the commissioners that the tribes refused to enter into an agreement because of the failure of the government to fulfill earlier promises:

> Washington has lots of money while these Indians are living from hand to mouth as best they can. Indians are starving while waiting for money promised to them. The Flatheads have always been friendly to whites and have clean hands while the Government has been kicking them around. Other tribes that have fought the Government have been treated much better than the Flatheads. The Indians feel this way and are afraid to sign an agreement, for fear they will be treated as heretofore. In a few years the Government will want to make another treaty and buy more land.

Presumably Duncan played an important background role in the negotiations that did not show up in the transcripts of the meetings.[80]

Between May 1, 1899, and June 5, 1903, Duncan maintained an account at C. A. Stillinger's general merchandise store. Duncan purchased calico material for his wife, machinery, and other items over the period. He paid on the bill with cash, cattle, and at least 170 boxes of apples in 1901 and 1902. In 1907, Duncan still owed $650 on the bill and was sued by Stillinger in the Missoula District Court.[81]

Duncan made his first trip to Missoula in months in June 1901. On this trip, Duncan brought news about smallpox that was then epidemic on the reservation.[82] On February 9, 1901, Smead had ordered a quarantine of the reservation for fear of smallpox. No cases of smallpox had yet appeared on the reserve, but by the next month sixteen or eighteen cases were reported among a band of Canadian Cree camped near Ronan. Permits to leave the reservation were to be granted only when "absolutely necessary."[83] Missoula County authorities also declared a quarantine on the reservation.[84] By May 6, 1901, Smead reported that only six smallpox cases remained and predicted the quarantine would be lifted soon.[85] The permit system was discontinued on May 18, 1901.[86] On May 25, 1901, George S. Lescher, the agency physician, found eleven more smallpox cases and the quarantine was reinstated.[87] A quarantine camp was established near St. Ignatius to isolate the infected and exposed.[88] This second quarantine lasted through the middle of August 1901.[89]

While Duncan was in Missoula in early June 1901 — despite the smallpox quarantine of the reservation — he was interviewed about the problems in containing the disease. Duncan called for the quarantine and destruction of infected property to be rigorously implemented: "The chief difficulty lies in the fact that the Indians resist the destruction of their property that has been infected. The hiding of blankets when cabins have been ordered burned has been responsible for much of the spread of the disease. Mr. McDonald's opinion is that only the most stringent measures will be sufficient."[90] Duncan told of his uncle, Grizzly Bear, who tried to use traditional Indian medicine to cure the disease. Duncan refused to allow Grizzly Bear to enter his house, because Grizzly Bear had been exposed to smallpox. In two weeks, Grizzly Bear came down with smallpox and died. In another case an Indian woman saved some "trinkets" belonging to her husband who had died of smallpox. Despite burning her cabin and the rest of her belongings, these trinkets brought the infection to the family that gave her shelter.[91]

On June 25, 1901, Agent Smead submitted a report on Indian school pupils who had returned to the Flathead Reservation. According to this report, Peter Colville McDonald was 19 years old, single, and in good physical condition. He had spent two years at Fort Shaw Indian School.[92]

Duncan joined D. Dowd and the Sisters of Providence in September 1901 in suing to recover 16 head of cattle "now in the possession of others, but supposed to have been unlawfully taken from the plaintiffs."[93] A month later, on October 12, 1901, Duncan stopped in Missoula on his way home from Butte where he had been a witness before the federal grand jury.[94]

Two *Anaconda Standard* reporters were waiting for the train at Ravalli station on October 16, 1901. The train was delayed, but they found Duncan and six other Indians waiting outside near the station. Duncan waxed philosophical about the negative impact of civilization on Indian life. The new foods resulted in decayed teeth, poor digestion, and other health problems. Before the whites came, the country was full of wild game. Duncan claimed that Indians in 1901 were "not as contented with all that we have these days as we used to be when all that we owned was a horse and a buffalo robe." He told of a preacher who listened to Indian tales, only looking for parallels in the Bible. The train finally came, but the reporters wrote that they had enjoyed Duncan's monologue during the delay.[95]

On November 12, 1901, C. A. Stillinger requested permission to visit the Flathead Reservation and confer with Duncan about some mining properties they owned jointly. No record was found to identify the properties or how their development turned out.[96]

Chapter 7

Cattleman and Tribal Spokesman
1901-1908

The first decade of the twentieth century was a time of turmoil and controversy on the Flathead Indian Reservation. Duncan was active in promoting the interests of the major stockmen on the reservation. During the first part of this period, they tried to prevent the imposition of a resident grazing tax but failed. Duncan opposed a 1903 Montana state attack on tribal hunting rights, though it was the traditional chiefs who hired a white lawyer to fight the law in court. He did not approve of the allotment program forced on the tribes, but was not actively involved in the battle against the policy. Samuel Bellew, the Flathead Agent who succeeded W. H. Smead in 1904, introduced fewer new policies at the agency, but the tribal community was continually roiled by each new step in the allotment program Congressman Joseph M. Dixon imposed on the tribes. By the end of this period in 1908, the government was forcing the reservation open to white homesteaders and the tribal economy began years of decline.

In November 1901, about 50 reservation stockmen met in St. Ignatius and organized a Flathead Reservation Stockmen's Association. Seven directors were elected for the association, most were mixed blood cattlemen with large herds. Duncan was selected as the association secretary. The association was formed to police their herds against rustlers and look out for the financial interests of the members. In 1903 they were especially active in opposing grazing fees for the use of the open range on the reservation.[1]

Duncan was a character witness and interpreter for the December 1901 murder trial of Baptiste Robieau or Robillard in Missoula. Robieau claimed self-defense in the October 28, 1901, murder of Antoine Michel on the road from Plains to the reservation. Robieau was a Chippewa mixed blood from Canada who had been working as a laborer on the Flathead Reservation for eight years. While drinking whiskey on the trip, a fight broke out, and, according to Robieau, Michel attacked him with a knife. Duncan and a number of other witnesses testified to Robieau's good reputation on the reservation. Despite Duncan's testimony, the jury found Robieau guilty of manslaughter and sentenced him to eight years imprisonment.[2]

In May 1902, Duncan commented on a report that buffalo bones had been found in Grass Valley near Missoula. Duncan wrote that both Salish Chief Arlee and Pend d'Oreille Chief Michelle had told him about hunting buffalo in Grass Valley and Frenchtown in the middle 1830s. Duncan also claimed he had found buffalo bones in his orchard in Ravalli.[3] A few months later in the run up to the 1902 Fourth of July Powwow, Duncan was involved in negotiations to try to unite the St. Ignatius and Arlee celebrations into one big powwow. Duncan wrote Agent Smead at Jocko that the St. Ignatius camp was willing to move south to meet Chief Charlo and the Jocko Valley Indians halfway.[4]

During a visit to Missoula in middle July 1902, Duncan made some comments that seemed to indicate, that, under certain conditions, he might support the allotment and opening of the Flathead Reservation:

> Mr. McDonald expresses great interest in the proposed opening of the Flathead Reservation and says that if the government will go about it in the right way it will not be hard to accomplish. The trouble is that the men who have been sent out to negotiate a treaty with the federated tribes have been unfamiliar with the red men and the latter have had such disastrous experiences with treaties that they are naturally suspicious of any attempt to negotiate a new one.

Duncan also reported in 1902 that his orchard was "flourishing" and would have a large crop that year. He claimed, however, that the orchard was "not in his line and that he does not have much to do with it."[5]

While on a trip to Missoula and Stevensville in August 1902, Duncan received a report that Charlo had died. It turned out to be Victor Charlo, Chief Charlo's 24 years old son, who had died. The unexpected death was an especially hard blow to Chief Charlo.[6]

Duncan's brother-in-law Michel was a well-known rich Kalispel Indian living on the reservation. About the first of November 1902, while Michel was in Plains, a gang of three men robbed the strong box at his home on the reservation and got away with a reported $22,000. The theft was even reported in *The New York Times*. Flathead Agent W. H. Smead sent out a number of inquiries trying to get evidence in the theft, but no one was ever convicted and the money was not recovered.[7]

Charles S. McNichols, a Special Indian Agent, had been sent to the Flathead Reservation to compile the first official enrollment of Indians entitled to tribal rights on the reservation. On February 6, 1903, as he was completing work on the roll, he wrote to the Commissioner of Indian Affairs for instructions regarding Indians and mixed bloods from other reservations who had been adopted into the tribes over the years. Chief Charlo, Judge Lewison, and Judge Ki-ka-she opposed the enrollment of the Courville, Clairmont, and Couture families. Their enrollment was supported by Pend d'Oreille Chief Pierre and Kootenai Chief Gusta. Since the Flathead Agency building had burned in 1898, no paper documentation of their adoptions had survived. Despite these contested cases, all the chiefs agreed on the enrollment of Michel Pablo (Blackfeet/Mexican), the McDonald brothers (Nez Perce/white), and the Matts (Piegan/white).[8]

Between 1898 and 1904, Flathead Indian Agent W. H. Smead tried to rationalize the Flathead Reservation livestock industry according to white American economic values. The first part of his campaign was to reduce horse herds on the reservation,

W. H. Smead, Flathead Indian Agent, 1898-1904.
Source: Photograph by W. H. Taylor Studio, Helena, Montana, Montana
Historical Society Photograph Archives, Helena, PAc 99-36.67.

so more grass would be available for cattle. Duncan and the other Indian cattle owners supported these efforts. However, in 1903 Smead announced a resident grazing fee on larger cattle and horse herds on the reservation, and this precipitated intense opposition from the reservation stockmen. On March 15, 1902, Inspector Jame E. Jenkins had recommended a resident grazing tax on Flathead. Jenkins argued that since much of the open range was "monopolized by large cattle owners," stockmen with more than 100 head should pay a $1.00 per head annual grazing tax into the tribal fund.[9] Chas. S. McNichols, a Special Indian Agent then working on the first enrollment of tribal members on the Flathead Reservation, submitted a report to the Commissioner of Indian Affairs on January 5, 1903, on the largest cattle owners on the reservation. Duncan was listed as having 300 acres fenced and 800 cattle and horses.[10] In response to McNichol's report, the Secretary of the Interior approved a grazing tax on herds of more than 100 head owned by tribal members. The annual tax of one dollar per head over 100 was to start April 1, 1903.[11]

Smead wrote to the Commissioner of Indian Affairs on February 24, 1903, that he had a talk with some of the leading Indians on the subject of a grazing tax on resident stock: "They favor the taxation of the stock belonging to the whites, mixed bloods, and such Indians as may have no legal rights on this reservation, but are seriously opposed to the full bloods who have rights here being taxed." Smead recommended that the tax on horses be modified to reduce the impact on full blood Indian horse owners. He wanted the Commissioner of Indian Affairs to send him written instructions that he could have read to the tribal leaders suggesting that horse herd owners sell their poor stock and keep only their best mares. Then the government could provide a carload of good stallions to improve the horse stock on the reservation.[12]

Opposition to the tax was immediate and intense. On March 17, 1903, the house diarist at St. Ignatius Mission said the Indians were "rather excited" over the tax.[13] A Missoula law firm, Woody and Woody, wrote the Commissioner of Indian Affairs

asking for information on the legal basis for the tax.[14] On March
18, 1903, Smead wrote to the Commissioner of Indian Affairs
requesting permission for a Flathead Reservation delegation to
visit Washington, D.C.[15] The permission was denied, but Smead
repeated the request by telegram on March 22, 1903.[16] Finally
on March 24, 1903, the Bureau of Catholic Indian Missions in
Washington, D.C., obtained permission for the Flathead delegation to visit Washington, D.C., at their own expense.[17] The St.
Ignatius Mission was also upset about the proposal to apply the
grazing tax to part of the Mission owned herds grazing on the reservation.[18] Two separate rival delegations from Flathead headed
for Washington, D.C., to argue against the resident grazing tax.
Duncan accompanied one of the delegations as a "guide."[19]

The rival delegations met and reconciled before reaching
the capital in order to present a unified protest.[20] An April 4,
1903, letter written by the delegation to the Secretary of the Interior protesting the grazing tax on the St. Ignatius Mission herds
listed the members of the unified delegation. The list included
four traditional chiefs: Charlo and Antoine Moise of the Salish tribe, Koostata of the Kootenai, and Charlie Michelle of the
Pend d'Oreille. Five agency judges were also included: Louison,
Baptiste, Joseph, Celot, and Pascale Antoine. Two mixed blood
cattlemen were listed as interpreters: Alexander Matt and Duncan
McDonald.[21] Agent Smead also accompanied the delegation.[22]

A little over a week later, the delegation returned to the reservation without getting any changes in the tax. The Secretary of
the Interior refused to make any modifications and the President
and Commissioner of Indian Affairs were both out of town.[23] On
his return, Duncan was very upset and complained:

"Oh, it was a hard trip. I had all kinds of trouble with
the Indians. It was the first time that most of them had
ever been east or in any large city, and they wanted everything that they saw. They would simply rush at whatever
pleased them, regardless of rules or laws. Twice I had to
call upon the police for aid to prevent them from getting
into trouble. It was interesting enough to watch them,

but the trouble of keeping them out of mischief was too great and I didn't enjoy the trip.

"We called upon the secretary of the interior and upon Commissioner Jones of the Indian bureau. These gentlemen listened to the protest of the Indians, but they wouldn't do anything for us. When we asked the secretary of the interior what we could do with all the ponies, which are not worth paying taxes upon, he advised us to kill them. This, of course, the Indians will not do. Before we had finished our interview I told the secretary that he would never get a cent of taxes out of me. He looked hard at me, but didn't know what to say.

"Some of the Indians have paid their taxes under this new order of the bureau, but there are many who have not paid and who never will pay. I suppose the matter will have to be settled by the courts, for we feel that the tax is not legal and that we should not be made to pay it. The treaties give us the absolute and exclusive right to the reservation and it does not seem right to make us pay this tax. The secretary of the interior would not yield an inch but simply settled down like a mired mule and wouldn't even answer us."[24]

The only adjustment was that the grazing tax on horses was reduced to fifty cents per head for the first year only.[25] Duncan was even disgusted with the sculptures he saw in the capital:

There are some statues there that they call art that I don't think much of. In front of the congressional library there is a statue of Neptune, I think they called it, and I swear that statue wouldn't be allowed on the reservation. There was too much nude about it for even the Indians and those people down there call it a-r-t.[26]

Smead immediately moved in May 1903 to collect the grazing tax.[27] On May 13, 1903, he received permission from the Commissioner of Indian Affairs to remove William Irvine from the reservation for refusing to pay his grazing tax.[28] By June

1, 1903, Irvine had paid his grazing tax and Smead reported that consequently Irvine had not been removed.[29]

Smead did request that buffalo be exempted from the tax in the interest of conservation. The Commissioner of Indian Affairs did not respond to this request.[30] On July 2, 1903, Smead reported having collected more grazing tax, but said he was not pushing it with ponies owned by full bloods. He asked that the money collected be paid out in a per capita as soon as possible to make the tax more popular with the full bloods.[31] The per capita payment was authorized on July 14, 1903.[32] The Commissioner of Indian Affairs instructed Smead on August 3, 1903, "not to urge the collection" of the grazing tax on St. Ignatius Mission cattle until further notice.[33]

But opposition to the tax was continuing to build. On August 25, 1903, Smead asked the Commissioner of Indian Affairs if an opinion had been received from the Department of Justice about enforcing the grazing tax in court. He expected some mixed blood cattle owners to seek legal representation in the matter.[34] The Commissioner of Indian Affairs replied that no decision had yet been received from the Assistant Attorney General, but those who refused to pay would still be removed from the reservation.[35] Despite Duncan's vow to the Secretary of the Interior, on October 23, 1903, Agent Smead reported that Duncan had paid his grazing tax on 300 head of cattle and 10 head of horses. The tax did not apply to the first 100 head of stock.[36]

Smead requested authority on October 22, 1903, to remove Joseph Morrigeau from the reservation for refusing to pay his grazing tax.[37] Morrigeau refused to obey the Indian police when ordered to leave the reservation and Smead requested a U.S. Marshall or soldiers be sent to enforce the removal.[38] On November 27, 1903, soldiers left Fort Missoula to forcibly remove Morrigeau from the reservation.[39] Two days later, Smead wired that, after being removed from the reservation by the soldiers, Morrigeau agreed to pay his grazing tax and was allowed to return.[40]

In January 1904 a $5 per capita payment was made to all tribal members from the grazing tax collections.[41] Opposition to the tax continued and was one of the charges brought against Smead in 1904. Smead was dismissed as a result of other charges, however, and the Commissioner of Indian Affairs supported Smead on the grazing tax.[42] Agent Smead worked hard to rationalize the livestock industry on the reservation according to white American economic standards. In the course of this effort he managed to antagonize many of the chiefs and influential tribal members and spawned fierce opposition.

While the controversy over the resident grazing tax was unfolding in 1903, several other events occurred affecting Duncan. On April 20, 1903, Duncan's son, Peter, inquired about getting a trader's license to set up a store at Ravalli. Agent Smead denied Peter's request because, "Few of the traders here have ever made much money and I feel sure if you were to embark on it you would loose your money. I advise you to go into the cattle business. It is a paying industry..."[43] Smead might have been influenced by the fact that M. H. Prideaux, who owned part of the trader's store at St. Ignatius, was his nephew.[44]

Agent Smead and the national Office of Indian Affairs supervisor of Indian education toured the Flathead Reservation in middle March 1903 looking for a location for a new government school.[45] After the survey, they were especially interested in purchasing Duncan's hotel building at Ravalli for school use. On May 17, 1903, Agent Smead turned down a request from John Weightman, who was then operating a stage line out of Ravalli, to lease Duncan's property at Ravalli, because of the prospective sale to the government.[46]

Duncan, however, wanted more for the building and improvements than the government was willing to pay. The matter dragged on, and on March 3, 1904, Smead wrote Duncan asking him to reduce his price because the property would be put to educational use. On March 6, 1904, Duncan replied that he had about $17,000 invested in the property, but he would be willing to sell the improvements to the government for $13,000.

Duncan pointed to the money and sweat he had invested over the years in developing the property: "I have spent the best of my life improving it. And actually it stands me about $17,000.00. Selish Station would never amount to any thing had I not beautified it with my sweat and money. And now you know how it looks."[47] No further information about the proposed sale has been found, but the government did not go through with the purchase.

In 1903 the Montana Legislature passed a law prohibiting Indians from carrying firearms off their reservations. Any arms and ammunition they had were to be seized and sold with the proceeds going to the state.[48] The law sparked a legal confrontation between the Flathead Reservation tribes and the State of Montana in the fall of 1903. Duncan spoke out in defense of the tribes' right to hunt off the reservation:

"It is a bad law," said he. "The Indians have a right under their treaty to hunt wherever they want to. Some of them need to hunt. I don't care about it. In 25 years I haven't killed more than one deer. That was once when I had lived on beans and bacon for three weeks, and I wanted some fresh meat. But I do want to carry a gun when I travel in the mountains. A man needs one for protection. This law is passed to prevent game from being destroyed, they say. I tell you, it isn't the Indians who spoil the game as much as it is these hunters and trappers — white men — that spend so much time in the mountains. I have seen trappers slaughter moose and deer and elk and not touch the carcass at all, except to leave it for bait for their bear traps. That is what spoils the game."[49]

There is no evidence Duncan played any role in the Alex Bigknife case, but this case showed the determination of the traditional chiefs to protect tribal rights and their willingness to use the white legal system to this end. In September 1903, Deputy Game Warden Arthur Higgins confiscated Alex Bigknife's guns when Bigknife was in Missoula shopping for his fall hunt. According to the newspaper report, Bigknife "was much surprised and put out." Bigknife returned to the reservation.[50] Bigknife and the traditional tribal chiefs were outraged and immediately hired a Missoula lawyer, Harry H. Parsons, to sue the game warden over the confiscation.[51] About the same time Higgins seized a pistol carried by Austa, a tribal policeman pursuing an Indian outlaw off the reservation.[52] The game warden returned the pistol to the policeman a few days later.[53]

On September 8, 1903, W. F. Scott, the State Game & Fish Warden, wrote Smead a contrite letter saying he was "sorry that Deputy Higgins has inconvenienced you or your Indians in any way." Scott instructed Higgins to attempt to return the weapons to Bigknife and Austa. Bigknife refused to accept the return, because he was "angry." Despite the new state law, Scott promised: "I shall get out instructions in a few days to my deputies covering this matter; stating that when Indians have permits from their agent to leave their reservation to hunt during the open season that they are not to be molested." Scott added, "I am sorry that this unfortunate instance has been taken and hope that no more of a like nature shall occur."[54]

Bigknife and the chiefs, however, were in no mood to drop their legal suit over the confiscation. The chiefs raised a purse of $1,000 to pay the legal expenses for the suit. Bigknife asked for $100 damages and that the act be declared unconstitutional and null and void.[55] On September 27, 1903, attorney Parsons traveled to the reservation to confer with the chiefs on legal strategy for the case.[56] Montana state officials attempted to get the case dismissed on a technicality to avoid having the court rule on the constitutionality of the law. First they argued that Bigknife could not sue in his own name because he was a ward of the government.[57] After the tribal complaint was amended to accommodate this problem, the case came before the court in November 1903. Montana Attorney General James Donovan came to Missoula to personally argue the case. He said the case should be dismissed because the game warden was originally sued as a deputy game warden and in the amended complaint he was sued as an individual.[58] In December 1903 the state took their arguments over the form of the complaint to the Montana Supreme Court.[59] The state was successful in keeping the suit tied up in court, but they did stop enforcing the law. The law remained on the books and was not repealed until 1953.[60]

Duncan complained to Agent Smead on September 16, 1903, that Eli Paulin had taken hay that Vetal Revais had sold to Duncan. Smead held a hearing at the agency, but Paulin failed to show up or explain his actions. Duncan presented witnesses and evidence to support his argument that the hay rightfully belonged to him. Smead decided that the evidence justified Duncan's claim and ordered Paulin to turn the hay in question over to Duncan.[61] In another transaction, in 1903 Duncan and Tom McDonald either sold or traded their hay and pasture to George Beckwith who operated the Missoula Mercantile store in St. Ignatius. C. H. McLeod, who ran the Missoula Mercantile business enterprises, instructed Beckwith to see if he could sell the hay to Michel Pablo.[62] That fall Duncan spent a week in October 1903 hunting off the reservation, but complained that he found very little game.[63]

That same month, Duncan received a visit from John McDonald, his cousin. This was a different John McDonald than the one who visited Duncan in June 1889. This John McDonald was a 32 year veteran in the Hudson's Bay Company and had been Chief Factor at Norway House in Manitoba.[64]

Duncan was upset about whiskey entering the reservation through the Jocko or Dixon railroad station in November 1903. He wrote Agent Smead that Pete Caye was still drunk at five in the afternoon on November 8, 1903. Duncan accused Caye of being one of the leaders of the bootleggers. Smead had Caye arrested and put in the agency jail. Caye denied the charges, and Smead requested Duncan come to the agency at once as a witness against Caye.[65]

Nez Perce Chief Joseph was Duncan's house guest for about a week in late 1903. Joseph stopped at Ravalli while waiting for an interpreter who was to accompany him to Washington, D.C. Duncan related they

had many long talks together about the troubles that over-
took the Nez Perces, but he seemed sad and taciturn.

He brooded over the unjust treatment of his
people.

He told me he would die satisfied, if the government would only permit him to go back to his old
hunting grounds even though he had to live on roots.

Joseph left Ravalli for Washington, D.C., and New York City
to plead his case, but he was still not allowed to return to
Idaho. He died in 1904 in exile and was buried at Nespelem,
Washington.[66]

On December 19, 1903, newly elected Montana Congressman Joseph M. Dixon sent copies of his Flathead Reservation
allotment bill to Duncan, Allen Sloan, Angus P. McDonald,
Michael Pablo, and Joseph Allard for comments. Dixon made
a point of emphasizing that the recent Lone Wolf decision of
the U.S. Supreme Court meant congress no longer needed tribal
approval to change treaties. Only Duncan, Pablo, and Allard
replied. Pablo begged off because he was busy with his cattle.
Allard replied that allotment "could not take effect any too soon
to suit me....I have spoken to quiet [sic] a number of the leading
members of the tribes and all they could say is that we don't want
to open our reserve."[67]

Duncan's response to Dixon's bill was resigned: "I have no
suggestions to make only that I am dissatisfied and disgusted
and have to take my medicine." Duncan repeated his frequent
criticism that reservations were designed to fleece the Indians and
make agents rich. He wanted agents to be selected by general
councils of tribal members. Regarding the Lone Wolf decision of
the U.S. Supreme Court, Duncan pointed out previous decisions
had upheld tribal rights and over time changes in the court could
reverse the decision.[68]

Despite the lack of tribal approval, Dixon was able to get
his Flathead allotment bill through congress and it became law
on April 23, 1904. Allotment was an economic and social disas-
ter for the Flathead Reservation tribes. Since it was done without

consent, the tribal communities were wrenched apart by futile attempts to oppose the policy. Allotment had two principal economic impacts on the reservation. First, it redistributed the land and reduced the large ranches that had been controlled by some mixed blood tribal members. Second, it provided for the sale of unallotted or "surplus" land under the provisions of the homestead and other laws meant to dispose of public lands. Since the homestead laws had been designed to transfer public land to private ownership as cheaply as possible, the "surplus" lands were sold to white homesteaders for only a fraction of their value.[69]

After the tribes were forced to dispose of their principal asset — land — at less than its market value, their future income declined. By the start of the twentieth century, the tribes had grown their livestock and farming to fill the hole left by the declining hunting and gathering resources. In the early 1900s, the tribes were self-supporting and reasonably well-to-do. In 1903, Arthur M. Tinker, a United States Indian Inspector, reported that, "From all indications they appear to be in good financial condition. No supplies or rations are issued except to a few aged and infirm....A large majority of them are good farmers for Indians and cultivate quite good sized farms, which usually produce good crops."[70] Research by economist Ronald Trosper suggested that in 1900 tribal members were about as well off economically as the average rural white community in Montana, and their subsequent poverty was largely the result of land loss through the allotment policy.[71] In the twentieth century, the land loss, drought, and national economic depression in the 1920s and 1930s reduced many tribal members to poverty.

By August 1904, Duncan was despairing for the livestock business on the reservation. A general drought in the country was flooding the cattle markets and depressing prices. On the reservation, the drought had severely curtailed the hay crop, limiting the ability of ranchers to feed their herds over the coming winter. In addition, the resident grazing tax on the reservation cost the cattle owners one dollar a head per year. Duncan planed to "sell off as many of his cattle as there is a good market for."[72]

On a personal note, Duncan's son, Peter, was hospitalized in Missoula in September 1904 for typhoid pneumonia. On September 7, Father John Post went to Ravalli on a sick call to the boy and Dr. W. Buchanan Parsons was summoned from Missoula by telegraph. The next day Peter was moved to the Parsons hospital in Missoula.[73] By September 14, 1904, Peter was reported to be "considerably better." Duncan stayed in Missoula to look after him.[74] Peter was well enough by September 16 to be seen on the streets of Missoula and left for home in Ravalli on September 22, 1904.[75]

Sometime during the autumn of 1904, probably September, Duncan moved from Ravalli or Selish to Dixon.[76] While in Missoula on a September 1904 visit, Duncan told of an Indian fisherman who recently caught a 40 inch char at the mouth of the Jocko River. It was the largest char caught in the region and was estimated to weigh over eighteen pounds.[77]

Duncan and the Dupuis brothers combined on October 3, 1904, to ship two train loads of cattle to the Chicago market. Peter went to Livingston, presumably to see to feeding the cattle while they were enroute.[78] A month later, Duncan shipped a railroad car of reservation horses to central Wisconsin. Duncan accompanied the train to sell the horses.[79] In December 1904, C. H. McLeod was concerned about the large amount owed to the Beckwith store by Duncan and other reservation residents.[80]

Duncan's younger brother, Donald McDonald, and Donald's daughter from Marcus, Washington, were house guests of Duncan at Dixon in March 1905.[81] A month later, Duncan sold some property adjacent to Dixon to Eli Paulin for an undisclosed sum.[82]

Duncan employed Peter Magpie in 1905 to take care of his cattle, but some disagreements arose. Magpie complained to Agent Samuel Bellew in March 1905 that Duncan had assaulted him. Bellew called for both Duncan and Magpie to come to the Agency to straighten the matter out. The correspondence did not explain what the fracas was about. Whatever happened to the assault charge, on July 18, 1905, Magpie complained to Bellew

Duncan McDonald and his son, Peter Colville.
Source: Toole Archives, Mansfield Library, University of Montana, Missoula,
Montana Photographs by Subject MS 562, folder 13/3.

that Duncan was five months behind on paying Magpie's salary for taking care of Duncan's cattle.[83]

While Duncan and Magpie were having their disputes in July 1905, *The Anaconda Standard* newspaper carried a series of articles about Tzi Kal Tzae, the Nez Perce son of William Clark of the Lewis and Clark Expedition, and Mary, Clark's granddaughter. Tzi Kal Tzae lived in western Montana but was caught up in the Nez Perce War and taken prisoner after the Battle of the Bear Paw. In 1905, Mary lived on the Flathead Reservation with her husband. Duncan was one of the authorities quoted in the articles to verify the relationships.[84]

Another tragedy struck Duncan and Louise on July 28, 1905, when Peter Colville, Duncan and Louise's only remaining child, died of rheumatism of the heart at 23 years of age. Father Louis Taelman had visited Peter the day before. Dr. Parsons of Missoula was called and had Peter moved to his hospital in Missoula. Peter was accompanied to the hospital by his parents, but he died a few hours after his arrival.[85] His funeral was at St. Ignatius Mission on July 31, 1905. According to Father D'Aste it was "a very large burial."[86] On August 12, 1905, Duncan and his wife held "a big dinner" in memory of Peter at their place in Dixon.[87]

Some time earlier in 1905, Peter had attempted to purchase whiskey at a saloon in Missoula. Edward Hockey, the bartender at the saloon was charged with selling liquor to an Indian, but he produced several witnesses who swore he refused to serve Peter. Charges against Hockey were dropped.[88]

A friend of Duncan's presented him with a pair of wooden shoes in January 1906. Duncan took them home to add to his collection of curios.[89] During a cold spell in March 1906, Duncan temporarily moved to Missoula to enjoy the steam heated buildings. While in Missoula he visited *The Anaconda Standard* office to regale the reporter with stories about the reservation. When a granddaughter of Chief Arlee, Mary Sooa-sah, passed the office, Duncan called her in and she posed with Duncan for

a photograph. Duncan related the story of Chief Arlee's life start-
ing with his first exploits as a warrior.[90]

A month later Duncan visited Missoula and reported there
was dissatisfaction over the allotments made to tribal members
and cattle losses on the reservation during the 1905-1906 winter had been extensive.[91] In August 1906, Duncan wrote a letter
to *The Missoulian* newspaper to provide background information on John McLean who had recently been sentenced to prison
in Washington State. McLean's father had been a Hudson's Bay
Company trader in British Columbia. Two of his older brothers
had been hung for killing a sheriff. For a short time, McLean had
worked for Alex Morregeau on the Flathead Reservation. Some
tribal members suspected McLean of stealing $22,000 from
Duncan's brother-in-law Michel in November 1902.[92] In February 1907, Michel was seriously ill at Camas on the reservation.
Duncan's wife, Louise, paid him a visit.[93]

In early December 1906, Duncan made a trip to St. Regis.
Shortly afterwards, on December 26, 1906, he returned to Missoula from a trip to Iron Mountain or Superior.[94] C. A. Stillinger
sued Duncan in early 1907 for an overdue account dating back
to 1903.[95] About the same time, Duncan was a patient in the
Parsons & Smith hospital in Missoula in January 1907. He had
run a spike through his foot and needed a cane to get around.[96]
A correspondent for *The Kalispell Bee* newspaper noted in June
1907 that Duncan's big two story house in Ravalli was being operated as a hotel by John Weightman.[97]

The 1907 Fourth of July Powwow at Arlee had a special
visitor: Secretary of the Interior James R. Garfield, the son of
Congressman and President James A. Garfield, who negotiated
with Chief Charlo in the Bitterroot Valley in 1872. Garfield,
Senator Joseph M. Dixon, and a crowd of some 500 white people took the train from Missoula to the Jocko Valley. The train
was met by several hundred mounted warriors dressed in their
Indian outfits. Carriages and wagons driven by other tribal members conveyed the visitors to the dance pavilion. Duncan was

one of the mounted warriors and was introduced to Secretary Garfield.[98]

Years later, Duncan recounted how he had lobbied Garfield to permit traditional Indian dances on the reservation:

"Yes, those were some dances we had in those days," he said. "Someone had informed the government that the dances should not be permitted and they were prohibited by law, until Secretary of the Interior Garfield visited the reservation some years ago. I believe he was accompanied by Senator Dixon.

"I was dressed in my warrior costume, eagle feathers and all, and he approached me and asked me about the Indian dances — a dance was in progress at the time for his benefit.

"'What about these dances?'" asked Garfield. 'What means this paint and feathers?'

"I looked at him for a moment, then I said. The red woman paints her skin red. Your white woman paints her skin white. Is there any harm in that?

"Your young man goes to a dance. He goes first to the barber shop and gets shaved and powdered. Then he borrows a white shirt and a diamond ring, and a dress suit and goes to the dance. When he puts his arm around a beautiful, attractive young lady, do you think he is thinking about killing anybody then?"

"With a sweep of my hand toward the dancing Indians, I said:

"Look at them. Look at their faces. Do they look like they want to kill? (And every darned Indian was a hoeing it down like the devil)," chuckled Duncan.

"Garfield took in the situation and understood what I was trying to convey to him, and from that time on we were not molested with our Indian dances."[99]

The prohibition against traditional Indian dances on the Flathead Reservation had actually been relaxed almost a decade earlier, but presumably Duncan pointed out to Garfield in 1907 that they were not dangerous or evil.

Despite the continued political controversy in Montana over tribal hunting rights, Duncan came to Plains in August 1907, to purchase a state hunting license.[100]

Sometime in the summer or fall of 1907, Duncan accompanied University of Montana Professor Morton J. Elrod on a tour of the reservation to select a location for the proposed National Bison Range. The recent sale of Michel Pablo's herd of buffalo to the Canadian government had finally prodded the Americans into action. The American Bison Society commissioned Elrod to do the survey, and Senator Dixon supported legislation to purchase the land from the tribes.

Duncan and Elrod recommended the Ravalli hills and meadows just above Duncan's old hotel at Ravalli. The plan was for the government to purchase the land for the range and the American Bison Society would raise the funds to purchase the animals. Duncan assured Elrod that, if the range could be established, the tribal members would be pleased:

[Elrod:] "If we can get the range, the animals will be put on it," I stated.

[Duncan:] "Do you think so?"

[Elrod:] "I am sure of it."

[Duncan:] "Professor Elrod, I hope they will do it. We all hope so. The Indians are very sorry to see the Buffalo go. They all love them. They all think the Government should keep them. They don't want to kill them. They love to see them roam over the hills and plains. Every Indian will be glad if the Government can and will save them, and keep them where they can be seen. And if there is anything in this world I can do to help, I want to do it."[101]

On May 8, 1908, one of the St. Ignatius Mission priests made a sick call on Duncan's wife, Louise. No further information was found explaining her condition.[102] A month later, on June 1, 1908, Duncan sold 35 tons of hay to John Weightman's

Stable and Stage at Ravalli for $9 a ton. Duncan took the proceeds in cash.[103]

The allotment that Duncan received overlapped the Northern Pacific Railroad station at Ravalli. On July 21, 1908, the Commissioner of Indian Affairs insisted that Duncan be compensated with lieu or replacement lands to make up the difference. On August 14, 1908, and December 1, 1908, the Commissioner of Indian Affairs repeated the instructions to either give Duncan another allotment somewhere else on the reservation or allow him to select 15 acres of lieu land to make up the difference.[104] Apparently the mistake was not corrected, because, in 1910, when Duncan received his patent for his allotment, it only covered 133.71 acres.[105]

In October 1908, Duncan hired V. S. Kutchin, a Missoula lawyer, to defend him against a suit over a promissory note he had given in payment for an insurance policy. Duncan had paid the first installment of the premium and then declined to make further payments, causing the policy to lapse. The insurance company still wanted their money despite the lapse of the coverage. Duncan argued that since he was a government ward any note or contract he signed was not valid without government approval. No record has been found about how the suit turned out.[106]

Duncan visited Missoula again just before Christmas 1908. He said most tribal members were anxious to get the reservation opening over with, even many of those who had opposed the opening. The exceptions were Sam Resurrection and a few others who still believed the opening could be stopped: "somebody is deceiving them and getting their good money under false pretenses and the opening will put a stop to this." Duncan also noted the Pablo buffalo on the reserve needed to be shipped to Canada so they would not cause damage or injury to the new settlers.[107] One newspaper article soon after said Duncan was a patient at the Parsons & Smith hospital in Missoula on December 23, 1908. The source did not identify his health problem.[108]

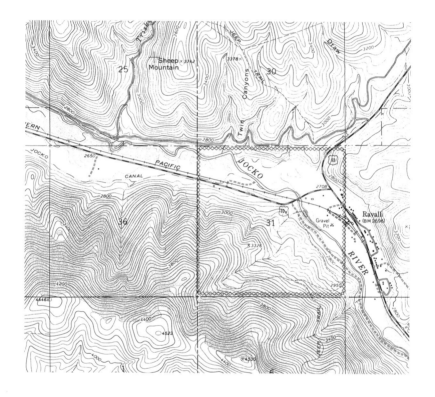

Duncan's allotment, Ravalli, Montana.
133.71 of the 160 acres in section 31, Township 18 North,
Range 20 West.
Source: Base map, "Ravalli Quadrangle, Montana," .5 minute series
(Topographical), United States Geographical Survey, Washington, D.C.,
1964.

Chapter 8

Chairman of the
Flathead Business Committee
1909-1916

Between 1909 and 1916, Duncan emerged as an officially recognized tribal leader on the Flathead Reservation. He was elected chairman of the Flathead Business Committee, which the federal government accepted as the governing body of the tribe. Duncan made trips to the Indian Office in Washington, D.C., to express tribal concerns to the government. He was also frequently interviewed by various newspaper reporters about tribal customs and viewpoints. He had the chance to keep alive tribal claims against the government for surveying errors in the southwest corner and northern boundaries of the reservation. Along the way he ignited a lively controversy over whether white homesteaders were entitled to buy tribal land for less than its real value. Protecting tribal interests in the 1910s was not easy, but he spoke up for what he thought was right.

In November 1908 a new younger man, Fred C. Morgan, was appointed Flathead Indian Agent. Samuel Bellew, the agent from 1904 to 1908, was a retired military man whose relaxed administration had stirred less conflict on the reservation than W. H. Smead. The new agent approached his job with a reformist zeal and determination to "improve" the morals of the Indians. Morgan was particularly concerned about couples who were living together without being legally married. He was supported in his efforts to stamp out unmarried cohabitation by Father Louis Taelman, S.J., a young priest at St. Ignatius Mission. Morgan also tried to shut down the bootleg alcohol trade. According to

Fred Morgan, Flathead Agent/Superintendent, 1908-1917.
Source: *The Daily Missoulian*, Dec. 12, 1915, ed. sec., p. 1, c. 1-7.
Thanks to Frank Tyro, SKC Media.

Thomas Downs, a Special U.S. Indian Agent, on January 30,
1909:

> Mr. Morgan is a young man full of ambition, pluck
> and energy. When he took charge of the reservation,
> two months ago, things were in a deplorable condition;
> drunkenness and immorality being openly practiced by
> the Indians without any apparent effort at control by the
> proper authorities. Mr. Morgan at once started a refor-
> mation movement, using all the force at his command
> to arrest and punish the offenders. Owing to his efforts
> order and discipline are rapidly taking place.

Duncan became a close ally of Morgan and worked with Morgan
and his successors for over fifteen years.[1]

Duncan's work with Morgan's administration of the Flathead Agency began in the spring 1909 election of a Flathead
Business Committee. On February 17, 1909, Morgan called a
general council of tribal members to meet at St. Ignatius on March
10, 1909. Any tribal member could attend a general council and
vote on tribal business matters under consideration. The March
10, 1909, council was called to elect a Business Committee to
represent the different tribes on the reservation. The Business
Committee would conduct tribal business "at the call" of the
Flathead Superintendent. (After the reservation was opened the
agent, a political appointee, was replaced by a Superintendent,
who was a civil service government employee.) No detailed account of the March 10 council has been found, but nine men
were elected for two year terms on the new Business Committee.
The members included Duncan, Charles Allard, Angus P. Mc-
Donald, and Chief Martin Charlo.[2]

Superintendent Morgan and his successors were quite happy with the results of the Business Committee election. A 1920
inspection report on Flathead concluded: "The personnel of this
Business Committee is perhaps the best that could be selected
on the reservation and I would be glad to see them continued in
office. Several of the members are men of large business affairs
and are not in any sense agitators and demigogues." In 1921,

Buffalo at Ravalli waiting for rail shipment north.
Source: Toole Archives, Mansfield Library, University of Montana, Missoula,
photograph 77-0283.

Flathead Superintendent Charles Coe advised against holding an election for a new Business Committee because it might result in a committee controlled by people who "do not want to co-operate with the local officials or with the [Indian] Department."[3] As a result, the 1909 Business Committee continued in office for more than a decade and a half. When members died or resigned, the rest of the committee selected new members as replacements. The lack of regular elections to the Business Committee and its willingness to work with the Flathead Indian Agency led to a divisive power struggle on the reservation after 1916. Duncan served as chairman of the Business Committee during the 1910s and 1920s. Charles Allard was secretary.

On a personal note, on February 26, 1909, Duncan visited Missoula for dental treatment. He had been unable to sleep for several nights.[4]

The biggest event on the reservation during the summer of 1909 was the roundup of the Pablo buffalo herd for shipment to Canada. Michel Pablo was forced to sell his herd because of the impending opening of the reservation to white homesteaders and the end of the open range. He sold the buffalo to the Canadian government and had to round them up for rail shipment north to their new home. The roundup was a colorful show and attracted national attention. Journalists and spectators from Canada and across the United States assembled to witness the show. Extensive corrals were erected near Ravalli to collect the buffalo and herd them into railroad cars.[5] Duncan was one of the principle local characters at the event.

One of the journalists attending the roundup was M. O. Hammond, a photographer for the Toronto *Globe* newspaper. Hammond spent about three weeks at Ravalli between May 19, 1909, and June 3, 1909, and recorded his experiences in his diary. He observed the roundup and took photographs. Getting the wild buffalo into the corrals proved an exciting challenge for the cowboys. The artist Charley Russell was one of the riders trying to herd the animals. Hammond described Russell as "a star as a swearer" and his language was "a succession of oaths and petty exclamations."

Duncan worked as a cowboy in the buffalo roundup and told stories at camp in the evenings:

> Duncan Macdonald came along & regaled us with Indian stories & reminiscences of his own for upwards of two hours. It was most interesting we had quite a discussion over the relative standards of morality of the white & red men. He is well read & bright, though somewhat stolid, as befits men with a red man's blood.

A few days later, "We had beefsteak & onions. After that a lot of Indian lore from Duncan Macdonald."[6]

The roundup continued after Hammond left. About June 27, 1909, a four year old cow fought so hard while being loaded into a railroad cattle car, that she broke her neck. The carcass was removed to the backyard of the Ravalli hotel where Duncan tried to get some of the young Indian men to skin the animal, but "They couldn't do it; they didn't know how. They made an excuse that they didn't like buffalo meat. The fact was, they didn't know whether they did or not." Duncan finally found three old Indian women who soon had the animal skinned and ready for cooking. Buffalo steak was served to all for Sunday dinner.[7]

Five months later Duncan returned to Missoula in November 1909 to observe the auction of reservation town lots. Most of the lots sold for considerably more than their appraised value. Duncan was a bidder and bought at least one lot, possibly in Dixon where he then lived.[8]

At the end of January 1910, Duncan made a trip to Missoula and was interviewed by several newspapermen. Some "malcontents" on the reservation had complained that the money from the sale of the land for the new bison range had been diverted from the "use of the Indians." Duncan assured the reporter that the "money, paid by the government for the bison reserve, goes into the general tribal fund and will be handled exactly as the rest of that fund." Either Duncan was being disingenuous or his meaning was distorted by the reporter. The 1908 law estab-

Duncan McDonald skinning buffalo killed while loading
at Ravalli, Montana.
Source: *The Daily Missoulian*, July 4, 1909, pt. 2, p. 4, c. 5-7.
Thanks to Frank Tyro, SKC Media.

lishing the Flathead Irrigation Project clearly stated that money
from land and timber sales and grazing charges would be used
to pay for the construction of the irrigation project. Only after
the construction costs were paid would any remaining money be
expended by the government for the benefit of the tribe or per
capita payments.[9]

During the same visit to Missoula, Duncan endorsed a proposal to allow tribal members to sell their allotments down to
twenty acres each. Duncan emphasized that the money must be
held in trust so that improvident Indians would not waste the
money.[10] Another newspaperman interpreted Duncan's remarks
differently. According to this reporter, Duncan complained that
government coddling was preventing the ambitious tribal members from accomplishing their potential:

"There is no inducement held out to the Indian of
today," he continued. "He is expected to live much in the
same any as any other public charge and to be coddled
and taken care of like a child and like any other being not
thrown into the world to have the rough edges knocked
off and learn the value of a dollar, he is rapidly becoming
indolent and useless. He is not naturally lazier than his
white brother. In every country and among all human
beings we find two classes of men — the shiftless and the
ambitious. Like all other races the Indian has these two
classes. Some of our people will always be indolent and
accomplish nothing, even as there are such characters
among the white race. Others would be ambitious and
accomplish great things if they only had the chance.[11]

Duncan's views might have favored having the government use
the trust status to protect those Indians who would not manage
their money well while freeing the more capable tribal members
from supervision.

A few months later, on March 10, 1910, Duncan was one
of the first tribal members to receive his patent in fee for his
allotment. His patent was in the second batch to be approved
by the Commissioner of Indian Affairs. Due to a conflict with

the Northern Pacific Railway station land at Ravalli, he ended up with only 133.71 acres.[12] At the same time he sold his cattle holdings on the reservation. The opening of the reservation to white homesteaders ended the open range for tribal cattlemen. The sale price for the cattle was not made public.[13]

On March 30, 1910, Duncan was in Missoula just after Halley's comet passed near the earth. He reported that the view of the comet was very impressive from Ravalli. Many tribal members were terrified at the sight.[14] The next month, according to an April 17, 1910, report in *The Daily Missoulian*, Duncan was appointed a tribal judge by Superintendent Morgan in place of Lewison. This was apparently in addition to his role as chairman of the Flathead Business Committee.[15]

A general council of about 200 tribal members was held at St. Ignatius Mission on May 9, 1910, to select members of a delegation to Washington, D.C. Superintendent Morgan reported that most of those at the meeting were full bloods, as many of the mixed bloods were occupied with plowing and planting crops and could not attend. However, many of the old full bloods present refused to vote, because they objected to allowing mixed bloods to vote for the delegation members. According to the public notice, the delegation was to confer "with the Indian Office on matters of general interest to the tribes." At the general council, Martin Charlo and Duncan were elected to represent the Flathead tribe; Charles Allard and Thomas Antiste were selected as Kootenai representatives; and Charlie Michel and Michel Pablo were to represent the Pend d'Oreille tribe. Mose Auld was voted in as interpreter for the delegation. Sam Resurrection was not chosen. He received only 8 votes out of 217 for Flathead representative.[16] The selection of Duncan and Michel Pablo as delegates was lauded in *The Daily Missoulian*.[17] The diarist at St. Ignatius Mission also approved: "Fortunately they had sense enough to select fairly good delegates."[18] William Irvine replaced Michel Pablo on the delegation due to the illness of Pablo's wife.[19]

The delegation left by train on June 7, 1910. Duncan noted, "There are some pleasant things about the trip but it is very

tiresome and the ride is so long and hot at this time of year that
I do not anticipate much pleasure." Duncan stated his goal for
the trip:

> "I am going to Washington with the firm intention of
> doing all I can for the Indians. I know Uncle Sam is poor,
> but the Indian is a whole lot poorer, and I will try, to the
> best of my ability, to wrest the last possible nickel from
> the reluctant grasp of the government. I regret greatly
> that Sam Ressurection [sic] cannot accompany us on this
> trip; we shall miss him very much."[20]

Sam Resurrection and some of the full blood tribal members were unhappy about the composition of the delegation. On
June 13, 1910, Resurrection wrote a letter to the Commissioner
of Indian Affairs. The letter was signed by Martin Charlo, who
was on the delegation, and Resurrection, who was not. Along
with complaints about the delegation and general complaints
about how the Flathead Reservation tribes had been treated by
the government, Resurrection charged that Duncan "wants to
open up our Reservation." A few days later, Resurrection wrote
President William Taft a ten page treatise on the mistreatment
of the Flathead Reservation Indians. Resurrection complained
that Duncan had been selected as a delegate by Superintendent
Morgan and Duncan was Scotch/Canadian and Nez Perce rather
than Flathead. The Commissioner of Indian Affairs defended the
delegate selection.[21]

In Washington, D.C., other topics probably came up in the
meetings, but one that was associated with Duncan was the complaint about the survey of the southwest corner of the reservation
boundary. Duncan had previously raised the matter as early as
the 1890s. Duncan brought the boundary up with the Indian
Office and with Senator Joseph M. Dixon. On June 17, 1910,
Dixon wrote the Commissioner of Indian Affairs asking for an
investigation into the matter. The Commissioner of Indian Affairs checked the Indian Office files and made an information
request to the the General Land Office, but after seven months of
correspondence seemed to have dropped the matter.[22]

In addition to meetings at the Indian Office, Senator Dixon made arrangements for the delegation to visit Mt. Vernon, Arlington National Cemetery, the Washington monument, the U.S. Navy Yard, and the Capitol. According to *The Daily Missoulian*, "Duncan McDonald was, for the most part, spokesman for the delegation and his thorough conversance with reservation people and affairs made the visit very different in its impression from that of the ordinary delegation. It was a helpful trip."[23]

A few days after Duncan was elected as a delegate to Washington, D.C., on May 11, 1910, Duncan went to Missoula to observe the Missoula Land Office filings for Flathead Reservation lands. Duncan commented on the quality of the land at the various locations being considered by the white homesteaders.[24]

Duncan's other interest in May, before he left for Washington, D.C., was prospecting on the reservation. White prospectors were combing the hills around Ravalli, looking for minerals. Duncan brought some specimens into Missoula to be assayed.[25] According to one account, Duncan had located a ledge of rich copper ore just west of Ravalli on his allotment.[26] Apparently Duncan joined with Clarence Rae, a white man, to file on a water power site near Dixon for use in developing a mine.[27] In December 1910, Duncan leased the copper prospect to a group of Coeur d'Alene mining men. The report claimed Duncan had discovered the copper ledge in the middle 1860s but had to wait until the reservation was allotted before he could develop it. The agreement provided for monthly payments to support Duncan and his wife for the rest of their lives.[28]

In September 1910, Duncan made another trip to Missoula to view the Flathead land selection at the Missoula Land Office. He also brought samples of his apple crop to be exhibited at an apple show.[29] A month later, Duncan shipped a four and half pound potato from his farm to the editor of *The Daily Missoulian*.[30] In December 1910, Duncan came to Missoula to attend court. No mention was made of the case in which he took part.[31]

In February 1911, Duncan provided background information on the victims of a recent fire. A Bitterroot Salish woman named Terese and Andy Triplett, a Black man, died in a house fire south of Missoula in late February 1911. Terese's common law husband, Paul Goin, a Canadian Cree, threw gasoline in a stove. According to Duncan, Terese had deserted her husband, Gerome, at the agency, and she was a sister of Pierre Paul who was hanged in 1890 for murdering a white men.[32]

Shortly after, in March 1911, Duncan swore out a warrant for the arrest of Lester Martin who broke into a house Duncan owned at Ravalli. Martin was captured by a Deputy Sheriff after a long chase and taken to the Missoula jail.[33]

Duncan also came to Missoula to take part in one of the biggest events in the town's history: the visit of ex-President Theodore Roosevelt on April 11, 1911. Duncan was part of a crowd of thousands of people who greeted Roosevelt. The city fathers, the Missoula band, Fort Missoula soldiers, and other dignitaries assembled to receive him.[34]

In Duncan's family life in May 1911, Duncan's wife, Louise, gave a memorial feast in memory of her mother and aunt who had passed away the previous winter. According to *The Ronan Pioneer*, it was largely attended by people from across the reservation.[35] That same year the Fourth of July celebration and St. Ignatius Indian dance also included baseball games and races in 1911. Duncan wore his Indian outfit and was prominent participant.[36]

Since Duncan had received his fee patent for his allotment in 1910, he was a United States citizen. In November 1911, he came down to the Missoula County Courthouse to register to vote. While at the courthouse he expressed his disgust with the paintings of Indians on the walls. They had been done by an artist from Iowa. The paintings had Indians riding horses with bridles and oxen with strange wooden legs.[37] In 1912, the Missoula Women's Club made an arrangement with Edgar S. Paxson to replace the paintings Duncan objected to with more accurate work by the Missoula artist.[38]

On November 1911, Arthur L. Stone published an installment of a series he called "Following Old Trails." This installment
included much interview material from Duncan. Duncan first
got sidetracked into complaints about young Indians who could
not skin a buffalo and stories about the establishment of Fort
Connah in the Mission Valley. Then Duncan related how the
Salish tribes got yellow paint from Wolf Creek in the Judith Basin; vermillion paint from the East Helena–Townsend area; green
paint from Lincoln Gulch; and black paint from Canada.[39]

As soon as the Flathead Reservation was opened to white
homesteaders, the state of Montana moved aggressively to im-
pose state jurisdiction. A particular flash point was their attempt
to enforce state fish and game laws. After the bulk of the reservation buffalo had been rounded up and shipped to Canada, a
small number of "outlaw" buffalo remained who could not be
captured. Michel Pablo allowed hunters who paid him a fee to
kill these buffalo. In 1910 the Montana Attorney General ruled
that the outlaw bison were wild animals under state control and
not Pablo's personal property. Pablo argued that the outlaw bison
were a public health hazard; they had already attacked several
white homesteaders. Pablo allowed the paid hunts to lapse, but
in 1911 a white sportsman, Lincoln Ellsworth, paid Pablo $225
to hunt and kill a buffalo bull in the northwest portion of the
reservation. Ellsworth killed the buffalo and wrote a description
of "The Last Wild Buffalo Hunt." The American Bison Society was outraged and on February 7, 1912, W. J. Hornaday, the
President of the society, wrote to Duncan for information about
the hunts. Unfortunately Duncan's reply was not found.[40]

The St. Ignatius Commercial Club hosted a meeting of
representatives of reservation and surrounding communities in
March 1912. The meeting was called to request policy changes
that would help the white homesteaders on the reservation. Duncan and John Matt were the only tribal members who attended,
and Duncan conspicuously wore moccasins with his white man's
clothes. Three topics were discussed: (1) getting assignable titles
for homesteads so the owners could mortgage them; (2) securing

rights of ways through Indian allotments for roads; and (3) selling and leasing of lands of "aged, infirm and incompetent" Indians without their consent. The first and third resolutions were passed and sent to the Montana congressional delegation. The provision to expand reservation roads was referred to a committee for further study. According to newspaper reports, Duncan spoke twice at the meeting. He objected when someone proposed using tribal funds from land sales to pay for the construction of new roads on the reservation. Duncan argued that the money was needed to help starving Indians and to pay for schooling of tribal members: "All I ask is justice." At the conclusion of the meeting, Duncan made a speech asserting that Indians needed the right to vote: "'Give the Indian a vote.' he said, 'and it will be all right. All your troubles will be ended there.'" Indians had been corrupted by the materialism and greed of white Americans: "All we want is a fair chance."[41]

In 1912, Duncan continued his long career as a historical consultant and sage on western Montana history. In June 1912, T. C. Elliott, a Washington state historian, consulted Duncan about descendants of fur trader David Thompson on the Flathead Reservation. Duncan pointed out two grandsons of Thompson living on Crow Creek.[42]

Duncan and Superintendent Morgan toured the reservation with an agent from the Indian Office in Washington, D.C., to select a new site for the Flathead Agency in early November 1912. The old location of the agency in the Jocko Valley was not centrally located. Ronan and Post Creek were surveyed, but the town of Dixon was chosen for the new agency. No record was found specifying Duncan's role in selecting the site so close to his home.[43]

Duncan began two very eventful roles in the autumn of 1912. He was a candidate for the Montana Legislature on the Progressive Party ticket and also a tribal member representative on an appraisal committee to set prices on forest land, abandoned irrigation reservoir land, and other miscellaneous tracts that had not been appraised by the first appraisal committee before the opening of the reservation to white homesteaders in 1910.

In the fall of 1912, Duncan was caught up in the political conflict between President Howard Taft and former President Theodore Roosevelt. Roosevelt had anointed Taft as his successor in the 1908 election, but, by 1912, he felt Taft was not progressive enough. Roosevelt competed with Taft for the 1912 Republican Presidential nomination but lost. After the bitter convention battle, Roosevelt led his supporters out of the Republican Party and established a new third party, the Progressives. The Progressives nominated Roosevelt for President to oppose Taft and Woodrow Wilson, the Democratic nominee. Joseph Dixon ran Roosevelt's campaign at the Republican convention and as the Progressive candidate in the national election. Dixon was also a candidate for reelection to the United States Senate from Montana in 1912, but he was mostly occupied with running Roosevelt's campaign for President.[44]

The Missoula County Progressive Party nominated candidates for the 1912 election at a September 5, 1912, meeting in Missoula. Duncan was one of the five candidates selected to run for the Montana House of Representatives from Missoula County. He spoke at the convention and endorsed Roosevelt for President and Dixon for the U.S. Senate: "No man's done more for the people than Teddy Roosevelt. There's not a man in this state who's done more for this state than Joe Dixon."[45]

From late September through October, Duncan joined his fellow Progressive candidates in a series of rallies in various Missoula County communities. On September 24, 1912, they met with over a hundred supporters at St. Ignatius. Duncan was the first speaker at the meeting, but news reports did not quote his speech.[46] On the evening of October 26, 1912, the Progressives held a rally at the town of Dixon where every available seat was occupied. The newspaper report did not mention Duncan specifically, but presumably he was there.[47] Finally on October 29, 1912, the Progressive campaign rally at Ronan was touted as a roaring success. The St. Ignatius band played at the meeting.

According to *The Daily Missoulian*, "The crowd tonight was the largest for the present campaign. The speakers were well received. The hall where the rally was held was filled to over flowing and there were cheers, loud and long, for Theodore Roosevelt and Senator Dixon. The meeting was the best of the campaign from every standpoint." Duncan was one of the speakers at the Ronan rally.[48]

The results of the November 5, 1912, election, however, were a disappointment for Duncan and the Progressive Party. Duncan received 1238 votes for the Montana House of Representatives, but six other candidates received more votes for the five available seats. Only one of the winning candidates for Missoula County seats in the Montana House was a Progressive, J. B. Henley, who received 1294 votes. Two other elected Missoula County Representatives were Republican and two were Democrat.[49]

In 1912 and 1913, Duncan was a member of a land appraisal committee or commission which ignited a storm of protest from white homesteaders on the reservation. The commission was to appraise timber lands along the Mission Mountains that did not contain valuable timber, and land held back in 1908 for reservoir and power reserves which had since been released. They were also charged with reappraising lands which white settlers felt had been overvalued in the 1908 appraisal. Many of the timber lands and abandoned reserves had been occupied and improved by white squatters whose filings were being held in abeyance at the land office. In September 1912, the Flathead Reservation Business Committee selected Duncan to represent the tribes on the commission. The other two members were Superintendent Fred C. Morgan and J. C. Van Hook of the surveyor general's office in Helena. In May 1913, Waldo G. Brown of Ronan was appointed to the commission to replace Morgan.[50]

The commission could not complete the appraisals in 1912 and returned to the work in the spring of 1913. When the white community thought Duncan would look out for their interests, *The Ronan Pioneer* praised Duncan highly:

Being a man of upright character, he endeavors to do what he considers right by everybody. This fact sometimes brings him in conflict with the members of the tribe who accuse him of working in and with the white man, and on the other hand, he is censured as being all for the Indian by the white men. The Pioneer has known Mr. McDonald during all the time it has been published and feels that there is not a man in all this section who could or would serve his people better and at the same time do what is absolutely right as he sees it, all the time.[51]

In May 1913, the commission members were thrown out of their vehicle when it overturned in the timber east of Ronan. They were shaken up but not seriously injured. In July 1913, they were working in the vicinity of St. Ignatius.[52] Things remained calm until November 1913 when the appraisals were filed at the local land offices and the white homesteaders learned the prices set for the land.

While the appraisals were still underway, a general council of Flathead Reservation Indians was held in Ravalli on February 13, 1913. Duncan was selected as one of the interpreters at the meeting. The meeting voted unanimously to send Louie Pierre and John Charley as Flathead Reservation representatives to the laying of the cornerstone of the Wanamaker monument to American Indians at Washington, D.C. Alex Matt and Angus McDonald were chosen as interpreters. The travel expenses of all four tribal members and Superintendent Fred Morgan were to be paid for out of tribal funds. Three days later on February 16, 1913, forty three tribal members, led by Martin Charlo, put their marks on a petition complaining about the selection procedure and the use of tribal money for the delegation expenses. Apparently the Indian Office ignored the complaint.[53]

At least some of the meetings of the Flathead Reservation Business Committee must have been informal affairs. On May 10, 1913, a meeting was called at Duncan's home at Ravalli and the notice went out only to members of the committee.[54]

Later on May 16, 1913, Duncan was the only tribal member who attended a meeting of the reservation commercial clubs held in Ronan. The meeting aired the grievances of the white settlers and passed resolutions telling what the government could do to help the homesteaders. The newspaper reports did not describe the contributions Duncan made to the discussions. The resolutions were a laundry list of actions the government could take to speed up issuance of patents, sales of Indian allotments, and leasing land to white farmers. The most controversial proposal was to give the Flathead Superintendent authority to lease allotments without the consent of the Indian owners. According to *The Ronan Pioneer*: "All [the resolutions] would help in the development of the country and none would injure anybody."[55]

On May 24, 1913, Duncan and the other members of the Flathead Reservation Business Committee met at St. Ignatius and passed a series of resolutions of their own. The first resolution called for tribal members who had poor allotments to be given first chance to exchange their allotments for better land on abandoned power and reservoir reserves. The second resolutions asked that the law covering white homesteads on timber land be changed to better protect tribal timber reserves. Number three was to allow the Flathead Superintendent to lease allotments without the consent of the allottees, and that land sales be conducted at public auction rather than with sealed bids. The first part of this request paralleled the recent resolution of the white commercial clubs on the reservation. Number four was an appeal for Congress to pass legislation allowing the tribes to sue the government in the United States Court of Claims for errors in the survey of the reservation boundaries. This had been a frequent complaint of Duncan's since the 1890s. Five was to have the irrigation project recognize the water rights of tribal members who had constructed irrigation ditches before the federal irrigation project was built. Six was for Congress to appropriate a half million dollars for a tribal per capita, since, under the present law, all the money from land and timber sales was being diverted to pay for irrigation project construction.[56]

Between 1909 and 1916 tribal funds from land sales, grazing, and timber sales were used to reimburse the federal government for the construction costs of the Flathead Irrigation Project which mostly benefitted white homesteaders. This was the funding method Joseph Dixon had written into the law authorizing the irrigation project. Duncan does not seem to have publicly complained, but the sixth resolution above from the Flathead Business Committee and a passing reference in a speech Duncan gave at the University of Montana in 1915 suggested he did not favor this use of tribal money. The use of tribal funds to pay for the irrigation construction was stopped in 1916.

Oscar H. Lipps, Supervisor of Indian Schools, attended the May 24, 1913, meeting of the Flathead Business Committee and composed a long report to the Commissioner of Indian Affairs endorsing the Business Committee resolutions. He wrote that he had "assisted the Committee in formulating the Resolutions adopted." Lipps said that the first resolution to allow tribal members with poor allotments to exchange them for new allotments in abandoned power and reservoir reserves had been suggested by Duncan, the Business Committee Chairman. Indian Office memos filed with the Business Committee resolutions reiterated the fact that, as of the end of 1913, every dollar raised from the sale of tribal land and timber had been deposited in the United States Treasury to reimburse the government for construction money spent on the Flathead Irrigation Project.[57] In response to a Business Committee complaint that white men were running cattle on tribal land without paying for grazing, the Commissioner of Indian Affairs agreed to send a livestock inspector to investigate.[58] *The Ronan Pioneer* applauded the Business Committee resolutions. According to the newspaper, the Business Committee was "working in harmony" with the white community to develop the reservation economy.[59]

Sometime in early July 1913, a white man named S. K. Williams from Spokane was on the Flathead Reservation recruiting Indian people to take part in the "First National Indian Congress." The congress was to take place in Spokane in autumn

1913. Williams claimed he had met with an enthusiastic response on the Flathead. He spent "a great portion of his time" on the reservation with Duncan. When Williams wanted to photograph Duncan on a horse, Duncan insisted on first changing from a white man's saddle to an Indian saddle. According to Williams, in addition to Duncan, Mose Auld and Cecille Tellier were supporting the congress.[60]

Duncan rode a horse leading the procession at the Fourth of July celebration at Polson in 1913. *The Ronan Pioneer* described him as "fully equipped in the most beautiful headdress one ever saw."[61] In September 1913, Duncan took part in the annual meeting of the Society of Montana Pioneers held in Missoula. The meeting was partly sponsored by W. A. Clark, who was not in attendance. Clark treated the pioneers to a trip to Bonner over his streetcar line. Duncan was one of the few Indian people attending the meeting. He did complain that the society badges only went back to 1856, when he should have one dated 1849 when he was born.[62]

Hamlin Garland, the author, met Duncan on the reservation about September 15, 1913. Garland, Duncan, and the agency doctor rode by automobile to the new National Bison Range. Garland described Duncan:

....a sad old man with a wistful droop in his voice.

His scotch blood showed and so did his Indian.

At times he was all scotch. at others he was all Indian. the coming of Settlement was a sad thing to him.

He has a house just outside Ravalli, and a fruit farm. "they took away my beef" he said meaning the buffalo "and they gave me a wormy apple to eat." This referred to his orchard.

He had one son who died. He wife is Indian. His home is fairly well kept....

Duncan was so cold. His blood is thin. His heart faint....

He is alone. His world is gone....

Old Duncan McDonald, half Scotch, a sad old figure.[63]

Ronan community leaders organized an exhibit of Flathead Valley crops in Ronan for a visiting delegation of Northern Pacific Railroad officials on September 26, 1913. Unspecified contributions to the exhibit were made by Duncan and a number of other Indian and white farmers in the area.[64]

As mentioned above, in November 1913 the appraisals from the reappraisal commission Duncan was on were filed in the local land offices. In 1908 the first appraisal commission had classified the land according to categories such as grazing and first and second class agricultural land, but the prices had been set by the federal laws governing the sale of public lands. These laws did not attempt to get market value for the land, so the white homesteaders in 1910 got their land for considerably less than what it was worth. The new appraisal commission, on which Duncan served, tried to set the prices at what the land was really worth. The wails of outrage from the affected settlers were loud enough to be heard in Washington, D.C.

The plats with the new appraisals reached the Missoula and Kalispell Land Offices in the middle of November 1913. By the end of November 1913, the white homesteaders had already met and filed official protests complaining that the appraisals were unfair. The homesteaders insisted they were entitled to receive the same low prices that had been set in the 1908 appraisals.[65] *The Ronan Pioneer* newspaper opined that it had been unfair to even charge the white farmers $7 an acre for "Uncle Sam's free land." The new appraisals running from $7 an acre to $30 an acre were even more outrageous.[66] Montana's two Senators responded immediately that they would work to get the new appraisals reversed.[67]

The Commissioner of Indian Affairs wrote that the land was worth more in 1913 than it had been five years before. The Commissioner pointed out that Montana school lands had recently been sold for as much as $60 an acre: "If this is correct, it is not seen why an Indian should be expected to part with good agricultural lands for a nominal sum per acre." *The Ronan Pioneer* commented, "Who wants to pay actual value for the land and use a homestead right besides?" *The Ronan Pioneer* wanted a new approach, "A fair way would have been to have appointed [white] civilians who were unbiased and then the charge of unfairness to the homesteader and too much friendliness to the Indian could not have been made."[68]

In response to the complaints, the General Land Office suspended further entries on the reappraised lands.[69] The reappraisal commission had lowered the appraisals on some lands, however. Senator Henry Myers intervened and got the General Land Office to accept the filings of those homesteaders who were satisfied with their new appraisals.[70]

In June 1914, Senator Myers introduced a bill in Congress providing a maximum price of $7 an acre on any Flathead Reservation land sales. *The Ronan Pioneer* newspaper enthusiastically endorsed the bill.[71] In supporting the Myers bill, the newspaper emphasized that they did not want to impugn the good name of Mr. W. G. Brown, the local white Bureau of Indian Affairs employee on the reappraisal commission. The newspaper conspicuously did not defend Duncan's work on the commission. The words of praise for Duncan in May 1913 were not repeated in June 1914 after the new, higher appraisals were known.[72]

Montana's congressional delegation submitted various bills in Congress to reduce the new appraisals. In June 27, 1914, the Secretary of the Interior filed a report on one of the bills which would dictate that no appraisals over $7 an acres were allowed. The Secretary noted,

> Settlers have no doubt lost sight of the fact that the lands of the Flathead Reservation are tribal and not Government property....The Indians have strongly protested against any reductions in the appraisement under the act of 1910, supra, since lands of like character are selling from three to five times the prices fixed by the second appraisement commission.

The Secretary wrote that white settlers who had squatted on the previously unappraised lands had been given clear notice that they made improvements on unclassified land at their own risk. Their trespass did not give them any right to buy the land at less than the appraised value. The Secretary recommended that "the bill be given no further consideration."[73]

In early November 1914, Montana's entire congressional delegation arrived in Ronan and promised to seek increased appropriations for Flathead Irrigation Project construction and reduced appraisals for land sales.[74] A week later Father William Ketcham of the U.S. Board of Indian Commissioners was in Ronan to investigate.[75] Ketcham took testimony from both Indian and white witnesses. Duncan and the Flathead Business Committee complained later that when Duncan spoke before Ketcham, "the statements he [Duncan] made were not taken nor reported by the members representing the Board of Indian Commissioners, but rather the statements of all the white people or homesteaders [sic] and were made part of the record. The Committee feels this is unjust."[76] In his report to the Board of Indian Commissioners, Ketcham recommended that the whites be billed for the lower amounts from the first appraisal. The government would then pay the tribes the difference between the two appraisals.[77]

On December 8, 1914, Special Agent Fred Cook submitted an extensive report on the situation to the Commissioner of Indian Affairs. Cook complimented Duncan, "He is a progressive farmer, a hard worker, has a well improved farm, is held in high esteem by his tribe and the community at large, and I think is well posted concerning the value of lands on this reservation." Cook concluded: "It seems to me that the settlers have entirely lost sight of the fact that the lands on this reservation are tribal, and not Government property."[78]

In March 1915, the Secretary of the Interior assured Senator Myers that the Interior Department would hold off trying to collect the charges for land appraised by Duncan's appraisal commission.[79] For the next several years, Myers sponsored bills to reduce the new appraisals to less than $7 an acre. The government would pay the tribes the difference between the 1908 and 1913 appraisals. In the next Congress, he got his bill through the Senate but it was defeated in the House of Representatives in 1917.[80]

In 1914, while the reappraisal controversy was unfolding on the reservation, other events involving Duncan were recorded. In February 1914, Duncan visited Missoula and was queried about the weather. Many white people at the time seemed to think Indians had special powers as weather forecasters. Duncan gave a measured response: "Maybe there is an early spring coming and maybe there is not — nobody can tell until April."[81] Duncan's old friend Michel Pablo died in the middle of July 1914. Pablo was one of the most successful cattlemen on the reservation and was also famous for being co-owner, with Charles Allard, of the reservation buffalo herd. He was buried in St. Ignatius and his funeral was attended by a large crowd. Duncan was one of the pallbearers.[82]

Duncan's orchard was supplying apples to Dixon area residents in August 1914.[83] In fall 1914 Duncan visited the Missoula County Courthouse to see the new historical paintings by Edgar Paxson, the Missoula artist. Duncan had been critical of the earlier set of paintings at the courthouse created by an Eastern artist. Duncan's reaction to the Paxson paintings was positive: "That he [Duncan] was generally pleased with the paintings is no small compliment to the artist." Duncan did note, however, that the western Montana tribes did not usually use the travois: "These were not common on this side of the range because they were too slow. The Indians always had plenty of horses and because of danger of pursuit the women and children were always mounted on the best horses and the luggage was packed on other animals."[84]

On January 30, 1915, the Flathead Business Committee passed a series of six resolutions or requests of the Commissioner of Indian Affairs. The motions gave an insight into the thinking of the committee and the concerns on the reservation at the time.

The requests sought to protect reservation grazing as a tribal asset and looked for the continuation of the tribe as an economic player on the now open reservation. Resolutions one and five asked that cut over timber land and any other unhomesteaded lands be reserved as tribal grazing land under the control of the Business Committee. The second resolution asked the Commissioner of Indian Affairs to send an official to the reservation to interview the old Indians about problems with the survey of reservation boundaries. Resolution three asked that the islands in the Flathead River be set aside as nesting and feeding places for migratory and other birds. As mentioned above, the committee complained in resolution four that Duncan's testimony during the investigation of Father Ketcham on the reservation was not recorded or entered into the record. The final resolution dealt with the request of Emmet Gird for enrollment and allotment on the reservation.[85]

Duncan delivered a public lecture at the University of Montana in Missoula on February 22, 1915. Several articles in *The Daily Missoulian* publicizing the talk lauded Duncan's knowledge of tribal lore and call him a "Famous Indian Leader."[86] Duncan was accompanied on the podium by Arthur L. Stone, of the *Missoulian*, Edgar Paxson, the artist, and Judge Frank Woody and Major John Catlin, two old friends of Duncan.[87]

He opened the talk with some general comments on the poor record of the United States government in dealing with Indians and the value of Indian culture. Duncan then proceeded to summarize the history of the buffalo herd on the reservation. He used the story to chide Professor Morton Elrod of the University about the importance of practical knowledge over book-learning. Duncan argued:

> "Here, as smart as you are, and I am a savage and we are left here [in the mountains] alone without a dollar and without a nickle [sic] or anything, naked, with all the knowledge that you have got, why you will starve to death and I will be getting fat (laughter). Why anything

I can eat, the root of these flowers, a stem of that plant there, I can eat that."

Duncan made a point of the irony of establishing a "buffalo park" within sight of the corrals at Ravalli which had been used to ship the reservation buffalo to Canada. After Elrod and Duncan found a location for the new buffalo range, the government bought the land from the tribes and the money was used for the Flathead Irrigation Project rather than the tribes.

He continued with a sketch of his family background and comments on the origin of the name Missoula. Flathead Superintendent Fred Morgan had recruited Duncan to accompany Morgan and an official from Washington to visit the new buffalo range. They found the range looked over by a white man from Texas. Duncan lamented about the failure to hire an Indian to take care of the buffalo. Now the buffalo were penned up on the bison range much as the Indians had been penned up on the reservation. The Indian's land had been jammed into only a miserable 80 acre portion of the reservation, and the land sale money had been credited to the irrigation project rather than helping suffering Indians. Now that the Indians were in such reduced circumstances, the whites established an institution, the University of Montana, to study Indian Mythology. Duncan then related a story about Coyote attempting to bring salmon to western Montana. The transcript did not do justice to Duncan's skills as a storyteller. Duncan actually acted out his stories. When the story told of animals singing songs or dancing, Duncan would sing the song and perform the dance for the listeners.[88] In conclusion, Duncan related the story of the Nez Perce Indian in 1877 who pursued and wanted to scalp a black man. The Nez Perce thought the curly hair on a black man's scalp had medicinal value.

At the start of the talk, Duncan was greeted with "enthusiastic applause" and the transcript shows applause at the conclusion. The talk was praised in *The Daily Missoulian*:

> Duncan McDonald was all Indian last night....He was, as he declared, "just a savage"....

Then Duncan started with the narrative of some of the legends of The Coyote. These stories were charmingly told. Duncan, as has been said, was all Indian, and he told the stories with characteristic Indian gestures and with the intonation of the "real American"...

The largest audience of the winter greeted the speaker of last night and the talk was thoroughly enjoyed.[89]

Charles Allard, Jr., one of Duncan's fellow Business Committee members conveyed a series of complaints to the Commissioner of Indian Affairs through Montana Senator T. J. Walsh in March 1915. Allard complained that fee patents and land sales on the reservation were being used "too freely." Allard wanted the Business Committee to pass on all patent applications and land sales of "incompetent" Indians. The Commissioner of Indian Affairs replied that each application was considered by the Commissioner and Flathead Agency Superintendent and "It appears there are a number of very competent Indians on the Flathead Reservation." It is likely that Duncan shared Allard's concerns about the government policy of forcing fee patents on tribal members.[90]

In October 1915, Duncan was interviewed by the Kalispell newspaper, *The Interlake*. Duncan lamented that before the whites arrived the Indians were scrupulously honest. Anything that was lost was returned to the owner. Now everything must be locked up or hidden from view. When Duncan was prospecting in the Iron Mountain area near Superior, the whites even stole the lumber from an outbuilding when he left the claim for a short trip. The federal land office did not even bother to reply when he wrote them a letter, so he understood why white homesteaders were "disgusted with the treatment" they received from the land office. As a Bull Moose Progressive, he wished Joseph Dixon could become Secretary of the Interior. Duncan also complained about the loss of Indian names for landmarks in western Montana.[91]

On a personal note again, in early December 1915, Duncan spent several days in Missoula under the care of an eye specialist. He returned to Dixon on December 7, 1915.[92]

Duncan was consulted by Paul Phillips, a University of Montana history professor, in spring 1916 about who first discovered gold in Montana. Duncan wrote that a mixed blood named Francois Finley had traded gold at Fort Connah in the early 1850s. Both his father, Angus McDonald, and later John Owen decided to keep the gold discovery secret to avoid a rush of white gold miners to the area. The gold rush came in the 1860s, after James and Granville Stuart rediscovered gold at Gold Creek.[93] In October 1916, Duncan defended Finley's claims to the gold discovery in a letter to General Charles S. Warren of Butte, but in this letter Duncan identified Finley as Anthony rather than Francois. Duncan's letter was published in *The Daily Missoulian* and led to a series of letters about who should get credit for the first discovery. Frank H. Brown, the historian for the Society of Montana Pioneers, argued that since the Stuarts publicized and developed their discovery, the "honor" should go to them.[94]

During May 1916, Duncan was put on the Flathead Agency payroll as a temporary agency farmer. He served for four weeks.[95]

The Indian Appropriations Act approved May 18, 1916, in Washington, D.C., changed the financing for Flathead Irrigation Project construction. The original legislation called for the money from tribal land sales to be used to reimburse the U.S. Treasury for the construction costs. As a result, no tribal funds were available to help tribal members. In 1916, Congress directed that the tribal funds be returned to tribal accounts and the land owners — Indian and white — were made liable for the construction costs. The prorated construction costs were to be a lien on allotments.[96] Duncan and the Flathead Business Committee had made several muted complaints about the old financing method for irrigation construction on the reservation. The new financing was to become a point of contention in later years due to objections by the Flathead Tribal Council, which was formed in opposition to the Flathead Business Committee headed by Duncan.

On September 13, 1916, Duncan, his wife, and his cousin, Daniel McDonald of Middleton, Conn., visited *The Ronan Pioneer* newspaper office. They were on an outing to the Mission Mountains east of Ronan. His cousin had traveled to Montana by automobile and was exploring the country. After regaling the newspaper staff with stories and politics, the McDonald party headed off to the mountains.[97] Daniel was probably the son of the John McDonald who visited Duncan in June 1889.

Duncan paid a similar visit to *The Daily Missoulian* office in November 1916. He had just returned from attending federal court in Butte as a witness. Duncan related the story of Laurent, a mixed blood Frenchman who had lived with the Salish in the early 1830s. His name was pronounced "Lolo" by the Salish, and the name was given to Lolo Creek in the Bitterroot Valley. Lolo was a coward who abandoned his wife and child at the first sign of trouble in the 1830s, when Blackfeet Indians visited their camp in the Salmon River country. Lolo was later killed by a grizzly bear in the mountains near Fort Benton in about 1846.[98]

When the weather turned cold in December 1916, Duncan visited Missoula to keep warm. In an interview, Duncan noted that the buffalo herd on the new bison range was healthy and multiplying.[99] In another interview on the same visit to Missoula, Duncan related a story about an elderly Indian woman near Fort Colville who used a hair louse to make a weather prophecy in the 1850s.[100]

Between 1909 and 1916, Duncan found a role as a tribal leader on the Flathead Reservation. A new younger and aggressive Flathead Agent, Fred C. Morgan, was a close associate. Duncan worked to get the best deal he could for the tribe in the new era of allotment and white homesteaders. In 1917, a time of conflict entered the tribal community as the Flathead Tribal Council fought against the Business Committee and Agent Morgan's administration of reservation affairs.

Chapter 9

Tribal Business Committee vs. Tribal Council
1917-1924

Duncan's work as chairman of the Flathead Business Committee had always involved some controversy, but much more was to come in the last seven to eight years of his tenure. The Business Committee was willing to work with the Flathead Indian Agency and federal Indian policy in the 1910s. Many tribal members, however, had deep-seated objections to government policies that were designed to destroy Indian tribes and force Indian people to live as United States citizens. These policies had run roughshod over tribal economic interests to benefit white settlers on the reservation. Duncan and the Business Committee tried to work around the edges to help the Indians, but other tribal members wanted more dramatic changes.

Duncan McDonald's tenure as chairman of the Flathead Business Committee continued from 1909 to 1924. Beginning in 1916, however, the Business Committee was opposed by the newly formed Flathead Tribal Council. The Tribal Council was much more militant in opposing federal policies on the reservation than the Business Committee was. The Tribal Council was led by tribal members Marie Lemery and Max Barnaby, Blackfeet tribal member Robert Hamilton, and the Polson Catholic priest, Father William O'Maley. Some of the most bitter disagreements between the two groups were over who should represent the Flathead Reservation tribes at the Indian Office in Washington, D.C., but other battles were over use of tribal funds and tribal claims against the federal government.

The leader of the Flathead Tribal Council, and Duncan's principal antagonist, was Marie Lemery, who was 39 years old in 1916. She had been born in Oregon to Ellen Gagnon Lemery, who was enrolled as one half Flathead. The family moved to the Flathead Reservation in the early twentieth century to be enrolled and get allotments. In 1918, Lemery was raising grain on her allotment. Much to the consternation of Senator Henry Myers of Montana, who was trying to increase the reimbursable appropriations for Flathead irrigation construction, Lemery traveled to Washington, D.C., and testified against further construction money. Not surprisingly, government officials railed against her as "a professional agitator, a critic without constructive criticism and an allowed trouble-maker who will not hesitate to exploit 'Her people.'" Duncan alleged to a U.S. Postal Inspector in 1916, that Albert Lemery, Marie's younger brother, "was not entitled to his allotment and that he obtained it by fraud."[1]

Marie Lemery's close associate in the Flathead Tribal Council was Maxime Barnaby, who was thirty years old in 1916. Barnaby was enrolled as three-quarters Flathead and had attended Chemawa Indian School in Oregon in the early twentieth century.[2] Another leader in the Flathead Tribal Council was Robert Hamilton, Sr., a member of the Blackfeet tribe. Hamilton had a long and very rocky relationship with Bureau of Indian Affairs officials on the Blackfeet Reservation, but he also became involved in promoting tribal concerns on the Flathead. He was one of the leaders of the Blackfeet Business Committee in the 1910s.[3] Rev. William O'Maley, a white man, was active in the Flathead Tribal Council. He was the Roman Catholic parish priest at Ronan and Polson between 1913 and 1927.[4]

At their January 6, 1917, meeting at St. Ignatius, the Business Committee approved a proposal to stock reservation reservoirs with catfish and Chinook salmon and encouraged tribal members to observe Montana state fish and game laws to conserve wildlife resources. The Business Committee vigorously protested against any agreements made by the Tribal Council in the name of the Flathead tribes. They specifically objected to the use of tribal funds to compensate attorneys hired by the Tribal Council. The Business Committee asked the reservation superintendent to telegraph the Commissioner of Indian Affairs to protest against the recognition of a Tribal Council delegation then in Washington, D.C. The Business Committee requested that all nine of their members be authorized to travel to Washington, D.C., with their expenses paid from tribal funds in the United States Treasury: "it is the opinion of the Business Committee that they should visit the Department [of the Interior] and the Bureau of Indian Affairs and become acquainted with the officers and officials in charge of the work, familiarize themselves with the records and work in said Department and Bureau connected with Flathead Reservation." On January 22, 1917, the Commissioner responded that he would refer the fish stocking request to the United States Bureau of Fisheries, but thought the Business Committee should submit their concerns by correspondence rather than in person in Washington, D.C.[5]

Later that winter in 1917, Duncan came down with bronchopneumonia. He spent some time in a Missoula hospital, but was able to walk around by April 6, 1917.[6] By May 6, 1917, he visited Missoula again and stayed at the Shapard Hotel.[7]

In the late 1910s and early 1920s, the Bureau of Indian Affairs used tribal money from grazing and land and timber sales to pay for the operating expenses of the Flathead Indian Agency. The Tribal Council complained about this use of tribal money and wanted the agency operations cut back. No record has been found that Duncan and the Business Committee objected to using tribal funds to pay agency expenses. At one point in 1920, an Indian Office memo argued against a per capita payment to tribal members, because the money was needed to pay agency salaries and operating expenses. On September 6, 1917, Walter West, an Indian Office Supervisor, reported that Duncan and the other Business Committee members complained to him that the Indian Office had listened to a Flathead Tribal Council delegation in Washington and used tribal funds to pay the expenses of the Tribal Council representatives. West reported that the Business Committee members claimed that

> although they are organized by authority and direction of the Indian Office and have been devoting themselves freely to bringing about harmony, contentment and good will, as well as material advancement among the Indians, the Office has recently appeared to have overlooked them and has recognized as representatives of the Flathead tribes an organized gang of mixed bloods, some of them having rights on the reservation and some of them having no such rights and none of them being authorized in any way to represent the tribe, whose chief occupation and interest in life is to create a feeling of discord, discontent and dissatisfaction among the Indians.[8]

That same year, Duncan's wife Louise spent a month in the fall of 1918 on a hunting and fishing trip on the White River, now in the Bob Marshall Wilderness. She traveled with Mr. and Mrs. Frank Bass of St. Ignatius.[9] In December 1918, Duncan reported his orchard had an unusually good apple crop in 1918 and the fruit had sold well.[10]

In February 1919, Duncan's younger brother, Donald, died in Dixon. Donald had lived in Marcus, Washington, before returning to the Flathead Reservation to get an allotment early in the twentieth century.[11] About a week after the funeral, Duncan visited Missoula "to consult physicians about his health, which has been failing lately." Duncan was 70 years old. While in Missoula, he objected to a proposal to give all Indians pensions. He feared it would make younger Indians lazy: "As soon as you begin to pension a person that is where you fail. How can you expect the Indian to amount to anything when you make him feel that he will be taken care of for the rest of his life."[12]

A couple of months later, Duncan accompanied a *Missoulian* reporter to an Indian camp digging bitterroot south of Missoula. Duncan met old friends and relatives at the camp and visited before returning to town and the Shapard Hotel. On the way back he lamented about the area landmarks that were no longer known by their Indian names.[13]

Two months later, on July 30, 1919, a pageant-masque entitled "The Selish" was presented at the University of Montana in Missoula. The presentation included enactment of several scenes from Salish history and a Salish Coyote story. The pageant was directed by Margaret Ganssle. The "Historical Material Committee" consisted of University Professors Paul C. Phillips and M. J. Elrod, newspaperman A. L. Stone, and Mrs. Peter Ronan, widow of a Flathead Indian Agent. According to an article in *The Daily Missoulian,* Duncan and tribal member Peter Paul had "given credence" to the Coyote story in the pageant. The Coyote story told of Coyote being led astray and drowned by a group of dancing maidens. An Indian in the story approached Coyote, white traders, a judge, a priest, and finally an Indian agent searching to find the Great Spirit. The cast members were white Missoula residents or University of Montana students. It is not known if Duncan attended the performance.[14]

The newspapers again put Duncan in the role of weather prophet during the winter of 1919-1920. In December 1919, he predicted a chinook was coming and later, in April 1920, he saw spring on the way.[15]

By 1920, the Business Committee and the Tribal Council were locked in a vigorous struggle over funding of the Flathead Irrigation Project and who should speak for the tribe. On January 3, 1920, Duncan attended a meeting of white settlers lobbying for increased appropriations for construction of the irrigation project. In his speech at the meeting, Duncan claimed both Indians and whites on the reservation had been shortchanged by government promises. Duncan's view was:

> "Do you think the Indian is fighting the white man? He is not. He is merely fighting for his rights. We want what your government has promised us. That is what you want also. You have waited 10 years. We have waited since the treaty of Governor Stephens in 1853 [sic]."

He did not object to funding the irrigation construction by placing a lien on the land — homesteads and allotments:

> "I want the settlers to get their appropriation and their
> water. And I want the Indian to get what is coming to
> him also. You have taken away our country without our
> consent. If you want our country, then give us the cash. It
> has appeared that the white folks — some of them — are
> grafters, and the senators at last have got wind of it."[16]

Duncan took a similar position on June 1, 1920, at a U.S.
House of Representatives hearing held at Dixon, Montana. He
complained that a neighboring homesteader stole the water from
the irrigation ditch for Duncan's orchard:

> I had a ditch there years and years through my orchard.
> What did they do? People above me were helping them-
> selves to my ditch and my water, and my poor old wife
> packing water in a bucket to water her little corn. Now,
> is it fair, when here is a man got a garden drowned out
> with water and my wife packing water in a bucket? I went
> and shut off that water. He comes to me and says, "Here,
> I am not afraid of you. I will use all the water that I want
> from that ditch." But here I am without the water and
> there is my ditch. I had a notion to kill that man right
> there, but something prevented me from doing that. I
> came mighty near committing murder right there.[17]

Duncan's conclusion was that the government should provide
water for the homesteaders: "If the white man wants water to pay
his debt to the Indian [for the land], give it to him. If there is a
million dollars to be had [for irrigation construction], what is the
use of my kicking. That is the way I look at it."[18]

On the other hand, the Flathead Tribal Council vigorously
opposed continued funding of Flathead Irrigation Project construction as long as part of the cost was being charged against
tribal allotments. Many of the allotments were located in areas
that had some natural sub irrigation or had irrigation ditches
that predated the irrigation project. In consequence, the Tribal
Council people argued that the cost of the construction exceeded

the value of the increased production which would result from building the project. Making the construction costs a lien against tribal allotments would greatly reduce the value of the allotments to tribal members. In 1918, Marie Lemery, spokesman for the Flathead Tribal Council, testified,

> we do not mean to kill the project, but we wish to be exempt from the charges of construction, because we can not carry it through. It burdens us with too much debt, and it is too expensive....The Indians do not wish to pay for the construction charges of the ditch, either out of their [tribal] funds or as a lien on our property. If you wish to continue the ditch, continue it; we do not object.[19]

In the 1920 hearings at Dixon where Duncan spoke, Robert Hamilton, a Blackfeet tribal member, spoke for the Flathead Tribal Council:

> I am coming to the point that if the Government will give these homesteaders all the water they need, well and good. That is the sentiment of these Indians, but the Indians do not want to spend a dollar of the money toward the construction of these irrigation projects upon the reservation, but the Indians under the treaty rights want to hold the water rights for their benefit without cost to them. That is the position that the majority of the Indians take to-day. They feel that they ought not to be charged with the construction cost of these irrigation problems [sic].[20]

In June 1920, Marie Lemery requested that new elections be held for Flathead Business Committee positions. The present Business Committee having been elected to a two year term in 1909 — eleven years before. The Commissioner of Indian Affairs, however, saw no reason to hold another general council to elect a new Business Committee: "Office sees no need for disturbing present business committee as a whole, hence General Council unnecessary."[21]

June 1920 was also the month that Inspector H. S. Taylor submitted an extensive report to the Commissioner of Indian Affairs on Tribal Council charges against Theodore Sharp, the new Flathead Agency Superintendent. Much of the report consisted of concerns about reservation affairs that the Flathead Business Committee expressed to the inspector. According to Taylor: "The personnel of the [Flathead] Business Committee is perhaps the best that could be selected on the reservation and I would be glad to see them continued in office. Several of the members are men of large business affairs and are not in any sense agitators and demigogues."[22] The Business Committee complained about the leasing of tribal grazing land, the financing of irrigation construction, lack of protection of pre-1908 reservation water rights, payment of travel expenses of Flathead Tribal Council delegations to Washington, D.C., and the need for development of the tribal hot springs.[23]

Some of the complaints investigated by Taylor were against Sharp personally. Sharp had continued Duncan as chairman of the Business Committee but may not have been as close to Duncan as Morgan had been. According to Taylor, "Sharp does not purposely antagonize his employes, but he is absolutely devoid of that personality which attracts and ties men to him. He would not purposely be inconsiderate, yet he is the most inconsiderate man connected with the Indian Service so far as my knowledge goes. It is the result of a character that is reclusive, sullen and cold." Sharp was extremely frugal with his money, and was happy to personally benefit from free labor coerced from Indian prisoners at the agency jail.[24] It is not known what Duncan thought of Sharp. In July 1920, Sharp was killed at Ravalli by N. J. Perkins, a white agency employee. In December 1920, a jury found Perkins innocent of the murder on the grounds of self-defense.[25]

About the same time Superintendent Sharp was murdered, Duncan reminisced at a gathering of mostly white Montana pioneers in July 1920. He told how Ross' Hole had been named after a Hudson's Bay Company trader, how he disapproved of nudity in sculpture in Washington, D.C., how he had persuaded

Secretary of the Interior James R. Garfield in 1907 that Indian dances should be permitted, and his reoccurring theme that the golden eagle was the only true eagle.[26]

A few months later, Duncan, his wife, and Zephyr Gardepi, the chauffeur, set out in September 1920 on an auto and camping tour of Montana. The trip would also include visits to Edmonton and Calgary, Alberta.[27] They made it home before the end of November 1920. On a November 29, 1920, visit to Missoula, Duncan lamented about the scarcity of wild game since the white men and their rifles came to western Montana.[28]

In August 1920, in response to another request from the Flathead Tribal Council that a new Business Committee be elected, the Commissioner of Indian Affairs punted. According to E. B. Merritt, the Assistant Commissioner of Indian Affairs, "in view of the sad death of Superintendent Sharp, the [Indian] Office desires that the matter of the election of the new Business Committee be postponed until the affairs of the Agency can be straightened out."[29] The old Flathead Business Committee met at Dixon Agency on February 15, 1921, with Duncan presiding, to select three new members. Two were to replace members who had died and the third was to replace a member who had been removed "on account of his conduct."[30]

The next Business Committee meeting, on February 24, 1921, at St. Ignatius, was also presided over by Duncan. After a protest by Max Barnaby of the Flathead Tribal Council against the authority of the Business Committee, several Business Committee members withdrew from the committee, including Martin Charlo. (Charlo was back on the committee at the next meeting on March 8, 1921.) Since the Business Committee still had a quorum, Duncan proceeded to consideration of several dozen cases applying for tribal enrollment or adoption.[31]

The minutes of the Business Committee meeting on March 8, 1921, have also survived. Max Barnaby again protested, but Duncan directed the committee to proceed with the business at hand. The committee considered nineteen applications for enrollment or adoption. Then the committee requested land near

Polson be set aside as an Indian camping and fair grounds, and a proposal to sell ten or twelve acres of land to the Ronan School District was approved. They petitioned for clemency for Antoine Stasso who was in the federal penitentiary for murder, because "he had committed the crime while under the influence of liquor." The committee also requested that the agency investigate general Indian rights to water on the reservation and the return of unused reservoir sites to the tribes, and asked for information about the rumored leasing of the dam site near Polson. Finally, the committee complained about how fee patents were being issued.[32]

On April 22, 1921, Special Supervisor Frank E. Brandon filed a report with the Commissioner of Indian Affairs about the issues that divided the Business Committee and the Tribal Council. Brandon was in favor of the Business Committee led by Duncan: "The personnel of the Business Committee is good, and the men are conscientious, conservative, representative Indian men of the better class." Brandon's evaluation of the Tribal Council was quite different: "The personnel of the 'Supreme Council' is not such as to inspire confidence, and the leaders are principally mixed blood Indian agitators who desire publicity, though it appears they have committed no act for which they can be called to account."[33]

Duncan's brother-in-law Michel Yatellamee died in Camas Prairie on April 29, 1921, at 82 years of age. Louise McDonald's brother was famous for being the victim of a 1902 robbery when some $20,000 in gold was stolen from an outhouse where he had buried it. None of it was ever recovered. J. A. McGowan, the Plains, Montana, merchant, had put a $300 annual payment in his will to support Michel in his old age. According to the obituary: "He was noted for his charity and always gave liberally of his money and belongings to the poor and needy. Many elderly Indians were supported by him for years."[34]

At the age of seventy-two, Duncan spent several weeks in autumn 1921 prospecting for gold in the Clearwater country in

Idaho. He failed to find an old mine he had been told about, but promised to keep on looking.[35]

Charles Coe, the new Flathead Superintendent, on November 25, 1921, recommended postponing the election for a new Flathead Business Committee to replace the old one led by Duncan, because he feared

> the faction of Indians opposing the policies of the [Indian] Office might dominate the new Committee.
>
> The situation appears to be no better here now than it has been in the past and I feel certain that if a new Committee were to be chosen at this time that this element would be strong enough to control a majority of the delegates.[36]

Duncan spoke at an elaborate banquet and smoker held by the white settlers in Ronan on Friday evening December 2, 1921. The event was held in honor of two officials of the "Great Western Land Company" and included a playette entitled "Where Do We Head from Here." The news article did not elaborate on Duncan's talk.[37]

Both the Business Committee and the Tribal Council supported having the U.S. Congress pass a jurisdiction bill to allow the tribes to sue the government for mistreatment. But they fought over which lawyers the tribe should hire to prepare and pursue the claims. The Tribal Council submitted their claims request directly to Congress, while Duncan and the Business Committee sent their request through the Flathead Agency. On December 14, 1921, the Business Committee and a group of tribal elders formulated their claims. Most of the claims involved problems with the construction of the Flathead Irrigation Project. Other claims involved mistakes in the survey of the reservation boundaries and the loss of the common hunting ground on the Great Plains provided for in the Blackfeet Treaty of 1855.[38]

Will Cave, a local white historian, wrote a series of articles for *The Daily Missoulian* in May and June 1922 about the names of western Montana valleys, rivers, and streams. Reviving the Indian names for the Montana landscape had been a long-standing cause for Duncan. Cave acknowledged Duncan as his principle source for the Salish names for local landmarks. Cave summarized his long friendship with Duncan: "No man...has been a more steadfast and consistent friend to the white race.... at the same time he has been ever loyal to his mother's race.... and he does not hesitate to voice at any time a defense of his convictions."[39]

Later that year, Duncan had a prominent camp at the 1922 Fourth of July Powwow at Arlee. He had a large beautifully decorated tipi with linoleum on the ground. When the singers came to his tent in the evening, he treated them to pop and ice cream. Duncan delivered a speech at the powwow.[40]

In May 1923, as the Flathead jurisdiction bill was slowly making its way through Congress, the Flathead Tribal Council passed two resolutions abolishing the Flathead Business Committee. The friction was attenuated by the competition over which lawyers to hire to represent the tribe in the suit in the U.S. Court of Claims. The Business Committee supported the Washington, D.C., legal firm of Serven, Joyce and Barlow. The Tribal Council was working with Burton K. Wheeler, a Montana attorney who was later U.S. Senator.[41]

Duncan did not attend the 1923 Arlee Powwow but camped at a smaller gathering at St. Ignatius.[42] After the celebration was over, he stopped at the *St. Ignatius Post* newspaper office and proposed a large reservation-wide celebration be held near the Fort Connah site. He also asked that newly organized Lake County look into preserving the surviving buildings at Fort Connah.[43]

Just a month later, in late August 1923, Duncan and his friend Alex Kai-Too from the Flathead Reservation Kalispel, joined the Pend d'Oreille Pioneers Association in a picnic. The picnic was held on the shore of Lake Pend d'Oreille in the Hope-Clark Fork, Idaho, area, where fur trader David Thompson had established Kullyspell House in 1809. Kai-Too was blind, but, with Duncan's help, he located the remains of the post's chimneys, establishing its exact location. Kai-Too had visited the ruins

Duncan McDonald with double trailer eagle feather
war bonnet.
Source: Toole Archives, Mansfield Library, University of Montana, Missoula,
photograph 82-61a.

Louise McDonald on horseback, with Duncan McDonald and his friend Wuiuhachya.
Source: Toole Archives, Mansfield Library, University of Montana, Missoula, photograph 82-123.

of the trading post as a child. The discovery was celebrated in local newspapers and *The Washington Post*.[44]

The Bureau of Indian Affairs continued to drag its feet in holding new elections to the Flathead Business Committee, because they feared a new committee would be dominated by agency opponents. By late 1923, however, it looked like a bill would soon pass Congress to allow the Flathead tribe to pursue their claims in the U.S. Court of Claims. If the bill passed, the tribes needed to select legal representation to handle the claims case. Tribal claims against the federal government had been a continuing concern for Duncan since the 1890s and included the survey problems with the reservation boundaries. The tribe would need a governing body that was recognized by the federal government and considered legitimate by tribal members to hire the attorney to file the claims. No record has been found to establish exactly when a new election was held and Duncan left the Business Committee, but in the fall of 1923, Charles Coe, the new Flathead Superintendent submitted bylaws to govern a new tribal council for the Confederated Flathead Tribes of Indians of Montana.[45]

On March 13, 1924, the President signed legislation allowing the Flathead Reservation tribes to pursue their claims under the Hellgate Treaty of 1855 and the Blackfeet Treaty of the same year. The suit was to be brought in the U.S. Court of Claims and "the final judgment and satisfaction thereof shall be in full settlement of all said claims."[46] The language in the 1924 law did not allow the tribes to sue for any claims resulting from the 1904 allotment act or the act providing for the Flathead Irrigation Project. It only allowed claims arising from the two 1855 treaties. By April 19, 1924, the conflict between the Tribal Council and the Business Committee still flared, and a general council of tribal members was held at St. Ignatius to select the attorneys to pursue the claims. The result was a large and tumultuous meeting. Abram Serven and John Carter were members of a Washington, D.C., law firm that worked with the Business Committee group to lobby Congress and get the claims legislation passed. A. A.

Grorud of Helena had been part of Burton Wheeler's law firm that worked with the Flathead Tribal Council. Since Wheeler was elected to the U.S. Senate in 1922, he could not represent the tribe in a suit against the federal government. After a boisterous and noisy meeting that seemed to Carter to threaten violence, the general council selected Grorud to represent the tribe in pursing the tribal claims. This was the last reference found of Duncan playing an official role in tribal politics.[47]

The tribal attorneys and the tribal government never did sue for Flathead Reservation claims under the 1924 act, because it was so limited. The tribes pursued and obtained another act in the 1940s that was more broadly worded and allowed the tribes to sue in the United States Court of Claims for all their claims against the federal government.[48]

As a tribal leader, Duncan worked hard for justice for the tribe, but time moved on, and the sentiment among tribal members demanded more dramatic change. Duncan was honored and respected on the reservation, but the economic and cultural impoverishment of the tribe wrought by the allotment policy and the drought and economic depression in Montana forced tribal members to seek new, less accommodating, leaders in the tribal community.

Chapter 10

Elder and Tribal Sage
1925-1937

Duncan left the tribal political scene in 1924 or 1925. Epic battles over the development of the hydropower site at the foot of Flathead Lake and a new tribal government under the Wheeler-Howard Act of the 1930s loomed. One of Duncan's principle concerns — tribal claims against the government — would take decades to work out. Even the convoluted fight over funding the Flathead Irrigation Project continued to fester until a 1948 compromise ended up using profits from irrigation project electrical sales to pay the construction charges. Duncan had helped express tribal concerns during one of the darkest periods of American Indian history — the 1910s and 1920s — but it fell to other tribal members to fight to preserve the tribe and tribal assets in the final three quarters of the twentieth century.

While Duncan may have been out of tribal politics between 1925 and his death in 1937, he was hardly out of the public eye. His role as consultant in tribal history and culture grew over the years. As a cultural broker, he became the go-to authority for white scholars and journalists seeking information or stories about tribal history and concerns.

For example, on March 19, 1925, Duncan wrote University of Montana professor Paul Phillips about trader John Owen in the Bitterroot Valley in the 1850s. Phillips was in the process of editing Owen's journals and letters for publication in 1927. Duncan related the story of a mixed blood named Batiste who was asleep on a load of hay being hauled to Fort Owen by John Dobson in 1850. The Blackfeet attacked, killed, and scalped

Dobson. Batiste slept through the attack and survived to relate the story to Duncan.[1]

Sometime in the summer of 1925, Duncan was interviewed several times by Martha Edgerton Plassmann, a historical journalist and daughter of the first governor of Montana Territory. Most of Plassmann's questions were about Duncan's life story. During the meetings with Plassmann, Duncan talked about the surrender of Chief Joseph and the Nez Perce at the Battle of the Bear Paws and Duncan's 1878 interview with Nez Perce chief White Bird in Canada. Duncan showed Plassmann how to make a wooden arrow and related the story of the founding of the Hudson's Bay Company's Fort Connah on the reservation. Given Duncan's ability to speak and write in English, Plassmann found it hard to believe he had almost no formal schooling. Duncan also related some of the tribal names in sign language. During one visit, Plassmann toured the Fort Connah site with Duncan's brother, Joseph McDonald.[2]

Duncan attended the First and Second National Indian Congresses held at Spokane, Washington, in November 1925 and July 1926. No program has been located for the 1925 congress, but Duncan was scheduled to speak. However, due to a misunderstanding, he was not able to give his talk. The Flathead Reservation delegation in 1925 consisted of thirty tribal members including Charlie Michelle, chief of the reservation Kalispels; Victor Vanderburg; and other representatives of the older, more traditional families as well as Duncan. According to Duncan, the most enjoyable part of the conference was watching the police trying to keep a "flock" of boys between 12 and 14 years old out of the football game between Gonzaga and Haskell. The boys cut the ropes holding the Flathead horses, so they could sneak into the game in the resulting confusion.[3]

The Second National Indian Congress in Spokane, in July 1926, was a bigger event. The Commissioner of Indian Affairs Charles Burke was master of ceremonies. The Flathead Reservation delegation was accompanied by superintendent Charles E. Coe. Duncan was one of many Indian people at the congress

Duncan McDonald
Source: Manuscripts and Special Collections,
Holland Library, Washington State University, Pullman, Wash., Historic
Photo Collection, PC2 box 30, folder 52.

who gave speeches. His talk was "The Indian as a Citizen," given in the afternoon of July 21, 1926. No transcript of his talk has been found, but according to one newspaper account, he called for the government to settle tribal claims quickly, because the Indians needed the money now rather than later.[4]

Between the two Indian Congresses, in 1925, Charles Russell's book, *More Rawhides*, with Duncan's story about holding a buffalo by its tail in the early 1870s, was published. The story was accompanied by a Russell drawing of Duncan holding the buffalo's tail. Presumably Duncan related the story to Russell in 1909 when they were both at the roundup of the Pablo buffalo shipped from Ravalli to Canada.[5]

In 1926, the Boy Scout Troop in St. Ignatius was named the Duncan MacDonald Scout Troop.[6] That same month, in July 1926, Maurice Ricker, the editor of motion pictures for the U.S. Department of the Interior, visited the Flathead Reservation to take motion pictures of the Flathead Irrigation Project. Ricker had visited the reservation previously in about 1901 and in 1910. In 1925, he renewed his friendships with Joe Allard and Duncan. It is not known if he made any movies of Duncan while visiting Flathead.[7]

Duncan disagreed with Will Cave, a local Missoula historian, in 1926 about the exact location of David Thompson's early nineteenth century trading post, Saleesh House. Cave thought he had located the remains near Thompson Falls, but Duncan insisted Cave's location was different from the site he had visited as a child with his father Angus.[8]

That fall, in October 1926, John H. Chisolm, a historical researcher from Canada and Duncan's distant cousin, interviewed Duncan about the Hudson's Bay Company activities in the Pacific Northwest. Duncan and Chisolm visited St. Ignatius on October 11, 1926.[9]

Duncan was in a storytelling mood in February 1927 when he was interviewed by a *Daily Missoulian* reporter. He told how the Indians had killed birds and other animals only when they needed to eat — not for fun or sport: "Indians, when young are taught to protect animal life and not to harm needlessly."[10]

The next summer, in July 1927, Duncan's old house/hotel in Ravalli burned to the ground. The house was then occupied by the Ellis Connerly family. Duncan lived in Dixon in 1927.[11]

Duncan attended the August 1927 meeting of the Society of Montana Pioneers in Missoula. While in Missoula for the meeting he enjoyed an automobile trip to Stevensville.[12] The late Missoula banker J. H. T. Ryman wrote an article about the name of the Bitterroot Salish Indians which was published in 1927. Duncan had written Ryman that the proper name was Salish, not Flathead.[13] Several months later, at the last 1927 meeting of the Lake County Commissioners in Polson, the commissioners received right-of-way deeds from Duncan and five other land owners. The deeds were for the construction of Bushman Road.[14]

Beginning in early 1928 and extending at least through 1932, Duncan carried on an extensive correspondence with Lucullus V. McWhorter. McWhorter devoted much of his life to collecting and preparing for publication Nez Perce testimony about the tribe's history and their war with the United States government in 1877. Some of Duncan's letters preserved by Mc-Whorter have been used earlier in this biography. McWhorter used Duncan's material in his classic history of the Nez Perce: *Hear Me, My Chiefs!: Nez Perce History and Legend.*[15]

The Daily Missoulian for August 13, 1928, related a Duncan McDonald story about the planned death of an Indian from another tribe living with the Salish in Stevensville. In the late 1850s or early 1860s, the elderly and helpless Indian feared he was putting his family and the Salish in danger from lurking enemies. He had himself tied to a horse, led into the river, and then the horse was shot, drowning the old man.[16]

As was his custom, Duncan attended the fall 1928 meeting of the Society of Montana Pioneers in Butte. Martha E. Plassmann, the journalist who had interviewed Duncan in Dixon in 1925, saw Duncan visiting with his friends in the hotel lobby at the Butte meeting. Duncan was emphasizing the Indian belief that game should only be killed if needed for food or other use. — It should never be wasted.[17]

H. T. Bailey, a journalist, published an essay on December 22, 1928, on the contribution of the Flathead Reservation Indians to the quality of life in western Montana: "There may be just as good Indians but no better Indians than members of the Flathead Tribe in the Mission valley." Bailey emphasized Duncan's stories and teachings about the importance of treating the land and animals with respect.[18]

An especially sad event for Duncan was the November 25, 1928, death of his wife Louise, who died at the Holy Family Hospital in St. Ignatius of pneumonia. She was buried in the St. Ignatius cemetery. They had been married for over 53 years.[19] Duncan related in 1930 that,

> During the long years together there was never a quarrel. Life without her companionship, loving kindness and care is lonely and dreary. She was a wild Indian woman when we were married, and I am glad that she did not have a drop of white blood in her veins. Her kitchen, always clean, and emanating cheer and hospitality, was the haven of all hoboes, both white and Indian. Everyone was always sure of a welcome and plenty of good food.
>
> I remember one day when I was tired from working with pick and shovel. I noticed a hobo leaving our home with some bread and butter and meat. I remonstrated with her, saying, "Why do you feed all the lazy fellows, doing nothing." She answered, "I am a Christian. I will not refuse anyone asking for something to eat when he is hungry. A true Christian must be charitable and human[e]; these are the teachings of our Lord. We must pray for our enemies and help them."[20]

Later that year, Duncan made a special gift to the University of Montana museum at the end of 1928. He presented his friend, Professor Paul C. Phillips, with the "Indian war costume" of Angus P, McDonald, Duncan's half brother. The costume included moccasins, leggings, war shirt, a bonnet, a spine of feather, and a wig of jet black Indian hair.[21]

In January 1929, the Fort Connah site was sold by Miss L. B. Hamilton of Missoula to Daniel Maynard of Hamilton. It was not then owned by the McDonald family.[22] Later that month, Duncan made a trip to Missoula and was asked to forecast the winter weather. His reply was, "I will tell you in the spring."[23] During this visit to Missoula, Duncan asked the Missoula Chamber of Commerce to support having the Indian names of western Montana landmarks restored. Duncan explained the meaning of the Indian names for Mount Jumbo, the Rattlesnake Creek, and Clark's Fork River.[24]

Duncan visited Polson for several days in February 1929 and gave a talk to the Polson high school students. According to a newspaper report, Duncan spoke "on early day topics of interest."[25]

Yet another interview was with Al Partoll for the University of Montana student newspaper, *The Montana Kaimin*, in March 1929. Duncan talked about restoring the Indian names to western Montana locations, the paints used by Indians before the white man arrived, the sign language, tipis, and the Iroquois who settled among the Salish tribes during the fur trade.[26] A little later in the spring, Duncan was in Charlo conducting business at a local real estate agency in April 1929. The nature of the business was not described.[27]

William S. Lewis, the historian of the Spokane Pioneer Society, interviewed Duncan in Dixon in spring 1929. Lewis recorded some of the most detailed reminiscences of Duncan's childhood at Fort Colville. This interview was the source for many of the episodes of Duncan's childhood years related in the first chapter of this biography.[28]

One of the highlights of Duncan's later years was visiting old friends at the annual meetings of the Society of Montana Pioneers. Duncan attended the August 1929 meeting in Great Falls. He told a *Great Falls Tribune* reporter that now that his wife had died and he was alone, he wanted to travel and revisit the scenes he had seen as a young man.[29]

In October 1929, Duncan visited Ronan and called at the newspaper office to relate accounts of the early days. According to *The Ronan Pioneer*, Duncan at 80 years of age was "still hale and hearty and has a remarkable memory of interesting occurances."[30]

As was Duncan's custom, he spent part of the winter of 1929-1930 in a hotel in Missoula. While visiting with friends in the hotel lobby, Duncan related the story of an Indian hunter who shot a bear and crane with one bullet. Later the hunter was attacked by a beaver he had pursued into its den.[31]

Duncan was interviewed by Mrs. L. L. Marsh in 1930. He gave an account of his father's life as a fur trader for the Hudson's Bay Company. He also talked about his experiences on a Salish "scalping expedition" on the Great Plains as a young man in the early 1870s. Duncan lamented the death of his wife Louise and their two children. His various business enterprises during the years had made him wealthy, but in the 1920s one of the banks that held his savings failed:

> The loss of his family has saddened the closing years of a long life. He suffered financial loss when one of the banks failed in which he had his savings. Many of his loans to friends and relatives have never been paid but he does not regret the help he has given although it leaves him with little for his old age.

In his later years, Duncan enjoyed visiting with friends and following current events on the reservation. He "was anxious" to see the Flathead Lake dam site leased for development so that "he and other old Indians may benefit from the revenue."[32]

The Polson Chamber of Commerce held a banquet on June 21, 1930, to celebrate the leasing of the dam site to the Rocky Mountain Power Company and the economic boom the area expected from the construction of the dam. A number of Rocky Mountain Power officials and the governor of Montana attended with dignitaries from white communities across western Mon-

Duncan McDonald
Source: Manuscripts and Special Collections,
Holland Library, Washington State University, Pullman, Wash.,
McWhorter Papers, PC85, box 3.1, folder 45.

tana. Duncan seems to have been the only tribal member there. White officials from the Flathead Indian Agency and Flathead Irrigation Project attended. Duncan was pleased that the dam site was leased, but he did not say whether he supported giving the lease to the Rocky Mountain Power Company. The Flathead Tribal Council had supported a competing application from Walter Wheeler, a developer.[33]

Duncan attended the funeral of Mary Sahpish Shin Mah in St. Ignatius in August 1930. She died at about 90 years of age and her mother had been the wife of Pend d'Oreille Chief Sil-lips-too who had been a close friend and associate of Duncan's father Angus. Duncan provided biographical information on Mary for the newspaper.[34]

During the winter of 1930-1931, Duncan visited Missoula in January and March 1931. When he arrived at Missoula on March 1931, he learned of the death of Joe LaMoose in Arlee. LaMoose had been one of the Salish volunteers who joined the white settlers and soldiers at Fort Fizzle at the mouth of the Lolo Canyon during the Nez Perce War of 1877.[35]

C. O. Marcey, the historian for the Society of Montana Pioneers, gave a birthday dinner for Duncan at Marcey's home in Missoula on March 31, 1931. The newspaper account did not say who else attended, but did say Duncan renewed old acquaintances. Duncan was 82 years old.[36] During this visit to Missoula, reports were received that crews working on the highway just south of St. Ignatius had unearthed numerous skeletons while widening the road. Duncan explained to *The Daily Missoulian* that there was an old burial ground south of the mission. The bodies had been buried in buffalo robes and wrapped in birch or cedar bark. The graves were shallow because people had few digging tools in those days.[37]

Later that spring, on May 11, 1931, Duncan was hurt in an encounter with an automobile on North Higgins Avenue. Duncan had been staying in Missoula with the Marcey's when he fell trying to avoid the automobile while crossing the street. It was two days after the fall before he sought medical help. He spent a month in St. Patrick's Hospital with an injured hip. Duncan noted he had worked with buffalo and wild horses, but it was a gas machine that got him.[38]

Fortunately Duncan recovered in time to attend the August 1931 meeting of the Society of Montana Pioneers held in Butte. As normal, Duncan was the only one at the meeting who could trace his Montana residency back to 1849. In a newspaper interview, he related how his white father and Nez Perce/Iroquois mother had communicated in French at home. Duncan learned some Nez Perce and had since picked up some Salish from living on the Flathead Reservation. Duncan summarized his linguistic abilities:

> Most of my life, spent in close contact with my good friends of the various Salish tribes, gives me better command of their language. But I can still talk to the Nez Perces, using considerable "sign" language. I can talk to all Indians I have ever met, but the more remote their tribes are, the more "sign" I have to use. The sign language is pretty much the same — it is the inter-tribal mode of communication.

Duncan brought some historic souvenirs to show people at the meeting. These included his father's powder horn, a dagger, a flint-lock pistol, and the key to the lock at the old Fort Colville Trading Post. He also mourned the loss of his life savings and retirement funds in a northern Montana bank that failed and lost his money.[39]

The C. O. Marcey family held another birthday dinner for Duncan at their home in Missoula in 1932. It was Duncan's 83rd birthday. The newspaper account mentioned that Duncan was "still active" and "well versed on modern issues." Duncan had spent the cold winter months with the Marcey's.[40]

The 1932 meeting of the Society of Montana Pioneers was held in Missoula, and Duncan arrived early to help with the preparations. Almost 300 people, who had arrived in Montana before 1869, were registered for the meeting. Activities for the gathering ranged from a business meeting for the society to a reception with singing and tap dancing performances to a fiddler's contest and dance to a formal banquet. Duncan was one of those who gave talks at a noon luncheon hosted at the Florence Hotel by the Missoula Rotary Club.[41] Duncan was the senior Montana resident at the meeting.[42] Almost all the other guests registered at the convention were white people. Duncan was either the only, or one of the few, mixed bloods or Indians attending.[43]

An exhibit of "pioneer relics" was held in conjunction with the meeting. Duncan's contribution included his late wife's Indian dress and his war bonnet made of golden eagle feathers.[44] Right after the meeting, Duncan took a trip through Glacier National Park and Browning before returning home to Dixon.[45]

That same year, in the fall of 1932, Meilie Cooney retold some of Duncan's Indian legends at children's story hours at the Missoula Public Library. She also told the children the Indian names of western Montana landmarks as related by Duncan.[46] As was his habit, Duncan spent most of the cold weather during the winter of 1932-1933 in Missoula.[47]

Duncan took part in a June 1933 conference between tribal representatives and Montana fish and game officials at the Dixon Indian agency. The conference agreed that the reservation would stay open to non-Indian fishermen and the state would take measures to enhance and protect the fisheries.[48]

Duncan celebrated his 85th birthday at a Sunday dinner at the Marcey' Missoula home on April 1, 1934. He had spent the winter of 1933-1934 at Dixon.[49]

During the spring of 1934, Duncan visited Thompson Falls to attend the dedication of a monument to David Thompson. The committee erecting the monument decided to place it along the highway so travelers would see it. The alternative was to place it at the actual site of Thompson's fur trade post, Saleesh House. Duncan and the committee toured the area near Ashley Creek where the post had been located, but they could not be certain of the exact location. Several of the white Thompson Falls men on the committee were Duncan's personal friends.[50]

In July of that year, Dick West published an account of an interview he had with Duncan at a Missoula hotel. Duncan related his story about shooting a buffalo cow in the early 1870s. This was the story of him holding the tail of the wounded buffalo until it finally died from Duncan's rifle shot. He also told of hunting mountain goats in Glacier National Park, probably in the late 1870s. When Duncan had tried to retrieve a Big Horn sheep shot by another Indian hunter, he fell through the ice and rolled three or four hundred feet down the slope before hitting a pile of gravel and narrowly escaping death.[51]

Duncan took Claude Schaeffer, a young graduate student in anthropology, to the National Bison Range in June 1934. Duncan related how, during the 1909 roundup of the Pablo buffalo, Gen. Hugh Scott was crawling towards some buffalo to photograph them. Duncan accidentally tossed a lighted match into the grass and the fire started the buffalo off on a gallop.[52] That same year in July, Duncan attended the Pony Express Days celebration in Missoula.[53] In August 1934, he attended the annual meeting of the Society of Montana Pioneers in Great Falls.[54]

He spent the 1935 New Years celebration in Missoula and in late January 1935 retreated back to Missoula until the cold weather passed.[55] Later that year, in September 1935, Duncan loaned his Indian dance outfit to be exhibited at St. Ignatius Mission. A three day celebration was held in honor of Father Louis Taelman's fifty year anniversary of entering the priesthood.[56] *The Daily Missoulian* on October 11, 1935, reported Duncan returned to the reservation after a stay at St. Patrick Hospital for an unspecified illness.[57]

Later that fall 1935, he came to Missoula for an extended visit and returned to Missoula again in February 1936 to remain until the cold weather was over.[58] Duncan had stayed in Dixon during the winter of 1936, but he woke one cold morning to find three feet of snow and a temperature of 20 below zero. More cold weather was coming, so he sought out the steam-heated comfort of Missoula.[59]

While in Missoula in March 1936, Duncan tried to take a bus to visit John R. Latimer, an old friend. After getting on the wrong route, Duncan disembarked and walked to Latimer's house. They had an extended visit.[60] He returned to Dixon in time for his 87th birthday on March 30, 1936. The Dixon Women's Club held a public birthday party in his honor.[61]

During January 1937, Duncan was asked to prophesy the winter weather. He said he would answer in the spring.[62] After spending much of the cold weather of 1937 at the Shapard Hotel in Missoula, he celebrated his 88th birthday in Missoula. He still regularly read daily newspapers and current magazines to keep up with events.[63] Duncan and Will Cave gave historical talks at the August 1937 "Pioneer Picnic." The event was held at the Jocko tourist camp at Arlee.[64] At the same time, *The Daily Missoulian* reported on Duncan's talk at Arlee, the paper was celebrating Duncan as the longest continuous reader of their newspaper. Duncan had subscribed to the paper since it was founded in 1870. Now he was 88 years old and still able to read without glasses.[65]

In his elder years Duncan rented out his house in Dixon and lived in a cabin in the back of the house. The end came quickly. Duncan fell seriously ill in October 1937 while in Thompson Falls. According to the McDonald family accounts, he was at Thompson Falls, the county seat, to start the eviction of his renters who he felt were not living up to their agreement with him. He died in a Thompson Falls nursing home on October 16, 1937. The news made headlines in Montana newspapers.[66] The body was brought to St. Ignatius and his funeral mass was attended by many friends from Missoula as well as tribal members. Father Louis Taelman conducted the rites. Pallbearers included tribal members Henry Matt, Louie Camille, Louis Combs, and Eneas Conco. The choir included Duncan's neice, Louise Dumontier, and her husband Harold.[67]

Duncan McDonald's journey was over.

Postscript

Duncan McDonald's life — 1849 to 1937 — ran from the fur trade to the automobile. He played many roles over the years. He was a fur trader, a hotel operator, a fruit grower, a historian, and a cattleman. A frequent critic of Flathead Indian Agency operations, he grew into a tribal leader and part of the establishment. During his years as chairman of the Flathead Business Committee from 1909 to 1924, he fought to defend tribal interests. His long advocacy for tribal claims against the government finally paid off years after he died. During his later years in office, he was overtaken by younger and more radical leaders. Over his life, he was a consistent voice advocating for the views and interests of the Flathead Reservation Indian community.

He was never a quiet Indian.

Appendix:

Address at the University of Montana, February 22, 1915
by Duncan McDonald

Duncan McDonald
In his address at the University of Montana Auditorium on the
evening of Monday, February Twenty-Second, 1915[1]
* * * * * * * * *

At twelve minutes after eight the speaker, accompanied by
Judge Woody, Major Catlin, Mr. Paxton, and Mr. A. L. Stone,
mounted the platform and Mr. Stone made the introductory
address.

* * * * * * * * *

Mr. McDonald was greeted with enthusiastic applause.
* * * * * * * * *

[Editors' note: Some typographical errors have been corrected and some paragraphing has been added to this manuscript.]

I am getting rattled.

Laughter.

You gentlemen (to the honorary guests on platform) better
come up closer so that you can hear.

To the Audience:

I have seen the day when my friend, honorable judge
Woody, he could hear long distances, like a bear, when he was
living on the indian diet, but now he has been living on what
you call "cultured diet" he is getting a little hard of hearing, and
I must get him close so he can hear.

Is there any full blood Selish indians in here? I spoke to
some of them. Is there any here, I wonder?

(By Mr. Stone: No, they did not come.)

We always start in with any opinion or sermon on the indian saying "There is the only good indian is a dead indian."
Now, we will see and I will tell you my ideas, the way we used to
live and our teachings to our children when the rivers were our
tubs and (Slavre ?) was our coffee, and we did not need doctors
or medicine. Are there any Doctors or lawyers here? There are I
see politicians and doctors and lawyers. I am in the box where we
all are. I don't care what impression you have I stand here alone,
the first aboriginal orator of the soil. Now, can anyone you say
"NO.?" Why should I be afraid of my blood, because I consider
myself once that I was a free North American Indian? And the
Great Bird, king of the birds in North America flies over my head
and still, today, you see it is our celebrations on the fourth of
July, that is the great American Eagle. Now, Uncle Sam, he says
to his agents, "If an indian wears feathers, starve him, don't give
him any rations, because I wear the great american eagle on my
head."

I never considered the American Eagle like a turkey or a
duck or a chicken or any of those nasty birds we have —— of
course I don't like to make some little remarks and I said to my
honorable friend, Professor Elrod; I was a little shy, when invited
first — I was a little shy of the ladies. I told him I might make
a break and the women will maybe chase me out from the place
of learning with a broomstick, but in his letter he said, "don't
be afraid, the ladies are good listeners and have more sympathy
and friendly feeling toward the red man." Well, on the strength
of that I had no more idea of being here standing on this here,
right here in this institution, that I believe is the great place of
learning of the state of Montana, —— But what does this "high
Culture" mean?

When, I the poor ignorant savage American Indian, stand
here and look east across the ocean at the carnage —— just think
for a minute what brutality it is no expression for those people
over there across the ocean to say, we are doing this for culture.
Culture! (Sneeringly). And I, the poor American indian, he is a
good indian if he is a dead indian. The German says, why, he is

cultured, by his firing of the mighty guns he is fighting for the smiting god with a sword in hand. That, with that weapon he says, "I am only fighting the french for pitty (?) and will make drakes of his institutions of learning, shoot those buildings down, and the little miserable islanders that pretend by her commercial holding that controls the world. Now I am going to fix him and I am going to wipe him out of existence; and why Uncle Sam here grinning and laughing with leg cocked up, the angel of neutrality, they are all turning on Uncle Sam, he is the angel of peace.

But what about the indian with this man?

Uncle Sam opens his heart in all directions and says, "come to my land of freedom, equality, and goes on with goodness only knows what else —

Here I am, standing trembling in my moccasins, stammering and Europe looks back to Uncle sam as a perfect gentleman and peacemaker and come to tell the truth I am obliterated. I am at a loss to know what culture means, and what is God and who is Adam. You all say "I come from Adam." As long as there is a little history about the white race, but you wont go to accomplish your proof and say that the red man is a decendant of Adam. But when you go over the ocean, no matter what land or island you come to you find there is a native there, there with long hair or short hair or straight or curling hair, black, or brown or maybe yellow or white.

Now, I don't want to detain you here. I know there are some people who are engaged to go to societies and card parties. I don't mean that every one of you. There is black sheep among the whole of you, and among the red men, and Kiotish [Scottish] children.

I come here —— I suppose you heard of the "blazing of old trail" by Mr. Stone? I had no idea when I saw him — I really will confess, I was in the brush, laying on my belly playing with insects, playing with ants, and the other insects, and amusing myself and looking around here to my surprise was Mr. Stone. So then we had a little friendly chat and in a kind of off handed way I told him a little story, but I never thought I was going to be

pulled in here for it. (Laughter) In this institution of knowledge.
It was a little bit of indian history I told him —— but before I
go any further it seems that we [should] mention the noble buffalo that was there. Sam Wilson and Walking Coyote, and all of
them, when they all crossed the mountains — Now I have to
explain all this gentlemen before I go into this little story of the
coyote, and the dragon so you can understand it. Two bull buffalo and a lot of heifers; that Sam was bringing over. (He died
here, I think, under the bridge here) He brought the buffalo, or
bison, to this country across the mountains. I don't know when
he died but he died here under the bridge of whiskey. Oh, that
is fine thing, eh, whiskey? What noble thing, fine thing to go to
heaven and face the almighty with it, and I doubt whether or not
we go there with a bottle. *applause*

Now a fellow Pablo bought the buffalo and begin figuring
and begins to negotiate with Uncle sam. He wanted certain land
for the buffalo so they could multiply. No. The employees of the
reservation they wanted a corner on it and so they say he was getting a little independent. And Pablo he has a little Mexican blood
and indian so you can immagine how stubborn he was when he
takes a notion and he did, too. Mr. Canadian comes around and
makes a talk. The American it seems does not want the Bison
in the country so a bargain is made and Pablo sell the buffalo to
the Canadian people and Mr. Pablo comes along with the bunch
— about four hundred head — Walking around there, watching
the fun. I come to a corner and to my surprise I met a gentleman from this house of institution, professor Elrod, with blood
in his eye. I spoke to him in a friendly manner, he answers but I
can see there was something wrong. I didn't know whether it was
the Devil or Culture was in him, but he says, Come on Mack,
go to Pablo and get horses and saddle them. WHY? Let us go up
this hill, here." I went and saddled up the horses and we went
up the ridge there at Ravalli. In a little bit he began to pick up
a little, pick a little flower and showed me and showed me and
kept going and looking at an instrument and was getting pretty
good, still I could see blood in his I [eye], but I didn't want to

ask him for fear, as he was a cultured man and not a savage. I might make a break that would be considered an insult and I did not feel like that, but he kept grabbing and grabbing at ants — and gray backs — *laughter* — every immaginable things all the insects, all the imaginable things, all the insects, all the flowers, all the grasses, why he was — I just wish I had a camera to snap him then — Finally we got on top and then he was asking me questions and I kept telling him and then I begin to talk and ask if he knows the "Ochell" as they call it Kouse. Ochello is an indian word and is right. We have no — I told him, — "here is something for you to learn." Then we argue and right on top of the mountain where we were arguing I said, — "Here, as smart as you are, and I am a savage and we are left here alone without an dollar and without a nickle or anything, naked, with all the knowledge that you have got, why you will starve to death and I will be getting fat (laughter) Why anything I can eat, the root of these flowers, a stem of that plant there, I can eat that; Well finally he said I want to go down here and I got tired and said "what are you driving at?" Well, "I am looking at this place. I want to see if we could get this for a buffalo park." Buffalo park! And it is right in plain view of Ravalli stock yard, you can see the dust in the yards where they are loading the cars with buffalo to go to Canada, but before we started one fellow comes to me and begin to curse a little, pretending he didn't like to see Canada getting them; he didn't like to see Uncle Sam get the worst of it on the buffalo. Oh! That tricky Yankee, what would they think of them! And he says, "Let us break the gates in the night and let the buffalo out." Then those few words of profane language, of course he don't like to see the noble buffalo go across the line and I said, "The owner of that buffalo I know well. We have been boys together and played together and I know he have worked, hard, hard, hard, for what he has made. Only for his native pride you would open the gates and let the buffalo go, but I decline and that is all. I started with Professor Elrod.

He said, — "What you say?" and I said, "What Buffalo? You can see the dust down there, don't you know where they are going?" He said, — "Never mind Mr. McDonald, if we get this place we will get a park" and that is the first time I ever knew there was such a thing as the "Bison Society" in New York, and I believe he told me he was a member of the society and Teddy Roosevelt, was the president, he was a member, and he said, — "I think I can manage it" and so we went down back of the place where it is."

("I want to get through with this, I wont take but a few minutes.")

He looked over the place and I guess he got it all right. Then they went to work and fenced in the whole country there — He got this through his letters to the head man of the society. I believe his name was Carnegie, wrote a letter explaining to him about the location and he seen Senator Dixon, I believe, he was Senator, and through schemes anyway they got a park from the indians I believe for thirty thousand dollars, something like that, and instead of the indian getting it they dumped it into that ditch what I think you call "Reclamation." (Laughter) So then they went to work and fenced it.

Ladies and Gentlemen I was here — born here — in this country in March 1849. My father, I believe, was from the Northern part of Wisconsin, a wild Brunswick Highlander [sic]. He was one. And my mothers father was from the state of New York and Canada. He was an Iroquois. He had more white blood in him than indian, but he come here with the rest of the fur traders, Hudson Bay Traders and Northwest Trading Company an American trading company, and got mixed up in these tribes here and it was then when they got intermarried with the Selish or the (?(Insoumi). That is the tribe that lived near the mission. That word means Flathead Lake — Near Broad Water — indians. What you call Pond E'Oreille is a French word which means, — "hang from here" and is changed — You know the Flathead lake is the biggest in the west, here, and so they call it "Broad Water."

I will make a few more remarks and then I will go ahead and tell you the story of the Coyote. You know we have it all about the great dragon and there is land marks down there, and he come up the river to Missoula and he was the man that named the river. He was the creature that called this river the In Missouletech. Now, I want some writers to write that down, In Missouletech. In Missoul — You ask some of them that were pioneers here what the meaning is. It seems these pioneers were a bunch of Missourians and they say it was corrupt pronunciation of Missouri. Well, these professors thought it was a fact and like all people got the impression that Missoula, — they lived in *In Messouletech* — was Missouri miscalled. Can you spell it? In Messoule — the *Etech* — well it is like two scotchmen and one said I betcha I can spell every word. And other scotchman says I betcha can't. And he said sure I can and the other fellow says, "Well spell *Tech*" and the other says I bet I can and he says I bet you cant and he says you cant do it and he says "T-A-*Ech*" "Tach" Then I tell you what is the meaning of Messoulettech. It is Selish — A little hesitating, I believe in speaking. I think Professor Elrod — you have no Idea of the ups and down I had with him and with My friend Mr. Stone, another friend of mine, and the Honorable Judge Woody, here, why he was a baby when I was a grown man. Many the time I wheeled him around. Now then they built a great fence around the land. And they never went around there when they finished it until last year. They were calling there and Major Morgan come to me and says: "Why there is a gentleman from Washington come on with me in the automobile, we want to go to the park and see buffalo. I was dirty, working and working, so I went. The gate was locked and we had to go to the warden. There was a warden there and he was a man with a long gun, he was from Texas I guess, that could shoot three thousand yards off and knock a man's eye out. There was a warden. I don't want to lay that part to Mr. Elrod but that was the Bison Society. They come in front to the gate, and there was that warden — They could not afford to get a full blood american indian to take care of that place. Now I went into the park and here I was, and here was the poor buffalo.

I saw the time when I had the state of Montana for my farm. All the animals, fish, everything was there before me. I can just lay there and see my "Washnuer" and everything was mine. I want deer, I get it; if I want Moose. I get it; I want sheep any kind or animals any kind of fur to wear, everything I wanted, and I feel that that [is] why God put us here, to enjoy ourselves and look to one another as brothers and sisters and respect one another. We have a way of respecting one another. We used to teach our girls, we used to tell them about virtue. I have known girls to go out of society because she was in love; I have known men quitting society because they was in love. That shows they must have a feeling. Now then, when I seen the buffalo from his "(?) Wigwam (?)" a mighty nice painted house, painted up, — when I saw the mighty buffalo so fenced and penned up my tears commenced running down my cheek when I see buffalo; Then days gone by when I see the day when I was free to the whole land and saw even the noble buffalo now penned up as I. I said, "Excuse me for asking a question" I could see that Major Morgan he was uneasy and supposed I was to create a scene, that I was going to give him a great "guff." But I was sore and I began to think that I had had Montana as my farm, when I ruled, and now they had put the buffalo into a park with a lock, and they lock them in there and here was a man with a long gun over them, from Texas. Why I guess I couldn't even come to look at the buffalo. He might shoot me. Just think for a moment! A man with a gun behind the poor savage. Look at the poor buffalo the fun he used to have with them. That is what the Bison Society did. Now, Uncle Sam, He draws around, now, eh.! You are a Nation you have been here before! We have to make treaties with you! Treaties! (sneeringly) Treaties before can do anything? Going to make treaties? Every treaty they made they broke it. Finally they made a treaty taking away nearly the whole section of the country, just but the reservation, and they pay the indian $120,000.00, and two-thirds of it they stole it back.

Now he kept on jamming me onto reservation and again was reservation too big and now he pen me down to a little miserable eighty acres, and then he commences to sell my land right and left to speculators. What is the money for? Now, confound you, you lazy indian, I ain't going to give you money. You have credit, and I am going to keep it. Now you starve to death unless you have lots of credit. Well, then, we begin to die — with starvation and neglect. With a credit — With a credit! (Sneeringly), and a promise.

Now a promise that is all we got now, a promise from Uncle Sam; also we have credit, that amounts to millions of dollars. Now what did he do then? He blew that credit in; that credit he spent for us but did not put into our hands, and here we are suffering for want of food and clothes, a lot of poor blind people, neglected and starving, and if they had not died they might have existed a few days longer. But that is not all of it. Now he went to work and established this institution, I believe they call it the University of Montana, planted some more people there and they see they haven't got that Indian Mythology. Now you will hear these professors wanting to get that Indian mythology from me now, but that is not all; Now they can have the Indian Mythology to the best of my ability. I have lots left, but I am very sure, now, that there is something else left here, that is the ghost we have, the ghost down at Fish Creek, and now they went down there, they sent a what you call psychologist, a man who studies the human mind, what you call him? (Mr. Stone — Psychologist)

They send your man down, he didn't believe in ghosts but he went there with an instrument. He put that instrument into place there in the cabin and he fixed everything all around and set it up in the shack; and he put strings on it — I don't know what kind of strings but some kind of strings that they use to catch ghosts with and when the ghost gets caught he sets off the trap and pictures is taken.

This man of science was a most stubborn kind of a fellow and did not believe in such a thing and he wakes up every once in a while. They was raising cain and having a lot of fun too; and finally they went to sleep and when they were asleep to my surprise that gentleman of science leaps over his friends, knocks the instrument out of kilter and later there appeared the picture of the ghost. Now what has the Indian got now only a promise that there is millions of dollars to his credit and the ghost; They could not catch the ghost — but they got his picture — I wish they could catch the ghost — but they got a fine picture of the ghost, yes they have even tried to steal the poor red man's ghost, and the picture, they have got that.

Now this story — the book I have is following old trails by Mr. Stone. Of course the land mark is down there yet. You can come down there every day, but this Coyote I am going to commence right from the Columbia River, from the Coast.

Mr. Coyote (Lione) He was a creature that had a certain amount of infinite power and could turn into everything and do lots of thing. He heard that Salmon could not go to the red man on the Columbia river because of the great dam that had fell across it, and he came to help the salmon and go to assist the indians to get the salmon up the river. He comes along up the Columbia and comes to the dams and to his surprise he saw four fine little maids swimming on the Columbia river. He said to himself, — "Now, how could I approach those maidens, as you would say "How can I make a mash" is the way they phrase it. How can I make a mash with those girls? So he studied there for the while and says, — "Now I am going to go up the river and find out where their camp is, and turn into a baby and lash myself onto a baby board — A baby board as you have seen lots of times — and float down the Columbia River, and crying hard, and see what they will do. So he turned himself into the baby and strapped himself onto baby board and floated down the Columbia river, squalling as hard as he could, and they heard him, and to their surprise here was a baby floating down the Columbia river. "Why we must save that baby, whoever gets there first shall be the owner of the baby." Alright, they answer and the sisters rushed and into the water they went and swum for the baby and the oldest girl reached it first and grabbed the board and went back to shore, took this baby back to the camp and nursed him and the baby began to grow. He was a nice fine little fellow, and he was growing fast. And at the same time he was winking at himself. They put the baby on their breast and he would crow and want to be there on the breast. The poor maiden didn't have no milk but at the same time, anyhow, made an attempt to make the baby suck, and it seems he liked it, and finally he grew up, but every morning he would bring in to the girls a big salmon, a fish, and they kept wondering and wondering how they could get the salmon and he grow up very quick; of course it was only a myth; He had gone one morning to bring the salmon for breakfast and —— he was getting bigger and bigger and demand a bigger supply of water and he would drink lots and throw rest, tip it on the ground, and then the girls would have to get more water and he would spill it again, and he was doing it [on] purpose. Finally they got tired and said they take him to the river to get water —— and he had begin to walk and they made him go to the river for water himself; He went down and then they seen what was there — they went down there too you see to see him — a great big trap right across the columbia.

Now I want to make a remark. Some little things there, of course Mr. Stone, you know at the time we was chatting I was careless — that is the true story. And they attempted to take up the trap so the salmon could come through and the girls begin to wonder what was the matter with the baby that he was not back. He must be drowned. And they got anxious and went to the walls of the bluff and to their surprise — he was already turned into Coyote again instead of a baby — a grown coyote — and he was just barking and jumping and they made a rush for him but they were too late he was hitting at the dam across the river and had already got the salmon going up the stream. The rush of the water and salmon was great and they rushed after him and everytime he made a motion with his yellow ——— the salmon come by millions and then they came to Spokane to see if they can get, if he can get a Spokane girl for his wife and he did and left the salmon there and he did and got a Spokane girl for his wife and the salmon come up and he got to the Falls there where it is covered by the city of Spokane now, but it was a deep cut there then and has been filled up by the people there, but then it was a deep gully or cut, and Salmon began to go up what is called the Coeur d'Alene river, but he thought he would see the Ronan girls and he came up there and they refused him and he quit the job, finished and went back and the Coeur d'Alene tribe was deprived of the salmon and he went up the river to Kalispell and he was deprived by the Kalispell girls of having a wife in that tribe and so he left the falls there and they got no salmon.

Then he come on to this place and when he got there he kept going until he there and he called this river In Messoul Etech.

Well I will read a part of this story of the dragon and the Coyote, about the great Yellow Dragon of the Selish and the Grizzely Bear, his dog.

"Here he read"

——————————

——————————

there had been a great land slide there, away down on the Columbia river ———

Well, that was the story I was telling Mr. Stone that day.

"Well there had been a great slide down the Columbia river which had cause a dam across the stream, a dam so high that the Salmon could no longer come up to the headwaters on its pilgrimages ——————

——————————

Out in the Jocko valley east of arlee ———

It is there yet, north of where, it is right at the place where the northern pacific crosses the bridge and near the place where the northern pacific crosses the Jocko, — and east of arlee and where between Arlee and the agency ———

"Resumes reading." to "Now the Lark was happy and she sang"

(Gives the song of the Lark) Encore.

(Above given at request of Judge Woody I believe) By Judge Woody: Tell them why there are no salmon in the Lo Lo.

Hold on, I have not come to that.

Now he went back and jumped up the Missoula river and kept going and come to the place (I will skip that though) There is another station there called Toole Station and he kept coming to the place called Carter.

Old Slooie, one of the old timers, he was coming along and heard the girls singing and he examined and looked around and every move he made was closer and until he could see distinctly what they were doing; and he seen that they were dancing and they invited him to come and join the dance and that was a fine song they were singing and it made him feel good, just as at times you know there is an air you like and other you don't wish to hear? So Mr. Coyote he comes over and grabs hold of them by the arm —— you know the way they dance, there is a man and a woman, and man and a woman, and a man and a woman, and so on, that is the way they were dancing. White people dance as man and woman and hug them tight but we dance that way, all in a ring; so he got in the ring and they commenced he noticed they were drawing toward the river, they kept coming and he liked it, he had is arms around the girl in front, he was hugging her in front, holding the girl and having a grand old time and they got to the edge of the river and he said, — "Girls I want to take my moccasins off" and they said, "No." And dragged Coyote into the river. Finally it kept getting deeper and deeper and that Mr. Coyote drowned. So they drowned him and turned him over and examined him. It seems he has a bad kind of smell so they did not care about eating him, so they threw him in the river and he floated down and they commenced dancing again, and he goes floating down the river dead. And cousin Fox comes along and finds cousin coyote and that he has got drowned. Ho, you FOOL, says he, you fool, never take my advice. I advised you but you never take advice. I have a notion to let you go ahead and stay there and he made a few steps and look around there and he found himself alone and pretty lonesome.

"I like old Coyote, even if he was so mischievous," because he had been great company to him. "I guess I bring you to life," and he jumped over him and he says "You having a long sleep."

And Coyote stretched and stretched and come awake again. They he remembered and he said "Wasn't I dancing and didn't they drag me into the river?" And Fox said, "Yes you was." And coyote was going to go back and Fox said "Don't" and Coyote said, "And wasn't I dead." and Fox said "Yes you was dead." "Now I tell you what you do, Mr. Coyote, you go back and you will find some bunch of grass and you will find them and they will dance again and you build a fire clear around those girls and light it and let them burn up, so he did and they tried to coax him back and have him dance again, but he set fire clear around them and finally these girls and it seems they were cannibals, all got burnt up and nothing left of them but shells, and the shells were kind of bright and sparkled. Now I was telling Mr. Elrod, now he takes and puts the shells to the river and heaves the shells into the river and he says when mankind is created I don't want you to eat up everybody that come here and while he heaves the shells into the river he says this river shall be called *In MessoulEtch*. Now the meaning of In Messoul Eteth, as near as I can make it, is "Quakemtes" there is a little tree called "Quakemtes" You know what you call it — you can see the leaves just glitter and sparkle and they are so pretty, and you know that shells are so pretty you know how when you throw them in the river they glitter and sparkle like this tree leaves? Now as near as I explain it he called it "Sparkling River" that is the meaning of "In Messoul Etech." Now you know what that tree is called, what is it? Can't you tell, some kind of an Ash. Quakemash — Sparkling or Quakem, that is the tree Quakem Ash. Of course then he comes along and kept on until he comes to those Sleeping Child. (And there are a lot of land marks down towards Frenchtown.) Of course —— I guess my time is too limited —— but I suppose that at any other times Professor Elrod or Mr Stone comes down the Ravalli I can tell them the rest.

I will tell another short story. Seeing my friend Mr. Catlin here puts me in mind of Chief Joseph's invasion of the Bitter Root Valley and marching through Big Hole and the battle of Big Hole. Now somebody was fishing or picnicing. A party was out and I don't know whether they was picnicking or fishing, or what, but they was out and the indians went after them, and among them was a colored man, I believe they got some of those people but the colored man got away and one of the indians took after him with a gun and the colored man, he looked back and he knew that he was doomed and he kept a going.

Now this is no "myth" that was a fact. I saw one of the party myself and heard it, who was on the war path during that invasion — and they come to that high place and there was short bush growing there, a little tree, not a big tree, and he looked ahead and it was to late for him, if he passed the tree. He thought if the indian didn't see him he could climb the tree and so he did and went up on the bush tree and rested. Of course the indian came along on the run and — Brother Catlin here was around the Bitter Root then and he can tell you this is the truth — and the indian come along under this tree and he looked around and could not find this colored man, or Ethiopian, whatever he is called — Now if there is any colored man here I don't want to make fun but it is so much fun and I cant help it, and I have to laugh every time I think of that fellow, — and I want to tell you this before I quit, and he looked around and could not find his man and here was the man in this tree above him, and he was holding his breath and could not make a move. Finally the indian went away and the colored man got down from the tree and hid and got away, and at that time I was corresponding with Captain Gray [Mills] at Deer Lodge, he was there and had a newspaper he was running, the —————— (?). Captain Gray wanted me to write a history and he told me to get him facts. So I had to go North and see White Bird, up in Canada, and he was there, and Sitting Bull. I got there and asked him all the questions that these newspaper men wanted — they have some great history, those newspaper men — You see I know myself, I was a newspaper man myself at the time, but this is no newspaper story or talk, it is a fact.

(Laughter.)

So I asked White Bird if such a thing had happened as one of the braves going after the colored man and he said it was and I asked where is he, and he said there he is over there, so I called him up and he said, are you the man who chased after that colored man? He said Yes. Did you consider him a white man? Well, no, I didn't think he was a white man. Did you know he was black? Yes, I knew that. Did you want to kill him? Yes. Why? I wanted to get his hair. Well, why did you want to get his hair? Well, he say — I think it was an Irishman or a democrat from the south — he got it into his head that the wool of the colored man was the best thing in the God's world, was the best thing for sore ears, that the wool if you put the ear it would cure it, because there was some magic cure.

Of course there are lots of such stories as that but I don't know. It is an old thing with me, but I think to you it is new. Thanking you for your attention, ladies and gentlemen.

(Applause)

Footnotes

Abbreviations Used in Footnotes

AS — *The Anaconda Standard.*

BCIM Papers — St. Ignatius Mission file, Bureau of Catholic Indian Missions Papers, Marquette University Library Archives, Milwaukee, Wis.

CIA — Commissioner of Indian Affairs.

DM — *The Daily Missoulian.*

FH Agency Papers, letters received — Flathead Agency Papers, letters received, 8NS-075-96-323, National Archives, Denver, Col.

FH Agency Papers, letters sent — Flathead Agency Papers, letters sent, local copy books, 8NS-075-96-318, National Archives, Denver, Col.

McWhorter Papers — Lucullus Virgil McWhorter Papers, collection 55, Manuscripts, Archives, and Special Collections, Holland Library, Washington State University, Pullman, Wash.

MDG — *Missoula Daily Gazette* and *Missoula Gazette* (daily).

MHS Archives — Montana Historical Society Archives, Helena.

NA — National Archives, Washington, D.C.

NA CCF — Central Classified Files, RG 75, National Archives, Washington, D.C.

NA CIA LR — Letters Received, Records of the Commissioner of Indian Affairs, RG 75, National Archives, Washington, D.C.

NA CIA LS — Letters Sent, Records of the Commissioner of Indian Affairs, RG 75, National Archives, Washington, D.C.

NAmf — National Archives Microfilm Publication.

NNW — *The New North-West* (Deer Lodge, Mont.).

OIA Letters Received — U.S. Office of Indian Affairs, "Letters Received by the Office of Indian Affairs, 1824-81," NAmf M234.

PNTMC — Robert C. Carriker and Eleanor R. Carriker, eds., "The Pacific Northwest Tribes Missions Collection of the Oregon Province Archives of the Society of Jesus" (Wilmington, Del.: Scholarly Resources Inc., 1987).

Ronan letters, vol. 1 — Peter Ronan, *"A Great Many of Us Have Good Farms":
Agent Peter Ronan Reports on the Flathead Indian Reservation, Montana, 1877-1887*, ed. Robert J. Bigart. (Pablo, Mont.: Salish Kootenai College Press, 2014).

Ronan letters, vol. 2 — Peter Ronan, *Justice to Be Accorded to the Indians:
Agent Peter Ronan Reports on the Flathead Indian Reservation, 1888-1893*, ed. Robert J. Bigart (Pablo, Mont.: Salish Kootenai College Press, 2014).

RP — *The Ronan Pioneer.*

Toole Archives, UM — Toole Archives, Mansfield Library, University of Montana, Missoula.

WM — *The Weekly Missoulian.*

Foreword

1. Duncan McDonald to L. V. McWhorter, Feb. 1, 1928, McWhorter Papers.

2. James Hunter, *Scottish Highlanders, Indian Peoples: Thirty Generations of a Montana Family* (Helena: Montana Historical Society Press, 1996, 1997), pp. 48-71.

3. Robert J. Bigart, *Getting Good Crops: Economic and Diplomatic Survival Strategies of the Montana Bitterroot Salish Indians, 1870-1891* (Norman: University of Oklahoma Press, 2010), pp. 18-46.

4. Ronan letters, vol. 1, pp. 351-353, 360-364.

Chapter 1

1. Susan Allison, *A Pioneer Gentlewoman in British Columbia*, ed. Margaret A. Ormsby. (Vancouver: University of British Columbia Press, 1976), p. 10.

2. Catherine C. Leighton, *Life at Puget Sound* (Boston: Lee and Shepard, Publishers, and New York: Charles T. Dillingham, 1884), pp. 75-76.

3. Albert J. Partoll, "Angus McDonald, Frontier Fur Trader," *Pacific Northwest Quarterly*, vol. 42, no. 2, (April 1951), pp. 138-146; Winona Adams, editor, "An Indian Girl's Story of a Trading Expedition to the Southwest About 1841," *The Frontier* (Missoula, Mont.), vol. 10, no. 4 (May 1930), pp. 338-351.

4. David H. Chance, I*nfluence of the Hudson's Bay Company on the Native Cultures of the Colville District*, Northwest Anthropological Research Notes, Memoir Number Two (Moscow, Id., 1973), pp. 57, 62, 64, 66, and 68.

5. J. Orin Oliphant, "Old Fort Colville," *Washington Historical Quarterly*, vol. 16, no. 1 (Jan. 1925), pp. 44-46.

6. David H. Chance, *Influence of the Hudson's Bay Company on the Native Cultures of the Colville District*, Northwest Anthropological Research Notes, Memoir Number Two (Moscow, Id., 1973), pp. 38-39, 52.

7. [John Keast Lord], *At Home in the Wilderness* (London: Robert Hardwicke, 1867), pp. 53-56.

8. Albert J. Partoll, "Angus McDonald, Frontier Fur Trader," *Pacific Northwest Quarterly*, vol. 42, no. 2, (Apr. 1951), pp. 138-146; Duncan McDonald to Mr. McWhorter, Dec. 11, 1931, box 9, folder 45, McWhorter Papers.

9. Samuel Anderson,"Letters of Lieut. Sam Anderson, 1859-1862," Samuel Anderson Papers, WA MSS S-1292, Beinecke Library, Yale University, New Haven, Conn., box 1, folders 17-20, pages 77-78 and 90.

10. "Louse Was Forecaster," DM, Dec. 30, 1916, p. 10, c. 2.

11. Charles Wilson, *Mapping the Frontier*, ed. George F. G. Stanley (Seattle: University of Washington Press, 1970), p. 135.

12. Samuel Anderson,"Letters of Lieut. Sam Anderson, 1859-1862," Samuel Anderson Papers, WA MSS S-1292, Beinecke Library, Yale University, New Haven, Conn., box 1, folders 17-20, pages 73-74, 82, and 88.

13. William S. Lewis, "Spent Boyhood Days at Old Fort Colville," *Spokesman Review* (Spokane, Wash.), Apr. 28, 1929, unpaged, c. 1-7.

14. Ibid; "Carrie Mears," *Washington Pioneer Project, Told by the Pioneers*, vol. 3 (1938), pp. 204-205; Carrie Mears interview, Washington Pioneers Project Papers, MS 31, Washington State Library, Olympia, Wash.

15. Alex McLeod, "Hudson's Bay Company," *Washington Pioneer Project, Told by the Pioneers*, vol. 1 (1937), pp. 87-88.

16. William S. Lewis, "Spent Boyhood Days at Old Fort Colville," *Spokesman Review* (Spokane, Wash.), Apr. 28, 1929, unpaged, c. 1-7.

17. Christina MacDonald McKenzie Williams, "The Daughter of Angus MacDonald," Washington Historical Quarterly, vol. 13, no. 2 (Apr. 1922), p. 109.

18. "Indian Colony Is Paid Visit," DM, May 11, 1919, p. 7, c. 1-2; "The Grizzly's Home," *Daily Democrat-Messenger* (Missoula, Mont.), May 7, 1910, p. 1, c. 6.

19. Ellen Nye, "Dixon Was Home of First White Woman to Live in Western Montana...," *Rocky Mountain Husbandman* (Great Falls, Mont.), Nov. 7, 1935, p. 7, c. 1-4.

20. "Victor Won the Race," AS, Sept. 13, 1898, p. 10, c. 2.

21. William S. Lewis, "Spent Boyhood Days at Old Fort Colville," *Spokesman Review* (Spokane, Wash.), Apr. 28, 1929, unpaged, c. 1-7.

22. Christina MacDonald McKenzie Williams, "The Daughter of Angus MacDonald," Washington Historical Quarterly, vol. 13, no. 2 (Apr. 1922), pp. 108-109; Thomas E. Jessett, *Chief Spokan Garry, 1811-1892: Christian, Statesman, and Friend of the White Man* (Minneapolis, Minn.: T. S. Denison & Company, Inc., 1960), pp. 107-152; Robert H. Ruby and John A. Brown, *The Spokane Indians: Children of the Sun* (Norman: University of Oklahoma Press, 1970), pp. 83-140.

23. Christina MacDonald McKenzie Williams, "The Daughter of Angus MacDonald," Washington Historical Quarterly, vol. 13, no. 2 (Apr. 1922), p. 113; Notebook, "Assistant Director of Museum, 1949-1953," Mary Elrod Ferguson Papers MS 205, series 3, box 1, folder 8, Toole Archives, UM.

24. "Duncan McDonald Tells of Early Days in the Northwest," *The Kootenai Times* (Libby, Mont.), Mar. 17, 1915, p. 1, c. 3-5; p. 3, c. 5; "Story of Mickey Hunt and Panama Pat, Two Refugees," *Rocky Mountain Husbandman* (Great Falls, Mont.), June 28, 1934, p. 7, c. 1-2.

Chapter 2

1. "Old Days at Flathead Post," DM, Dec. 19, 1915, ed. sec., p. 4, c. 6-7.

2. Ibid.

3. "Letter from Missoula Co.," *The Weekly Independent* (Deer Lodge, Mont.), Dec. 12, 1868, p. 2, c. 4.

4. Jan. 28, 1869, Daybooks, vol. 14, Francis Lyman Worden Papers, MSS 21; Subgroup 2, Worden and Company, Series 7, Financial, Toole Archives, UM; "An Old Set of Books," AS, Nov. 27, 1897, p. 10, c. 3.

5. Jan. 29, 1869, and Nov. 5, 1869, Daybooks, vol. 14 and 15, Francis Lyman Worden Papers, MSS 21; Subgroup 2, Worden and Company, Series 7, Financial, Toole Archives, UM.

6. Jno. Owen to Gov., Jan. 18, 1869, John Owen Papers, MS 44, box 1, folder 3, MHS Archives.

7. W. J. McCormick to CIA, Feb. 4, 1869, Montana M101/1869, OIA Letters Received, reel 489, fr. 368-370.

8. M. M. McCauley to CIA, Apr. 2, 1969, Montana M335/1869, OIA Letters Received, reel 489, fr. 419-421.

9. Oct. 2, 1869, Daybooks, vol. 15, Francis Lyman Worden Papers, MSS 21; Subgroup 2, Worden and Company, Series 7, Financial, Toole Archives, UM.

10. "George Young Killed at Frenchtown," NNW, May 20, 1870, p. 2, c. 4; Territory vs. John Stanley, murder, June 5, 1870, case 38, criminal, Missoula Court Records, Missoula County Courthouse, Missoula, Montana, Territorial, reel 1, frames 1472-82, 1487-94, 1503-05, 1512-13, and 1548-49.

11. July 12, 1870, Daybooks, vol. 16, Francis Lyman Worden Papers, MSS 21; Subgroup 2, Worden and Company, Series 7, Financial, Toole Archives, UM.

12. J. A. Viall to CIA, Jan. 13, 1871, Montana V13/1871, OIA Letters Received, reel 491, fr. 435-438.

13. "Old Days at Flathead Post," DM, Dec. 19, 1915, ed. sec., p. 4, c. 6-7.

14. "The Last of Montana's Wild Black Horses," *The Pioneer* (Missoula, Mont.), June 29, 1872, p. 1, c. 5-7; "'Wild Horse Island,'" *Missoula County Times*, June 15, 1887, p. 3, c. 5.

15. "Horse Stealing," *The Pioneer* (Missoula, Mont.), Nov. 9, 1872, p. 3, c. 3; "Capture of the Horse Thieves," *The Weekly Independent* (Deer Lodge, Mont.), Nov. 16, 1872, p. 3, c. 1.

16. Robert Bigart, "The Travails of Flathead Indian Agent Charles S. Medary, 1875-1877," *Montana: The Magazine of Western History*, vol. 62, no. 3 (Aut. 2012), pp. 32-33.

17. "Good Old Days," *Western Democrat* (weekly) (Missoula, Mont.), Sept. 2, 1894, p. 2, c. 4.

18. "More About Indian 'Medicine,'" NNW, Feb. 21, 1879, p. 3, c. 3.

19. Ibid.

20. "Duncan McDonald Nearly Lost Argument When He Wounded a Buffalo...," *Rocky Mountain Husbandman* (Great Falls, Mont.), July 26, 1934, p. 7, c. 1-4; C. M. Russell, *More Rawhides* (Great Falls, MT: Montana Newspaper Association, 1925), pp. 29-31.

21. Notebook, "Assistant Director of Museum, 1949-1953," Mary Elrod Ferguson Papers, MS 205, series 3, box 1, folder 8, Toole Archives, UM.

22. June 12,1873–Sept. 19, 1873, Daybooks, vol. 23, Francis Lyman Worden Papers, MSS 21; Subgroup 2, Worden and Company, Series 7, Financial, Toole Archives, UM.

23. Peter Whaley to CIA, Aug. 25, 1874, Montana W1441/1874, OIA Letters Received, reel 500, fr. 1138.

24. President to CIA, Nov. 18, 1874, Montana P681/1874, OIA Letters Received, reel 500, fr. 190-195.

25. Ronan letters, vol. 2, pp. 389-393.

26. "Sage of Reservation Says Trees Will Not Die," *St. Ignatius Post*, Mar. 6, 1925, p. 4, c. 3.

27. "Duncan MacDonald Dies at Age of 88," RP, Oct. 21, 1937, p. 1, c. 1.

28. Notebook, "Assistant Director of Museum, 1949-1953," Mary Elrod Ferguson Papers, MS 205, series 3, box 1, folder 8, Toole Archives, UM; U.S. Bureau of Indian Affairs, "Selected Records of the Bureau of Indian Affairs Relating to the

Enrollment of Indians on the Flathead Reservation, 1903-08," NAmf M1350, reel 1, fr. 25, nos. 883-884.

29. "Family Record," Duncan McDonald family Bible, xerox copy in possession of authors.

30. Mrs. L. L. Marsh, "Duncan M'Donald, Resident of Montana 81 Years...," *Great Falls Tribune*, Mar. 25, 1930, p. 6, c. 2-5; U.S. Bureau of Indian Affairs, "Selected Records of the Bureau of Indian Affairs Relating to the Enrollment of Indians on the Flathead Reservation, 1903-08," NAmf M1350, reel 1, fr. 59, no. 2100, and reel 3, fr. 44-55.

31. July 28, 1875, Daybooks, vol. 26, Francis Lyman Worden Papers, MSS 21; Subgroup 2, Worden and Company, Series 7, Financial, Toole Archives, UM.

32. "Buffalo Are Increasing," DM, Dec. 28, 1916, p. 10, c. 5; WM, May 17, 1876, p. 3, c. 2; Notebook, "Assistant Director of Museum, 1949-1953," Mary Elrod Ferguson Papers, MS 205, series 3, box 1, folder 8, Toole Archives, UM; Ronan letters, vol. 1, p. 239.

33. WM, Oct. 18, 1876, p. 3, c. 1.

34. Robert Bigart, "The Travails of Flathead Indian Agent Charles S. Medary, 1875-1877," *Montana: The Magazine of Western History*, vol. 62, no. 3 (Aut. 2012), pp. 27-41 and 93-94. Unattributed information about Medary which follows is from this article.

35. Charles S. Medary to CIA, Dec. 8, 1876, BCIM Papers.

36. Charles S. Medary to "My dear General," July 1875, BCIM Papers.

37. Robert Bigart, "The Travails of Flathead Indian Agent Charles S. Medary, 1875-1877," *Montana: The Magazine of Western History*, vol. 62, no. 3 (Aut. 2012), pp. 32-33.

38. Ronan letters, vol. 2, pp. 401-405.

39. Charles S. Medary to Gen. John Gibbon, Dec. 7, 1876, BCIM Papers.

40. U.S. Grand Jury to Hiram Knowles, Dec. 15, 1876, BCIM Papers.

41. Charles S. Medary to "My Dear General," Jan. 3, 1877, BCIM Papers.

42. Charles S. Medary to U.S. Attorney General, Jan. 5, 1877, BCIM Papers.

43. Duncan McDonald, "From Jocko Reservation," NNW, Feb. 9, 1877, p. 2, c. 8.

44. Charles S. Medary to CIA, Feb. 19, 1877, Montana M340/1877, OIA Letters Received, reel 508, fr. 233-238

45. Charles S. Medary to "My Dear General," Feb. 21, 1877, BCIM Papers.

46. Charles S. Medary to "My dear General," Feb. 27, 1877, BCIM Papers.

47. Charles Ewing to Charles Medary, Mar. 28, 1877, BCIM Papers.

48. Mary Ronan, *Girl From the Gulches: The Story of Mary Ronan*, as told to Margaret Ronan, ed. Ellen Baumler (Helena : Montana Historical Society Press, 2003), p. 183.

Chapter 3

1. Mary Ronan, *Girl from the Gulches: The Story of Mary Ronan*, as told to Margaret Ronan, ed. by Ellen Baumler (Helena: Montana Historical Society Press, 2003), pp. 155-156.

2. WM, July 6, 1877, p. 3, c. 2; "The Flatheads," *The Helena Independent* (daily), July 4, 1877, p. 1, c. 6-7.

3. Duncan M'Donald, "The Nez Perces War of 1877," NNW, Jan. 10, 1879, p. 2, c. 5

4. Duncan McDonald to L. V. McWhorter, Feb. 1, 1928, McWhorter Papers.

5. Joseph McDonald, interview, March 19, 2015; Camille Williams to Mr. McWhorter, June 21, 1937, box 12 folder 84, McWhorter Papers; Camille Williams to McWhorter, undated letter fragment, box 12, folder 80, McWhorter Papers.

6. Alvin M. Josephy, Jr., *The Nez Perce Indians and the Opening of the Northwest* (New Haven, Conn.: Yale University Press, 1965), pp. 573-633.

7. Ibid.

8. Angus McDonald to Hiram Knowles, before June 1878, Hiram Knowles Papers, MS 2, box 1, folder 3, MHS Archives.

9. Ronan letters, vol. 1, p. 239.

10. WM, Aug. 9, 1876, p. 3, c. 2;"Why Indians Abandon the Reservation," WM, Mar. 29, 1878, p. 3, c. 3-4; "An Open Letter," NNW, Apr. 26, 1878, p. 3, c. 6; "Precinct Officers," WM, Nov. 15, 1878, p. 3, c. 2; *Progressive Men of the State of Montana* (Chicago: A. W. Bowen & Co., 1902?), p. 1567.

11. "In Memorium," *Contributions to the Historical Society of Montana*, vol. 5 (1904), pp. 265-272; James H. Mills, "Reminiscences of an Editor," *Contributions to the Historical Society of Montana*, vol. 5 (1904), pp. 273-288; "Capt. Mills Crosses River," *The Helena Independent* (daily), Sept. 6, 1904, p. 5, c. 1-2; *Progressive Men of the State of Montana* (Chicago: A. W. Bowen & Co., 1902?), pp. 317-318.

12. "The Nez Perces Campaign," NNW, Apr. 19, 1878, p. 2, c. 2.

13. Duncan McDonald, "The Nez Perces," NNW, Apr. 26, 1878, p. 3, c. 5.

14. *Rocky Mountain Husbandman* (Diamond City, Mont.), May 9, 1878, p. 3, c. 2; NNW, May 10, 1878, p. 3, c. 6; NNW, May 17, 1878, p. 3, c. 6.

15. "The Nez Perce Papers," NNW, June 14, 1878, p. 3, c. 2; Duncan McDonald, "Indian Feeling," NNW, June 14, 1878, p. 3, c. 5-6.

16. "En Route," NNW, June 21, 1878, p. 3, c. 1.

17. *The Helena Daily Herald*, June 18, 1878, p. 2, c. 1.

18. Except as noted, this account of Duncan's July 1878 trip to Canada and meeting with White Bird is based on "Notes on Duncan McDonald and John Lebson," Joseph M. Dixon Papers, MS 55, box 99, folder 99-6, Toole Archives, UM; Duncan McDonald, "The Nez Perces War of 1877," NNW, Mar. 28, 1879, p. 3, c. 4-5; Duncan M'Donald, "White Bird and Sitting Bull," NNW, Aug. 9, 1878, p. 3, c. 4; Jerome A. Greene, *Beyond Bear's Paw: The Nez Perce Indians in Canada* (Norman: University of Oklahoma Press, 2010), pp. 134-153; Canada. Governor General's Office, "Papers Relating to the Nez Perce Indians of the United States, Who Have Taken Refuge in Canadian Territory," Numbered files, RG7-G21, vol. 323, file 2001-1, microfilm T-1387, frames 1178-1198, Public Archives of Canada, Ottawa.

19. Duncan McDonald, "Letters from Duncan McDonald," NNW, July 26, 1878, p. 2, c. 4.

20. John Rhone, *Wild Horse Plains* (Plains, Mont.: The Plainsman, n.d.), pp. 19-21; Bud Ainsworth, "Neptune Lynch Family Were First Settlers in Plains Valley...," *Rocky Mountain Husbandman* (Great Falls, Mont.), Aug. 4, 1932, p. 1, c. 1-3.

21. Duncan McDonald, "Letters from Duncan McDonald," NNW, July 26, 1878, p. 2,

22. NNW, July 26, 1878, p. 3, c. 3.

23. NNW, Aug. 2, 1878, p. 3, c. 2.

24. "The Return from Exile," NNW, July 19, 1878, p. 3, c. 2.

25. D. B. Jenkins, "The Murder of Joy, Elliott and Hayes," NNW, July 19, 1878, p. 2, c. 2-3.

26. Ibid.

27. "The Hostiles," *The Helena Independent* (daily), July 21, 1878, p. 3, c. 2.

28. C. S. Nichols, "Stevensville Pioneer Tells Interesting Story of the Chase After Chief Joseph's Renegades," DM, May 28, 1916, ed. section, p. 1, c. 1-7.

29. "Pursuit of the Murder Party," NNW, Aug. 2, 1878, p. 2, c. 5; "The Recent Battle on the Clearwater," WM, Aug. 2, 1878, p. 3, c. 3-4.

30. Duncan M'Donald, "An Appeal to Reason," NNW, Aug. 16, 1878, p. 3, c. 4.

31. Ibid.

32. NNW, Aug. 16, 1878, p. 2, c. 1.

33. Duncan McDonald, "'Friendlies' or 'Hostiles,'" NNW, Aug. 30, 1878, p. 3, c. 5.

34. "From Philipsburg," NNW, Aug. 30, 1878, p. 3, c. 4.

35. Angus McDonald to Hiram Knowles, Nov. 10, 1878, Hiram Knowles Papers, MS 2, box 1, folder 3, MHS Archives.

36. Ronan letters, vol. 1, pp. 82-85; "Wayside Notes," *The Helena Independent* (daily), Nov. 22, 1878, p. 3, c. 3; Society of Montana Pioneers, *Constitution, Members, and Officers, with Portraits and Maps* (Akron, Ohio, 1899), vol. 1, p. 266; U.S. Census Bureau, "Population Schedules of the Ninth Census of the United States, 1870," NAmf M593, reel 827, Montana, Missoula County, Cedar Creek Mines, p. 318A, #5.

37. "Notes on Duncan McDonald and John Lebson," Joseph M. Dixon Papers, MS 55, box 99, folder 99-6, pages 16-19, Toole Archives, UM; Jerome A. Greene, *Beyond Bear's Paw: The Nez Perce Indians in Canada* (Norman: University of Oklahoma Press, 2010), pp. 118, 135-150.

38. "Notes on Duncan McDonald and John Lebson," Joseph M. Dixon Papers, MS 55, box 99, folder 99-6, pages 19-21, Toole Archives, UM; Duncan McDonald to Mr. T. D. Duncan, undated, Duncan McDonald Papers, SC 429, vol. 1, p. 35, MHS Archives; James E. Murphy, *Half Interest in a Silver Dollar: The Saga of Charles E. Conrad* (Missoula, MT: Mountain Press Publishing Company, 1983).

39. Ronan letters, vol. 1, pp. 89-93

40. Duncan M'Donald, "The Nez Perces War of 1877," NNW, Jan. 24, 1879, p. 3, c. 4-6.

41. NNW, Jan. 24, 1879, p. 2, c. 1.

42. NNW, Feb. 7, 1879, p. 2, c. 1.

43. NNW, Feb. 14, 1879, p. 2, c. 1; "From Bannack," NNW, Feb. 14, 1879, p. 3, c. 1.

44. Duncan M'Donald, "The Nez Perces War of 1877," NNW, Mar. 21, 1879, p. 3, c. 3

45. Duncan M'Donald, "The Nez Perces War of 1877," NNW, Jan. 24, 1879, p. 3, c. 4-6; NNW, Jan. 31, 1879, p. 2, c. 1.

46. Duncan McDonald, "More About Indian 'Medicine,'" NNW, Feb. 21, 1879, p. 3, c. 3.

47. Ibid.

48. "Family Record," Duncan McDonald family Bible, xerox copy in possession of the authors; Notebook, "Assistant Director of Museum, 1949-1953," Mary Elrod Ferguson Papers, MS 205, series 3, box 1, folder 8, Toole Archives, UM.

49. "A Handsome Present," *The Helena Daily Herald*, Mar. 10, 1879, p. 3, c. 2.

50. Duncan M'Donald, "The Nez Perces War of 1877," NNW, Mar. 28, 1879, p. 3, c. 4-5.

51. NNW, Mar. 14, 1879, p. 3, c. 2.

52. "End of the Nez Perce War History," NNW, Mar. 14, 1879, p. 3. c. 1.

53. WM, May 23, 1879, p. 3, c. 2.

54. [W. H. H. Dickinson Variety Store, Missoula, Mont., Ledger, 1879-80], W. H. H. Dickinson Papers, LC 23, box 1, folder 7, Toole Archives, UM.

55. "An Indian Row," NNW, July 18, 1879, p. 3, c. 2; "The Murders Near Lincoln," NNW, July 18, 1879, p. 3, c. 2.

56. "Helena Letter," *Bozeman Avant Courier*, July 31, 1879, p. 3, c. 4; "The Lincoln Indian Affair," NNW, Aug. 8, 1879, p. 3, c. 2.

57. Duncan McDonald, "From Over the Line," NNW, Oct. 24, 1879, p. 2, c. 5-6.

58. Ronan letters, vol. 1, pp. 118-119, 123-125, 140.

59. Duncan McDonald, "From Over the Line," NNW, Oct. 24, 1879, p. 2, c. 5-6.

60. Ibid.

61. Ibid.

62. NNW, Nov. 7, 1879, p. 2, c. 1.

63. Duncan McDonald, "From North of the Line," NNW, Dec. 19, 1879, p. 2, c. 2.

64. "Wintering in the Far North," NNW, Feb. 6, 1880, p. 3, c. 1.

65. Duncan M'Donald, "Life in the Far North," NNW, Apr. 2, 1880, p. 2, c. 5-6.

66. NNW, Mar. 5, 1880, p. 2, c. 1.

67. Duncan McDonald, "From the North," NNW, Mar. 19, 1880, p. 3, c. 4.

68. Duncan M'Donald, "Life in the Far North," NNW, Apr. 2, 1880, p. 2, c. 5-6.

69. NNW, June 18, 1880, p. 3, c. 5.

Chapter 4

1. "Former Prices," DM, Nov. 21, 1911, p. 10, c. 2; "From Missoula County," *Helena Weekly Herald*, Jan. 6, 1881, p. 8, c. 3.

2. "A Stampede," The Helena Daily Herald, June 6, 1881, p. 3, c. 4.

3. "Aboriginal Items," WM, June 10, 1881, p. 3, c. 3-4.

4. Duncan McDonald vs. Joseph Ashley, June 21, 1881, debt, case 467, District Court Records, Missoula County Courthouse, Missoula, Mont., microfilm reel 7, frames 1090-1103.

5. U.S. Bureau of the Census, "10th Census, 1880," Montana, Missoula County, p. 458B, #29, NAmf T9, reel 742.

6. "From the Missoulian," *Rocky Mountain Husbandman* (White Sulphur Springs, Mont.), July 28, 1881, p. 2, c. 2-3.

7. Ledger, vol. 52, pp. 472-473, Charles H. McLeod Papers, MSS 1, Toole Archives, UM.

8. WM, Nov. 11, 1881, p. 3, c. 2.

9. WM, Dec. 16, 1881, p. 3, c. 1.

10. Duncan McDonald, "The Eagle Bird," NNW, Jan. 20, 1882, p. 3, c. 4.

11. WM, Feb. 24, 1882, p. 3, c. 1.

12. "The Weather," AS, Feb. 7, 1896, p. 10, c. 1; "Duncan Macdonald Recalls Cold Snap," DM, Jan. 25, 1927, p. 3, c. 2.

13. NNW, Apr. 7, 1882, p. 3, c. 3.

14. "Railroad Obstruction," NNW, Mar. 17, 1882, p. 3, c. 1.

15. Duncan McDonald, "Something of the Early Days," NNW, Mar. 24, 1882, p. 3, c. 4.

16. "Family Record," Duncan McDonald family Bible, xerox copy in possessin of authors.

17. WM, June 23, 1882, p. 3, c. 2.

18. U.S. President, "Message from the President of the United States, Transmitting a Letter from the Secretary of the Interior Respecting the Ratification of an Agreement with the Confederated Tribes of Flathead, Kootenay, and Upper Pend d'Oreilles Indians, for the Sale of a Portion of Their Reservation in Montana Territory," Senate Executive Document No. 44, 47th Cong., 2d Sess. (1883), serial 2076, p. 8-22, 24, 28, and maps.

19. WM, Dec. 8, 1882, p. 3, c. 2.

20. St. Ignatius Mission, Montana, Financial Account Book, 1878-1884, PNTMC, reel 7, frames 327-328.

21. "Down the Road," WM, June 22, 1883, p. 2, c. 1-3.

22. S. S. Benedict to Secretary of the Interior, July 10, 1883, U.S. Department of the Interior, "Reports of Inspection of the Field Jurisdictions of the Office of Indian Affairs, 1873-1900," NAmf M1070, roll 11, Flathead Agency, 3093/1883.

23. Ibid.

24. Ronan letters, vol. 1, pp. 232-236.

25. For Duncan's experiences with the Northern Pacific Railroad last spike tour on Flathead Reservation see Arthur L. Stone, "Following Old Trails: XXIV — The Villard Invasion," DM, Dec. 3, 1911, ed. section. p. 4, c. 5-7; Arthur L.

Stone, *Following Old Trails* (Missoula, Mont.: Morton John Elrod, 1913), pp. 165-172; WM, Sept. 28, 1883, p. 3, c. 3.

26. Ibid.

27. Geneva E. Wright, "A Double Decade in Dixon," in R. S. Bishop, Chairman, "Dixon-Agency Montana Study Group" (Missoula, Mont.: n.p., mimeo, 1946).

28. *The Northwest* (St. Paul, Minn.), vol. 3, no. 5 (May 1885), p. 10, c. 1.

29. C. H. Howard to Secretary of the Interior, Dec. 4, 1883, U.S. Department of the Interior, "Reports of Inspection of the Field Jurisdictions of the Office of Indian Affairs, 1873-1900," NAmf M1070, roll 11, Flathead Agency, 5061/1883.

30. Ronan letters, vol. 1, pp. 238-243.

31. WM, May 16, 1884, p. 3, c. 3.

32. Tom Jones, *The Last of the Buffalo* (Cincinnati, Ohio: Tom Jones Publisher Scenic Souvenirs, 1909), p. 2.

33. "Amusements," WM, Aug. 1, 1884, p. 3, c. 3; WM, Aug. 1, 1884, p. 3, c. 4.

34. Duncan M'Donald, "Indian Names," NNW, Oct. 24, 1884, p 3, c. 5.

Chapter 5

1. Duncan McDonald to W. H. Smead, Mar. 20, 1904, Flathead Agency Papers, letters received.

2. "The Indian Troubles," WM, Dec. 25, 1885, p. 2, c. 1.

3. Tom Stout, *Montana: Its Story and Biography* (Chicago: The American Historical Society, 1921), vol. 3, p. 1277; "Around the Town," DM, Feb. 28, 1923, p. 2, c. 3.

4. Ronan letters, vol. 1, pp. 369-371.

5. Ronan letters, vol. 1, pp. 372-373.

6. Ronan to CIA, Dec. 14, 1886, 33,614/1886, NA CIA LR.

7. D. M. McDonald, "Another Steamboat," *Missoula County Times*, Jan. 17, 1887 [i.e., Jan. 26, 1887], p. 3, c. 3; "Ravalli News Notes," *Butte Semi-Weekly Miner*, Jan. 15, 1887, p. 1, c. 7-8; *Butte Semi-Weekly Miner*, May 11, 1887, p. 2, c. 6.

8. "For Flathead!," *Missoula County Times*, May 4, 1887, p. 2, c. 3; "Flathead Travel," *Missoula County Times*, May 4, 1887, p. 3, c. 2.

9. "To Flathead Lake," NNW, May 6, 1887, p. 3, c. 6; "Selish Stage Line!," NNW, May 6, 1887, p. 2, c. 7.

10. *Missoula County Times*, June 8, 1887, p. 3, c. 3 (2 items).

11. "Still on Top," *Missoula County Times*, Oct. 5, 1887, p. 3, c. 4; NNW, Apr. 13, 1888, p. 3, c. 8.

12. *Missoula County Times*, Feb. 1, 1887, p. 3, c. 3; "After Judge Woody," *Missoula County Times*, Feb. 8, 1888, p. 3, c. 4.

13. "New Line," *Missoula County Times*, Mar. 7, 1888, p. 3, c. 4.

14. "Ho for the Flathead Valley!," NNW, Mar. 16, 1888, p. 4, c. 5.

15. E. J. Stanley, "A Trip to Flathead Lake," *The Montana Methodist* (Helena, Mont.), vol. 1, no. 1 (1888), p. 6.

16. "Pioneer Tells of Frontier Days," *Rocky Mountain Husbandman* (Great Falls, Mont.), June 30, 1932, p. 2, c. 3-4.

17. "Flathead Had to Import Its Potatoes in Pioneer Days," DM, Mar. 1, 1936, p. 7, c. 1-3; Oliver Vose, "Early Resident Tells of Arrival in Flathead," in Frank H. Trippet and L. L. Bain, *History of Kalispell* (Kalispell, Mont.: Trippet Publishers, 1956), pp. 33-44.

18. Jerome D'Aste, S.J., diary, Mary 7, 1889, PNTMC, reel 29, fr. 581.

19. "Notice," WM, June 12, 1889, p. 3, c. 6.

20. WM, June 12, 1889, p. 3, c. 1.

21. Christina Mead to "My Dear Cousin," July 16, 1889, letter in possession of McDonald family, authors have xerox copy.

22. Robert J. Bigart, ed., *Zealous in All Virtues: Documents of Worship and Culture Change, St. Ignatius Mission, Montana, 1890-1894* (Pablo, Mont.: Salish Kootenai College Press, 2007), p. 17.

23. "Land of the Flathead," *The Helena Journal* (daily), May 22, 1890, p. 7, c. 3.

24. "Notes From the Mission," MDG, June 30, 1890, p. 1, c. 6.

25. David R. McGinnis, "My First Trip to Flathead Valley," *Twelfth Annual Report of the Water Department, City of Kalispell, Montana, Year Ending December 31, 1925*, pp. 76-81.

26. MDG, Aug. 28, 1890, p. 8, c. 3.

27. WM, Dec. 10, 1890, p. 3, c. 1.

28. "The Fertile Flathead Country," *The Northwest Illustrated Monthly Magazine* (St. Paul, Minn.), vol. 9, no. 7 (July 1891), pp. 46-48.

29. Samuel William Carvoso Whipps reminiscence, 1933, SC 163, MHS Archives, pp. 108-109.

30. MDG, Mar. 25, 1891, p. 8, c. 2.

31. "The Flathead Country," *The Helena Independent*, May 12, 1891, p. 8, c. 1-2.

32. "The Flathead Country," *The Helena Independent*, May 24, 1891, p. 10, c. 1-2.

33. "The Great Northwest," AS, June 8, 1891, p. 6, c. 1-2.

34. Ronan letters, vol. 2, pp. 209-210, 217-218; CIA to Ronan, June 26, 1891, letter press, vol. 6, pt. 1, pp. 336-337, miscellaneous, NA CIA LS; CIA to Secretary of the Interior, July 15, 1891, letter press, vol. 6, pt. 1, p. 415, miscellaneous, NA CIA LS.

35. "Ravalli and Arlee," MDG, Aug. 12, 1891, p. 4, c. 1.

36. Leila Sawhill, "A Richland Girl in Montana," *The Weekly News* (Mansfield, Ohio), Nov. 5, 1891, p. 8, c. 3.

37. *Missoula Weekly Gazette*, Nov. 4, 1891, p. 3, c. 5-6.

38. Mildred Chaffin, "Smallpox Epidemic Recalled," *The Missoulian*, May 21, 1967, p. 11-A.

39. "Stage Line Change," MDG, Jan. 5, 1892, p. 1, c. 6; "Important Transfer," WM, Jan. 6, 1892, p. 1, c. 6; Bon I. Whealdon, et. al., *"I Will Be Meat for My Salish": The Buffalo and the Montana Writers Project Interviews on the Flathead Indian Reservation*, ed. Robert Bigart (Pablo and Helena, Mont.: Salish Kootenai College Press and Montana Historical Society Press, 2001), pp. 239, 254.

40. WM, Mar. 13, 1885, p. 3, c. 4.

41. CIA to Ronan, Sept. 4, 1885, letter press vol. 69, pt. 1, pp. 214-215, accounts, NA CIA LS.

42. Rosters of Indian Police, 1886-1887, vol. 7, p. 10, entry 982, Record Group 75, NA.

43. Duncan McDonald, "Big Bear," NNW, July 3, 1885, p. 3, c. 6; Hugh A. Dempsey, *Big Bear: The End of Freedom* (Lincoln: The University of Nebraska Press, 1984).

44. "Thompson Falls," WM, Nov. 6, 1885, p. 2, c. 3.

45. Citizen of Missoula to CIA, Dec. 17, 1885, 30,733/1885, NA CIA LR; Missoula Democrat to CIA, Jan. 7, 1886, 1,626/1886, NA CIA LR.

46. Ronan letters, vol. 1, pp. 354-356; Ronan to CIA, May 12, 1886, 13,265/1886, NA CIA LR; "The Kalispel Gold Region," *Missoula County Times*, May 26, 1886, p. 3, c. 2.

47. Geo. B. Pearsons to Secretary of the Interior, Nov. 11, 1886, U.S. Department of the Interior, "Reports of Inspection of the Field Jurisdictions of the Office of Indian Affairs, 1873-1900," NAmf M1070, reel 11, Flathead Agency, 6543/1886; Ronan letters, vol. 2, pp. 79-80.

48. Ronan letters, vol. 1, pp. 373-375.

49. Louisa McDermott, "Ethnology and Folklore, Selish Proper," unpublished masters thesis, University of California, Berkeley, 1904, pp. 40-41.

50. "Wild Horse Island," *Missoula County Times*, June 15, 1887, p. 3, c. 5.

51. "Drowned," *Butte Semi-Weekly Miner*, Sept. 15, 1888, p. 2, c. 1.

52. "A Mystery of the Blackfoot," WM, Oct. 31, 1888, p. 3, c. 3; "The Marias Pass," NNW, Nov. 9, 1888, p. 3, c. 6.

53. "A Dark Deed Discovered," *Great Falls Tribune* (semi-weekly), Nov. 3, 1888, p. 1, c. 3.

54. "Another Landmark Gone," *Missoula Gazette*, Feb. 6, 1889, p 3, c. 3; "Old Days at Flathead Post," DM, Dec. 19, 1915, ed. section, p. 4, c. 6-7.

55. MDG, Feb. 14, 1890, p. 4, c. 1; Angus McDonald, probate 187, 11-5-89, Missoula District Court Records, Missoula County Records Management, Missoula, Montana.

56. "Family Record," Duncan McDonald family Bible, xerox copy in possession of authors.

57. "Official," WM, Mar. 20, 1889, p. 3, c. 3.

58. WM, May 29, 1889, p. 3, c. 1; "Good," WM, June 5, 1889, p. 3, c. 5.

59. Ronan letters, vol. 2, pp. 48-60.

60. "The Indians," WM, Aug. 21, 1889, p. 2, c. 4.

61. WM, Oct. 30, 1889, p. 4, c. 3.

62. WM, Jan. 15, 1890, p. 3, c. 2; WM, Jan. 22, 1890, p. 3, c. 1.

63. "Ripple in the Springtide Boom," *The Helena Journal* (daily), Jan. 26, 1890, p. 1, c. 8.

64. WM, Jan. 29, 1890, p 3, c. 1.

65. WM, Jan. 22, 1890, p. 3, c. 1; "Missoula Gazette Extracts," *The Inter-Lake* (Demersville, Mont.), Jan. 31, 1890, p 4, c. 1.

66. MDG, Feb. 10, 1890, p. 4, c. 1.

67. "Murder at Flathead," AS, July 10, 1890, p. 1, c. 6; Ronan letters, vol. 2, pp. 142-145.

68. "After the Redskins," AS, Aug. 7, 1890, p. 1, c. 6; William Mooring, "When Houston Was Sheriff," DM, Nov. 21, 1915, ed. section, p. 1, c. 1-3, p. 3, c. 7.

69. Jerome D'Aste, S.J., diaries, Aug. 19-20, 1890, PNTMC, reel 29, fr. 615-616; Duncan M'Donald, "Duncan M'Donald Gives Version of La La See Capture," *The Daily Inter Lake* (Kalispell, Mont.), Dec. 1, 1915, p. 4, c. 2-4; Ellen Nye, "Stick Games Held Recently on Historically Gruesome Site...," *Rocky Mountain Husbandman* (Great Falls, Mont.), Aug. 5, 1937, p. 1, c. 2-6.

70. "Saunterings," *Missoula Weekly Gazette*, Aug. 27, 1890, p. 5, c. 2-3; "Friday," WM, Aug. 27, 1890, p. 4, c. 3.

71. MDG, Oct. 21, 1890, p. 8, c. 2; MDG, Oct. 30, 1890, p. 8, c. 2.

72. "News of the State," *Butte Weekly Miner*, June 18, 1891, p. 3, c. 7.

73. Ronan letters, vol. 2, pp. 168-169.

74. "Killed a Big Buffalo," AS, Sept. 14, 1891, p. 6, c. 1-2.

75. "A Bill and a Blow," MDG, Sept. 8, 1891, p. 1, c. 6; Missoula County Court Records, Series II, vol. 142, p. 139, MS 310, Toole Archives, UM.

76. "Missoula Notes," AS, Oct. 10, 1891, p. 1, c. 1; WM, Oct. 14, 1891, p. 4, c. 2; Marianne Farr, "Sisters of Providence and Health Care, at St. Ignatius Mission and St. Patrick Hospital, 1855-1900," unpublished student paper, Dec 12, 1997, Appendix G.

77. MDG, Oct. 30, 1891, p. 4, c. 1; MDG, Nov. 11, 1891, p. 4, c. 1; *Missoula Weekly Gazette*, Nov. 18, 1891, p. 8, c. 1.

78. MDG, Dec. 24, 1891, p. 8, c. 1.

Chapter 6
1. B. H. Miller to CIA, Dec. 15, 1891, 45,483/1891, NA CIA LR; Ronan letters, vol. 2, pp. 278-279.

2. "An Indian Murdered," MDG, Aug. 9, 1892, p. 1, c. 2; Ronan letters, vol. 2, pp. 317-318.

3. *Morning Missoulian*, Aug. 23, 1892, p. 5, c. 1.

4. WM, Sept. 7, 1892, p. 2, c. 3.

5. "A Montana Character," WM, Apr. 12, 1893, p. 1, c. 3; *The Evening Missoulian*, Apr. 13, 1893, p. 4, c. 1.

6. *The Evening Missoulian*, June 28, 1893, p. 4, c. 1 (2 items); "On Trial for Murder," AS, June 30, 1893, p. 1, c. 4; "Who Killed Stevens," AS, July 1, 1893, p. 8, c. 1-2; "Angus M'Donald's Tale," AS, July 2, 1893, p. 1, c. 4-5; "Angus M'Donald Free," AS, July 3, 1893, p. 8, c. 3.

7. "He Is a Very Bad One," AS, Mar. 15, 1894, p. 6, c. 1-2.

8. CIA to Ronan, July 14, 1893, letter book 262, pp. 26-27, land, NA CIA LS; Ronan letters, vol. 2, p. 370.

9. Granville Stuart, "Trip for the Purpose of Examining the Country Lying Between the Big Blackfoot River and Flathead Lake," Granville Stuart Collection, MSS 1534, box 6, folder 10, Perry Special Collections, Lee Library, Brigham Young University, Provo, Utah.

10. *Flathead Herald-Journal* (Kalispell, Mont.), Sept. 8, 1893, p. 8, c. 1.

11. Ronan letters, vol 1, pp. 219-222; Ronan letters, vol. 2, pp. 166-170, 225-228; Confederated Salish and Kootenai Tribes vs. United States, docket 50233, decision Nov. 12, 1965, U.S. Court of Claims, vol. 173, p. 398.

12. Ronan letters, vol. 2, pp. 194-197, 246; Confederated Salish and Kootenai Tribes vs. United States, docket 50233, decision Nov. 12, 1965, U.S. Court of Claims, vol. 173, p. 398.

13. Thomas P. Smith to CIA, Sept. 23, 1893, 36,376/1893, NA CIA LR.

14. *The Evening Missoulian*, Sept. 16, 1893, p. 4, c. 1-2.

15. "The Nez Perces Raid," WM, Oct. 18, 1893, p. 1, c. 2.

16. Joseph Carter to CIA, Feb. 6, 1894, 6,591/1894, NA CIA LR.

17. Ibid.

18. CIA to Joseph Carter, Feb. 21, 1894, letter book 274, pp. 394-396, land, NA CIA LS.

19. "That Only Flood," WM, June 13, 1894, p. 2, c. 3; "'About the Same,'" WM, June 13, 1894, p. 7, c. 4.

20. "Ruined By the Floods," AS, July 25, 1894, p. 6, c. 1-2.

21. "Good Old Days," *Western Democrat* (weekly) (Missoula, Mont.), Sept. 2, 1894, p. 2, c. 4.

22. "It's A Very Funny Bill," AS, Feb. 23, 1895, p. 6, c. 1; "A Bit of History," *The Kalispell Graphic*, Feb. 27, 1895, p. 2, c. 1-3.

23. DM, May 16, 1896, p. 2, c. 2.

24. "Working 'Em Out," DM, Mar. 10, 1895, p. 1, c. 4.

25. Hon. T. H. Carter, U.S. Senate, to CIA, Mar. 9, 1896, 9,381/1896, NA CIA LR; Ronan letters, vol. 2, pp. 399-401.

26. Joseph Carter to CIA, Mar. 4, 1895, 10,563/1895, NA CIA LR.

27. Hon. T. H. Carter, U.S. Senate, to CIA, Mar. 9, 1896, 9.381/1896, NA CIA LR; "A Flathead Fracas," *The Daily Democrat* (Missoula, Mont.), Mar. 5, 1895, p. 1, c. 8; "Went on the Warpath," AS, Mar. 6, 1895, p. 6, c. 3.

28. "Still in Jail," AS, Mar. 12, 1895, p. 6, c. 2; Habeas Corpus Swasa Michel, Quala Machea, and Louis Quilquili, Mar. 12, 1895, case 226, District Court Records, Missoula County Courthouse, Missoula, Mont.; "Two Jurists," AS, Mar. 13, 1895, p. 6, c. 3; "All At Liberty Again," AS, Mar. 14, 1895, p. 6, c. 3.

29. *The Daily Democrat* (Missoula, Mont.), Mar. 14, 1895, p. 4, c. 1; "Missoula Gossip," AS, Mar. 15, 1895, p. 6, c. 3.

30. "Those Three Bad Indians," AS, Mar. 23, 1895, p. 6, c. 3-4; "The Indians Held," AS, Mar. 26, 1895, p. 6, c. 2; Joseph Carter to CIA, May 7, 1895, 20,518/1895, NA CIA LR.

31. Joseph Carter, Helena, Mont., to CIA, telegram, May 2, 1895, 19,118/1895, NA CIA LR; Joseph Carter to CIA, May 7, 1895, 20,518/1895, NA CIA LR.

32. "Missoula News," AS, May 8, 1895, p. 6, c. 4.

33. "Will Walk Back," *The Kalispell Graphic*, May 15, 1895, p. 2, c. 3.

34. "Thompson Falls," AS, May 1, 1895, p. 6, c. 2.

35. Joseph Carter to CIA, Aug. 4, 1895, 33,331/1895, NA CIA LR.

36. CIA to Joseph Carter, Aug. 14, 1895, letter book 312, pp. 169-172, land, NA CIA LS.

37. *Evening Republican* (Missoula, Mont.), Sept. 9, 1895, p. 1, c. 4.

38. *Evening Republican* (Missoula, Mont.), Sept. 10, 1895, p. 1, c. 6.

39. "Briefs and Personals," AS, Jan .12, 1896, p. 10, c. 2.

40. Joseph Carter to CIA, Jan. 29, 1896, 4,996/1896, NA CIA LR; "Cory Is Cunning," DM, Jan. 29, 1896, p. 1, c. 2-3; "Corey a Queer Duck," AS, Jan. 30, 1896, p. 10, c. 1.

41. "Indians and Horses," AS, Nov. 2, 1895, p. 10, c. 3-4.

42. "The Nez Perce Cayuses," AS, Nov. 14, 1895, p. 10, c. 3-4.

43. "Notice," DM, Dec. 22, 1895, p. 2, c. 2.

44. Joseph Carter to CIA, Jan. 29, 1896, 4,996/1896, NA CIA LR; "Cory Is Cunning," DM, Jan. 29, 1896, p. 1, c. 2-3; "Corey a Queer Duck," AS, Jan. 30, 1896, p. 10, c. 1; "Stock-Owners Take Action," *The Plainsman*, Feb. 15, 1896, p. 3, c. 2.

45. Joseph Carter to CIA, June 15, 1896, 23,678/1896, NA CIA LR.

46. T. H. Carter to CIA, Mar. 9, 1896, 9,381/1896, NA CIA LR.

47. Ibid.

48. Joseph Carter to CIA, Mar. 14, 1896, 11,223/1896, NA CIA LR; CIA to Joseph Carter, Mar. 28, 1896, letter book 328, p. 338, land, NA CIA LS.

49. "In Memoriam," DM, Dec. 16, 1896, p. 4, c. 4.

50. Petition to Secretary of the Interior, received July 23, 1897, Joseph T. Carter file, charges files, Interior Department, RG 48, NA.

51. DM, Sept. 17, 1897, p. 4, c. 1; "At the University," DM, Oct. 4, 1897, p. 1, c. 2-3.

52. "University Notes," DM, Nov. 18, 1897, p. 4, c. 3-4.

53. *Daily Democrat-Messenger* (Missoula, Mont.), Mar. 8, 1898, p. 4, c. 1-2.

54. "They Must Pay Taxes," AS, June 11, 1898, p. 12, c. 2.

55. "In the Old Days," AS, July 27, 1898, p. 12, c. 3.

56. "Missoula Notes," AS, Sept. 17, 1898, p. 10, c. 1.

57. "Western Montana Fair," AS, Oct. 6, 1898, p. 12, c. 2.

58. "'Lo Lo' Is Right," AS, Mar. 22, 1899, p. 12, c. 3.

59. W. H. Smead to CIA, Mar. 13, 1899, 14,292/1899, NA CIA LR.

60. W. H. Smead to F. C. Campbell, Superintendent, Fort Shaw School, Mar. 18, 1899, FH Agency Papers, letters sent.

61. W. H. Smead to D. McDonald, Ravalli, July 1, 1899, FH Agency Papers, letters sent.

62. "Personal," AS, Sept. 4, 1899, p. 10, c. 3.

63. "Witnesses Summoned," AS, Oct. 20, 1899, p. 12, c. 4.

64. Louisa McDermott, "Ethnology and Folklore, Selish Proper," unpublished masters thesis, University of California, Berkeley, 1904, p. 40.

65. "They Have Bad Records," AS, Dec. 3, 1899, p. 14, c. 2.

66. W. H. Smead to Duncan McDonald, Ravalli, Jan. 27, 1900, FH Agency Papers, letters sent; Rosters of Indian Police, vol. 13, entry 982, RG 75, NA.

67. Duncan McDonald to W. H. Smead, Mar. 3, 1900, FH Agency Papers, letters received; W. H. Smead to F. C. Campbell, Ft. Shaw, Mar. 6, 1900, FH Agency Papers, letters sent; F. C. Campbell to W. H. Smead, Apr. 1, 1900, FH Agency Papers, letters received; Duncan McDonald to W. H. Smead, Apr. 6, 1900, FH Agency Papers, letters received.

68. "Brands All Right," AS, Apr. 19, 1900, p. 12, c. 3.

69. Cyrus S. Beede to CIA, Aug. 14, 1900, 40,931/1900, NA CIA LR.

70. Suzie Ogden to W. H. Smead, May 1, 1900, FH Agency Papers, letters received.

71. "The Grizzly's Home," *Daily Democrat-Messenger* (Missoula, Mont.), May 7, 1900, p. 1, c. 6.

72. W. H. Smead to F. C. Campbell, Superintendent, Ft. Shaw, June 12, 1900, FH Agency Papers, letters sent.

73. A. L. Stone, "Following Old Trails, XXVII — The Dragon of the Selish," DM, Dec. 17, 1911, ed. section, p. 4, c. 5-7; Arthur L. Stone, *Following Old Trails* (Missoula, Mont.: Morton John Elrod, 1913), pp. 179-186.

74. "Found the First Gold," AS, July 12, 1900, p. 12, c. 2. See also Paul C. Phillips and H. A. Trexler, "Notes on the Discovery of Gold in the Northwest," *Mississippi Valley Historical Review*, vol. 4, no. 1 (June 1917), pp. 92-95, where name is given as Francois Finley.

75. Cyrus Beede to CIA, May 14, 1900, 40,931/1900, NA CIA LR.

76. W. H. Smead to CIA, June 7, 1900, 27,744/1900, NA CIA LR; Cyrus S. Beede to CIA, Aug. 14, 1900, 40,931/1900, NA CIA LR.

77. W. H. Smead to Charles Wilkins, US Indian Agent, Apr. 29, 1901, FH Agency Papers, letters sent.

78. *Plainsman*, Aug. 10, 1900, p. 4, c. 4; *The Kalispell Bee*, Oct. 19, 1900, p. 3, c. 1.

79. "Says It Is All Wrong," AS, Aug. 19, 1900, p. 15, c. 1-2; "A Revision of Names," AS, July 30, 1900, p. 10, c. 2.

80. Crow, Flathead, Etc. Commission to CIA, Apr. 18, 1901, 22,670/1901, NA CIA LR.

81. C. A. Stillinger vs. Duncan McDonald, 1907, case 4217, Missoula County Court Cases MS 582, box 1, folder 5, Toole Archives, UM.

82. DM, June 8, 1901, p. 4, c. 2.

83. "To Avoid Contagion," AS, Feb. 9, 1901, p. 12, c. 3; W. H. Smead to Joseph Jones, Ronan, Feb. 9, 1901, FH Agency Papers, letters sent; "Danger of Epidemic," AS, Mar. 18, 1901, p. 12, c. 2.

84. *Daily Democrat-Messenger* (Missoula, Mont.), Mar. 19, 1901, p. 4. c, 1.

85. "Missoula Notes," AS, May 6, 1901, p. 10, c. 4.

86. W. H. Smead to Jos. Jones, Ronan, May 18, 1901, FH Agency Papers, letters sent.

87. George S. Lesher to W. H. Smead, May 25, 1901, FH Agency Papers, letters received; "Smallpox on Reservation," DM, May 25, 1901, p. 1, c. 6.

88. "Fighting Smallpox on the Reservation," AS, Nov. 10, 1901, p. 20, c. 1-5.

89. W. H. Smead (by Holland) to Mr. T. W. Longley, Blanchard, Mont., Aug. 13, 1901, FH Agency Papers, letters sent.

90. "Smallpox Is Epidemic," AS, June 8, 1901, p. 12, c. 3.

91. "Victims of Smallpox," AS, June 10, 1901, p. 10, c. 2.

92. W. H. Smead to CIA, June 25, 1901, 34,401/1901, NA CIA LR.

93. "Will Ask for Writ," AS, Sept. 5, 1901, p. 12, c. 6.

94. DM, Oct. 12, 1901, p. 8, c. 2.

95. AS, Oct. 20, 1901, p. 18, c. 1-7.

96. C. A. Stillinger to W. H. Smead, Nov. 12, 1901, FH Agency Papers, letters received.

Chapter 7

1. "Stockmen Organize," DM, Nov. 17, 1901, p. 8, c. 3-4.

2. "Threatens Him With Big Knife," DM, Dec. 11, 1901, p. 1, c. 5; "Robieau Tells His Tale," AS, Dec. 11, 1901, p. 14, c. 4-5; "Guilty of Manslaughter," AS, Dec. 13, 1901, p. 14, c. 2.

3. "Buffalo in Western Montana," DM, May 13, 1902, p. 4, c. 2.

4. F. J. Brown to W. H. Smead, June 29, 1902, FH Agency Papers, letters received; D. McDonald & headmen to W. H. Smead, July 5, 1902, FH Agency Papers, letters received; W. H. Smead to Duncan McDonald, July 5, 1902, FH Agency Papers, letters sent.

5. AS, July 17, 1902, p. 14, c. 2.

6. "Chief Charlot Not Dead as Reported," DM, Aug. 19, 1902, p. 4, c. 5-6; "Hard Blow to the Chief," AS, Aug. 20, 1902, p. 14, c. 2-3.

7. "Robbed on Reservation," AS, Nov. 3, 1902, p. 1, c. 4; "Indian Robbed of $22,000," *The New York Times*, Nov. 4, 1902, p. 1, c. 3; W. H. Smead to Duncan McDonald, Nov. 7, 1902, FH Agency Papers, letters sent; "Outlaw M'Lean Is Known Here," DM, Aug. 12, 1906, p. 2, c. 1.

8. Chas. S. McNichols to CIA, Feb. 6, 1903, 9,822/1903, NA CIA LR.

9. Jame E. Jenkins to Secretary of the Interior, Mar. 15, 1902, inspection reports, Office of the Secretary of the Interior, RG 48, NA, 2828/1902.

10. Chas. S. McNichols, Jocko, Mont., to CIA, Jan. 5, 1903, 1,789/1903, enclosure no. 1 of 6,311/1903, NA CIA LR.

11. CIA to W. H. Smead, Feb. 2, 1903, letterbook 582, pp. 68-71, land, NA CIA LS.

12. W. H. Smead to CIA, Feb. 24, 1903, 13,682/1903, NA CIA LR.

13. St. Ignatius Mission House Diary, Mar. 17, 1903, reel 3, fr. 227, PNTMC.

14. Woody and Woody, Missoula, Mont., to CIA, Mar. 12, 1903, 17,122/1903, NA CIA LR.

15. W. H. Smead to CIA, Mar. 18, 1903, 18,617/1903, NA CIA LR.

16. W. H. Smead to CIA, Mar. 22, 1903, telegram, 18,910/1903, NA CIA LR.

17. L. Van Gorp to W. Ketcham, Mar. 24, 1903, telegram, BCIM Papers; St. Ignatius Mission House Diary, Mar. 25, 1903, reel 3, fr. 227, PNTMC.

18. St. Ignatius Mission House Diary, Mar. 26, 1903, reel 3, PNTMC.

19. "Rival Indian Delegation," DM, Mar. 29, 1903, p. 5, c. 4; "Indians Are Going East," AS, Mar. 28, 1903, p. 14, c. 4.

20. "The Tax Levy Must Be Paid,"DM, Apr. 10, 1903, p. 3, c. 1.

21. Charlot, et. al., to Secretary of the Interior, Apr. 4, 1903, Sisters of Providence, "St. Ignatius Chronicle, 1864-1938," typescript, Provincialate Archives, St. Ignatius Province, Sisters of Providence, Spokane, Wash., 1975, p. 154.

22. Charlott, Helena, Mont., to CIA, Mar. 29, 1903, telegram, 19,946/1903, NA CIA LR.

23. "The Tax Levy Must Be Paid,"DM, Apr. 10, 1903, p. 3, c. 1; St. Ignatius Mission House Diary, Apr. 10, 1903, reel 3, fr. 228, PNTMC.

24. "They'll Have to Pay It," AS, May 4, 1903, p. 10, c. 1.

25. W. H. Smead to CIA, Apr. 21, 1903, 26,590/1903, NA CIA LR.

26. "They Who've Come Back," AS, Aug. 2, 1903, p. 12, c. 3.

27. W. H. Smead to T. G. Demers, Camas, May 5, 1903, FH Agency Papers, letters sent; W. H. Smead to Francis & Victor Dupuis, Ronan, May 23, 1903, FH Agency Papers, letters sent.

28. CIA to W. H. Smead, May 13, 1903, letterbook 603, pp. 105-106, land, NA CIA LS.

29. W. H. Smead to CIA, June 1, 1903, 34,876/1903, NA CIA LR.

30. Ibid.

31. W. H. Smead to CIA, July 2, 1903, 41,378/1903, NA CIA LR.

32. CIA to W. H. Smead, July 14, 1903, letterbook 614, pp. 89-90, land, NA CIA LS.

33. CIA to W. H. Smead, Aug. 3, 1903, letterbook 618, p. 220, land, NA CIA LS.

34. W. H. Smead to CIA, Aug. 25, 1903, 55,375/1903, NA CIA LR.

35. CIA to W. H. Smead, Sept. 22, 1903, letterbook 625, pp. 365-366, land, NA CIA LS.

36. W. H. Smead to CIA, Oct. 23, 1903, 69,397/1903, NA CIA LR.

37. W. H. Smead to CIA, Oct. 22, 1903, 68,996/1903, NA CIA LR.

38. W. H. Smead to CIA, Nov. 20, 1903, telegram, 75,236/1903, NA CIA LR.

39. "Soldiers Leave for Reservation," AS, Nov. 27, 1903, p. 12, c. 1-2.

40. W. H. Smead to CIA, Nov. 29, 1903, telegram, 77,120/1903, NA CIA LR.

41. "Stock Tax Collected," DM, Dec. 20, 1903, p. 8, c. 2.

42. W. H. Smead to CIA, Mar. 23, 1904, 21,470/1904, NA CIA LR; C. F. Nessler and Chas. M. McNichols to Secretary of the Interior, June 21, 1904, inspection report, Office of the Secretary of the Interior, RG 48, NA, 6655/1904.

43. W. H. Smead to P. O. McDonald, Apr. 20, 1903, FH Agency Papers, letters sent.

44. St. Ignatius Mission House Diary, Oct. 7, 1901, reel 3, PNTMC.

45. St. Ignatius Mission House Diary, May 16, 1903, reel 3, PNTMC.

46. W. H. Smead to John Weightman, May 17, 1903, FH Agency Papers, letters sent.

47. W. H. Smead to Duncan McDonald, Mar. 3, 1904, Flathead Agency Papers, letters sent; Duncan McDonald to W. H. Smead, Mar. 6, 1904, FH Agency Papers, letters received.

48. Montana Legislative Assembly, *Laws, Resolutions and Memorials of the State of Montana Passed at the Eighth Regular Session* (Helena, Mont.: State Publishing Company, 1903), pp. 157-158.

49. "They Who've Come Back," AS, Aug. 2, 1903, p. 12, c. 3.

50. "Indians Going After Big Game," DM, Sept. 9, 1905, p. 8, c. 4; "Alex Bigknife Loses His Gun," DM, Sept. 5, 1903, p. 8, c. 2.

51. "Indians on the Warpath," AS, Sept. 6, 1903, p. 12, c. 4; "Will Test the Law," DM, Sept. 6, 1903, p. 8, c. 2.

52. "Indians on the Warpath," AS, Sept. 6, 1903, p. 12, c. 4; "His Gun Taken From Him," AS, Sept. 5, 1903, p. 2, c. 3.

53. A. E. Higgins, Missoula, to W. H. Smead, Sept. 12, 1903, Flathead Agency Papers, letters received.

54. W. F. Scott, Montana Fish & Game Warden, Helena, to W. H. Smead, Sept. 8, 1903, Flathead Agency Papers, letters received.

55. "Indians Contest State Law," DM, Sept. 13, 1903, p. 1, c. 4; p. 8, c. 3.

56. DM, Sept. 27, 1903, p. 3, c. 2-3.

57. "Demurrer Is Filed," DM, Sept. 27, 1903, p. 8 c. 2; "Files Amended Complaint," DM, Oct. 22, 1903, p. 3, c. 4.

58. "Attorney General Here," DM, Nov. 4, 1903, p. 8, c. 1.

59. "To the Supreme Court," AS, Dec. 9, 1903, p. 12, c. 3.

60. Montana Legislative Assembly, *Laws, Resolutions and Memorials of the State of Montana Passed by the Thirty-Third Legislative Assembly in Regular Session* (Helena, Mont.: State Publishing Co., 1953), p. 13.

61. W. H. Smead to Eli Pauline, Sept. 18, 1903, FH Agency Papers, letters sent.

62. C. H. McLeod to George Beckwith, Oct. 7, 1903, C. H. McLeod Papers, Toole Archives, UM.

63. *The Missoula Democrat and Montana Home Journal*, Oct. 29, 1903, p. 8, c. 2.

64. "Duncan M'Donald's Cousin Visits Him," AS, Oct. 29, 1903, p. 12, c. 3; Alex Christie to Bob Bigart, Aug. 20, 2015, email.

65. D. McDonald to W. H. Smead, Nov. 10, 1903, Flathead Agency Papers, letters received; W. H. Smead to Duncan McDonald, Nov. 10, 1903, FH Agency Papers, letters sent.

66. "Notes on Duncan McDonald and John Lebson," Joseph M. Dixon Papers, MS 55, box 99, folder 99-6, pp. 24-25, Toole Archives, UM; D. McDonald to Joseph Dixon, Dec. 29, 1903, Joseph M. Dixon Papers, MS 55, Toole Archives, UM; M. Gidley, *Kopet: A Documentary Narrative of Chief Joseph's Last Years* (Seattle: University of Washington Press, 1981), pp. 37-38.

67. Michael Pablo to Joseph Dixon, undated [Dec. 1903], Joseph M. Dixon Papers, MS 55, Toole Archives, UM; Joseph Allard to Joseph Dixon, Jan. 2, 1904, Joseph M. Dixon Papers, MS 55, Toole Archives, UM.

68. D. McDonald to Joseph Dixon, Dec. 29, 1903, Joseph M. Dixon Papers, MS 55, Toole Archives, UM.

69. *U.S. Statutes at Large*, vol. 33 (1903-1905), pp. 302-306; Burton M. Smith, *The Politics of Allotment: The Flathead Reservation as a Test Case* (Pablo, Mont.: Salish Kootenai College Press, 1995).

70. Arthur M. Tinker to Secretary of the Interior, Sept. 20, 1903, Inspection Reports 9007/1903, RG 48, National Archives, Washington, D.C.

71. Ronald Lloyd Trosper, "The Economic Impact of the Allotment Policy on the Flathead Indian Reservation, unpublished Ph.D. dissertation, Harvard University, Cambridge, Mass., 1974, pp. 255-359.

72. "Cattle Market Looks Blue," DM, Sept. 2, 1904, p. 3, c.1.

73. Jerome D'Aste, S.J., diary, Sept. 7, 1904, reel 30, PNTMC; DM, Sept. 7, 1904, p. 3, c. 5; "Missoula Notes," AS, Sept. 9, 1904, p. 12, c. 4.

74. DM, Sept. 14, 1904, p. 3, c. 5.

75. "Missoula Notes," AS, Sept. 17, 1904, p. 12, c. 4; "Missoula Notes," AS, Sept. 23, 1904, p. 10, c. 5.

76. "Missoula Notes," AS, Sept. 17, 1904, p. 12, c. 4; DM, Sept. 30, 1904, p. 3, c. 4.

77. "Is Ill With Typhoid Pneumonia," DM, Sept. 10, 1904, p. 8, c. 3.

78. "Montana Cattle Go East," DM, Oct. 4, 1904, p. 8, c. 4; "Dixon," DM, Oct. 16, 1904, p. 10, c. 5.

79. "M'Donald Ships Horses," DM, Nov. 11, 1904, p. 6, c. 2.

80. C. H. McLeod to Geo. Beckwith, Dec. 5, 1904, C. H. McLeod Papers, Toole Archives, UM.

81. "Dixon," DM, Mar. 12, 1905, p. 7, c. 3.

82. "Dixon," DM, Apr. 2, 1905, p. 10, c. 2-3.

83. Samuel Bellew to Duncan McDonald, Mar. 27, 1905, FH Agency Papers, letters sent; Peter Magpie to Samuel Bellew, July 18, 1905, FH Agency Papers, letters received.

84. "It's a Link in Ancient History," AS, July 15, 1905, p. 1, c. 7; "Mary's Father Was Known To Be William Clark's Son," AS, July 16, 1905, p. 1, c. 3-5; "Three Generations of Clarks," AS, July 23, 1905, p. 9, c. 3-5.

85. "Family Record," Duncan McDonald family Bible, xerox in possession of authors; Jerome D'Aste, S.J., diary, July 28-30, 1905, reel 30, PNTMC; "Death Takes Only Son From Them," DM, July 30, 1905, p. 2, c. 1; "Dies Shortly After Reaching Hospital," AS, July 30, 1905, p. 13, c. 1.

86. Jerome D'Aste, S.J., diary, July 31, 1905, reel 30, PNTMC; "Funeral at the Mission," AS, July 31, 1905, p. 8, c. 4.

87. Jerome D'Aste, S.J., diary, Aug. 12, 1905, reel 30, PNTMC.

88. "Accused of Selling Whiskey to a Breed," AS, Sept. 15, 1905, p. 11, c. 2; DM, Sept. 28, 1905, p. 2, c. 4.

89. DM, Jan. 10, 1906, p. 2, c. 6.

90. "When the Indians Owned the Land," AS, Mar. 25, 1906, p. 13, c. 3-4.

91. "Indians on Flathead Object to Allotment," AS, Apr. 15, 1906, p. 13, c. 4.

92. "Outlaw M'Lean Is Known Here," DM, Aug. 12, 1906, p. 2, c. 1.

93. *Sanders County Signal* (Plains, Mont.), Feb. 14, 1907, p. 1, c. 3 (2 articles).

94. DM, Dec. 15, 1906, p. 2, c. 4; DM, Dec. 27, 1906, p. 2, c. 5.

95. C. A. Stillinger v. Duncan McDonald, 1907, case 4217, Missoula County Court Cases, MS 582, box 1, folder 5, Toole Archives, UM.

96. DM, Jan. 16, 1907, p. 2, c. 6.

97. "Across the Reservation," *The Kalispell Bee*, June 28, 1907, p. 3, c. 2-4.

98. "Red Men Are Visited by Secretary Garfield," AS, July 5, 1907, p. 11, c. 4; "Indians Entertain Mr. Garfield," DM, July 5, 1907, p. 3, c. 7.

99. "Old Timers Talk of Pioneer Days," DM, July 28, 1920, p. 3, c. 4-6.

100. *Sanders County Signal* (Plains, Mont.), Aug. 29, 1907, p. 1, c. 5.

101. Morton J. Elrod, "The Flathead Buffalo Range," *Annual Report of the American Bison Society (1905-1907)*, (New York, 1908), pp. 15-49; DM, Apr. 19, 1908, p. 8, c. 2.

102. Jerome D'Aste, S.J., diary, May 8, 1908, reel 30, PNTMC.

103. John Weightman Stable and Stage, Inventory, cash receipts ledger & bills payable, 1908, p. 199, Worden and Company Papers, Toole Archives, UM.

104. CIA, Livingston, Mont., to Indian Office, July 21, 1908, file 70,487/1907 Flathead 053, part 2, NA CCF; file 65950/1908 Flathead 313, NA CCF.

105. "Patents in Fee" book, p. 2, Flathead Agency Papers, National Archives, Denver, Col.

106. V. S. Kutchin to S. Bellew, Oct. 14, 1908, FH Agency Papers, letters received; V. S. Kutchin to Fred Morgan, Feb. 11, 1909, FH Agency Papers, letters received.

107. "Haste Is Waste," DM, Dec. 22, 1908, p. 10, c. 2.

108. *The Missoula Herald*, Dec. 23, 1908, p. 4, c. 2.

Chapter 8

1. "Fred Morgan Named as Agent," DM, Nov. 21, 1908, p. 10, c. 4; Thomas Downs to CIA, Jan. 30, 1909, file 9,444/1909 Flathead 150, NA CCF; Fred C. Morgan to CIA, May 8, 1909, file 27,058/1909 Flathead 154, NA CCF.

2. Theodore Sharp to CIA, May 11, 1920, file 109,764/1919 Flathead 056, NA CCF.

3. CIA to Fred C. Campbell, Dec. 24, 1920; and Charles Coe to CIA, Nov. 25, 1921, file 109,764/1919 Flathead 056, NA CCF.

4. *The Missoula Herald*, Feb. 26, 1909, p. 8, c. 2.

5. Newton MacTavish, "The Last Great Round-Up," *Canadian Magazine*, vol. 33, no. 6 (Oct. 1909), pp. 482-491; vol. 34, no. 1 (Nov. 1909), pp. 25-35; Agnes Deans Cameron, "Buying Buffalo on the Hoof," *The Pacific Monthly*, vol. 22, no. 6 (Dec. 1909), pp. 591-602; Morton J. Elrod, "The Passing of the Pablo Buffalo Herd," *Shields' Magazine* (New York), vol. 12, no. 2 (Feb. 1911), pp. 35-41.

6. M. O. Hammond, diary, 1909, SC 1218, MHS Archives.

7. "Many Enjoy Choice Steaks Cut From a Young Buffalo," DM, July 4, 1909, pt. 2, p. 4, c. 5-7; A. L. Stone, Following Old Trails, XXIII—Fighting for Paint," DM, Nov. 19, 1911, ed. section, p. 4, c. 5-7.

8. "Watching the Sale," DM, Nov. 17, 1909, p. 12, c. 2; "Flathead Townsites Sell Well," DM, Nov. 22, 1909, p. 3, c. 2-4.

9. "Bison Range Fund Is Intact," DM, Jan. 28, 1910, p. 3, c. 3; *U.S. Statutes at Large*, vol. 35 (1907-1909), pp. 448-450.

10. "Indians to Elect New Chief," DM, Jan. 28, 1910, p. 6, c. 5.

11. "M'Donald Deplores Conditions," *The Missoula Herald*, Jan. 28, 1910, p. 2, c. 4.

12. "Patents in Fee," Flathead Agency Papers, National Archives, Denver, Col., p. 2.

13. "M'Donald Disposes of All His Cattle," *The Missoula Herald*, Mar. 16, 1910, p. 2, c. 3.

14. "On the Reserve," DM, Mar. 31, 1910, p. 12, c. 2.

15. "New Tribal Judge Named," DM, Apr. 17, 1910, p. 7, c. 2-3.

16. Fred C. Morgan to CIA, May 10, 1910, file 47,604/1909 Flathead 056, NA CCF; "Indians in Council Pick Delegates," DM, May 10, 1910, p. 1, c. 5.

17. DM, May 11, 1910, p. 4, c. 2.

18. St. Ignatius Mission House diary, May 9, 1910, reel 3, PNTMC.

19. CIA to F. C. Morgan, June 15, 1910, file 47,604/1919 Flathead 056, NA CCF.

20. "Ready to Go East," DM, June 7, 1910, p. 12, c. 2; "Indian Delegation to Washington," DM, June 8, 1910, p. 14, c. 3.

21. Martin Sharlo and Sam Reserrection to CIA, June 13, 1910; Sam Res-selection to Mr. W. H. Taft, June 22, 1910; and CIA to Martin Sharlo, June 24, 1910, file 47,604/1909 Flathead 056, NA CCF.

22. File 49,688/1910 Flathead 304.3, NA CCF.

23. "Indian Delegation Starts Home," DM, June 20, 1910, p. 2, c. 1; "Home Again," DM, June 25, 1910, p. 12, c. 2.

24. "Forty Men and Women Pick Homes on Flathead Indian Reservation," DM, May 12, 1910, p. 9, c. 1-7 and p. 11, c. 3.

25. "Mineral Locations Numerous," DM, May 11, 1910, p. 2, c. 2.

26. "Big Copper Values on Flathead Reserve," *The Kalispell Journal*, May 30, 1910, p. 1, c. 3-4 and p. 6, 1-2.

27. "Dixon Power Sites Secured," DM, July 22, 1910, p. 2, c. 1.

28. "M'Donald's Mine Is Leased," DM, Dec. 10, 1910, p. 8, c. 1.

29. *The Missoula Herald*, Sept. 9, 1910, p. 6, c. 5; DM, Sept. 10, 1910, p. 2, c. 4.

30. "Duncan's Big Spud Is a Dandy," DM, Oct. 17, 1910, p. 2, c. 3.

31. DM, Dec. 13, 1910, p. 2, c. 3.

32. "Negro and Indian Woman Cremated When Gasoline Is Thrown in Stove," DM, Feb. 27, 1911, p. 2, c. 1-2; "Woman Was Outcast Says Mr. M'Donald," DM, Feb. 28, 1911, p. 6, c. 4.

33. "Deputy Is Hurdler of Prowess," DM, Mar. 22, 1910, p. 5, c. 1.

34. "Enthusiastic Thousands Extend to Mr. Roosevelt a True Western Welcome," DM, Apr. 12, 1911, p. 1, c. 3-5 and p. 7, c. 3; DM, Apr. 12, 1911, p. 12, c. 2.

35. "Mission Messages," RP, May 5, 1911, p. 1, c. 3.

36. "Mission Messages," RP, July 14, 1911, p. 1, c. 5-6.

37. "Ready to Vote," DM, Nov. 12, 1911, p. 12, c. 2; "Earnest Protest," DM, Nov. 12, 1911, p. 12, c. 2; "Duncan Praised," DM, Nov. 14, 1911, p. 10, c. 2.

38. "E. S. Paxson Makes Generous Offer...," DM, Mar. 17, 1912, p. 9, c. 1-2.

39. A. L. Stone, "Following Old Trails, XXIII—Fighting for Paint," DM, Nov. 19, 1911, ed. section, p. 4, c. 5-7.

40. W. J. Hornaday to Duncan MacDonald, Feb. 7, 1912, Series I, box FF3, Letterbox 1909-1915, American Bison Society Papers, Western History Collection, Denver Public Library, Denver, Col.; "The Pablo Buffalo," *Forest and Stream*, vol. 75, no. 22 (Nov. 26, 1910), p. 858; "The Outlaw Buffalo," *Forest and Stream*, vol. 75, no. 23 (Dec. 3, 1910), pp. 916-917; Lincoln Ellsworth, "The Last Wild

Buffalo Hunt," Explorers Club, *Explorers Club Tales* (New York: Tudor Publishing Company, 1936, 1940), pp. 90-101.

41. "Boosters Together in St. Ignatius Theater," DM, Mar. 10, 1912, p. 1, c. 3; "Mission Town Has Great Meeting," DM, Mar. 11, 1912, p. 1, c. 1 and p. 3, c. 3-4.

42. T. C. Elliott to Mr. J. B. Tyrrell, Feb. 11, 1913, J. B. Tyrrell Papers, Thomas Fisher Rare Book Library, University of Toronto, Toronto, Ontario, box P201.

43. "Government Agent Here Selecting Agency Site," RP, Nov. 8, 1912, p. 1, c. 3; "New Agency Is Located," RP, Mar. 21, 1913, p. 1, c. 1-2.

44. Jules A. Karlin, *Joseph M. Dixon of Montana: Part I: Senator and Bull Moose Manager, 1867-1917* (Missoula: University of Montana Publications in History, 1974), pp. 162-183.

45. "Progressives Foil Plan of Amalgamated Parties," DM, Sept. 6, 1912, p. 1, c. 1-2 and p. 5, c. 1-5.

46. "Progressives Have Rousing Rally at Mission," DM, Sept. 27, 1912, p. 1, c. 6.

47. "Dixon People Hear Bull Mooseers," DM, Oct. 28, 1912, p. 3, c. 2.

48. "Ronan Rally Scores Heavily for Moose," DM, Oct. 30, 1912, p. 6, c. 3; "Bull Moose Meeting Last," RP, Nov. 1, 1912, p. 1, c. 5-6.

49. "Official Returns, Missoula County (County Candidates)," DM, Nov. 14, 1912, p. 6, c. 1.

50. "An Indian Council Is Held," DM, Sept. 9, 1912, p. 2, c. 1; "Commissioners at Work," RP, Oct. 25, 1912, p. 1, c. 5-6; "Land Appraisal Has Commenced," RP, May 2, 1913, p. 1, c. 3.

51. "Indian Business Council Adopts Resolutions," RP, May 30, 1913, p. 1, c. 2-3.

52. "Appraisal Commissioners Meet Accident in Timber," RP, May 30, 1913, p. 1, c. 4; "Land Appraisers Are in Vicinity of St. Ignatius," RP, July 18, 1913, p. 3, c. 6.

53. File 20,951/1913 Flathead 056, NA CCF.

54. "Notice to Members of the Business Committee," Flathead Business Committee folder, box 143, 8NS-075-96-327, Flathead Subject Files, 1907-1935, Flathead Agency Papers, RG 75, National Archives, Denver, CO.

55. "Largest Meeting Ever Held on Reservation," RP, May 23, 1913, p. 1, c. 1-2; "Resolutions," RP, May 23, 1913, p. 2, c. 3-6; "Reforms Are Needed," RP, May 23, 1913, p. 2, c. 1-3.

56. File 70,964/1913 Flathead 054, NA CCF.

57. File 70,964/1913 Flathead 054, NA CCF.

58. File 75,531/1912 Flathead 301, NA CCF.

59. "Indian Business Council Adopts Resolutions," RP, May 30, 1913, p. 1, c. 2-3.

60. "Flathead Indians to Be at Congress," *Spokane Daily Chronicle*, July 7, 1913, p. 14, c. 5.

61. "Ronan Assists Polson in Big Celebration," RP, July 11, 1913, p. 1, c. 6-7.

62. "Delightful Hours for Pioneers' First Day," DM, Sept. 5, 1913, p. 5, c. 1-2; "Pioneer Notes," DM, Sept. 6, 1913, p. 10, c. 3; "Roll Call," DM, Sept. 5, 1913, p. 5, c. 5-7.

63. Hamlin Garland, Notes on the Flathead Reservation, 1913, Hamlin Garland Collection, Special Collections, University of Southern California Library, Los Angeles, item 63-9, pages unnumbered.

64. "Almost as Good as County Fair," RP, Oct. 3, 1913, p. 1, c. 3-4.

65. "Missoula Receives the Re-Appraisement Plats," RP, Nov. 21, 1913, p. 1, c. 6-7; "Settlers Protest Against the High Appraisement," RP, Dec. 5, 1913, p. 1, c. 6-7.

66. RP, Dec. 5, 1913, p. 2, c. 1.

67. "New Appraisement on Reservation Is Likely," DM, Dec. 16, 1913, p. 9, c.4.

68. "Commissioner Tells How and Why It Happened," RP, Dec. 19, 1913, p. 1, c. 1-3.

69. "Entries Suspended on Flathead Lands," DM, Dec. 28, 1913, p. 4, c. 5.

70. "Settlers on Flathead Notified as to Values," RP, Feb. 13, 1914, p. 1, c. 2-3; "Good News for Twenty-Three Homesteaders West of Ronan," RP, Apr. 3, 1914, p. 1, c. 6-7.

71. "Senator Myers Introduces Bill to Really Open the Flathead," RP, June 19, 1914, p. 1, c. 3-4; "A Good Bill," RP, June 19, 1914, p. 2, c. 1.

72. "A Good Bill," RP, June 19, 1914, p. 2, c. 1.

73. Secretary of the Interior to Senator H. L. Myers, June 27, 1914, file 132,598/1914 Flathead 150, NA CCF.

74. "Myers, Walsh, and Evans," RP, Nov. 13, 1914, p. 1, c. 1-3.

75. "Indian Representatives in Ronan," RP, Nov. 20, 1914, p. 1, c. 1-2.

76. Business Committee to CIA, Jan. 30, 1915, file 66,745/1923 Flathead 054, NA CCF.

77. William H. Ketcham, *Conditions on the Flathead and Fort Peck Indian Reservations* (Washington, D.C.: U.S. Board of Indian Commissioners, 1915), pp. 18-24, 63-65.

78. Fred S. Cook to CIA, Dec. 8, 1914, file 132,598/1914 Flathead 150, NA CCF.

79. "Second Appraisal Held in Obeyance [sic]," RP, Mar. 19, 1915, p. 1, c. 6.

80. "House Defeats Reappraisement," RP, Feb. 16, 1917, p. 1, c. 6.

81. "As to Spring," DM, Feb. 27, 1914, p. 8, c. 2.

82. "Funeral of Pablo Is Attended by Hundreds," DM, July 15, 1914, p. 1, c. 4; "Michel Pablo Dies Suddenly," RP, July 17, 1914, p. 1, c. 3.

83. "Dixon," DM, Aug. 24, 1914, p. 5, c. 2.

84. "Duncan Visits," DM, Nov. 20, 1914, p. 10, c. 2.

85. Flathead Business Committee to CIA, Jan. 30, 1915, file 66,745/1923 Flathead 054, NA CCF.

86. "Duncan M'Donald Will Lecture on Race," DM, Feb. 17, 1915, p. 10, c. 5; "Duncan M'Donald Lectures Tonight," DM, Feb. 22, 1915, p. 8, c. 3-4.

87. "Duncan McDonald," typescript, Carling I. Malouf Papers, MS 640, Toole Archives, UM, series II, box 18, folder 1.

88. Eileen Decker, interview, St. Ignatius, Montana, Feb. 26, 2008.

89. "Duncan, All Indian Charms His Hearers," DM, Feb. 23, 1915, p. 10, c. 3.

90. CIA to Senator T. J. Walsh, Mar. 9, 1915, file 19,459/1915 Flathead 320, NA CCF.

91. "White Man's Ways Puzzle Indian Leader," DM, Nov. 1, 1915, p. 2, c. 1-2.

92. DM, Dec. 7, 1915, p. 2, c. 2.

93. Paul C. Phillips and H. A. Trexler, "Notes on the Discovery of Gold in the Northwest," *Mississippi Valley Historical Review*, vol. 4, no. 1 (June 1917), pp. 92-95.

94. "Half-Breed First to Find Gold Here, Says M'Donald," DM, Oct. 27, 1916, p. 10, c. 3-4; Granville Stuart, "Stuart Describes Finding of Gold," DM, Nov. 12, 1916, ed. section, p. 1, c. 1-2; Frank D. Brown, "Stuart Deserves Honor Paid Him," DM, Nov. 13, 1916, p. 3, c. 1-3.

95. U.S. Office of Indian Affairs, Flathead Agency Diary, 1916-1918, MSS 823, Toole Archives, UM, pp. 35, 42.

96. *U.S. Statutes at Large*, vol. 39, pt. 1 (1915-1917), pp. 139-142.

97. RP, Sept. 15, 1916, p. 2, c. 3.

98. "How Lolo Was Named," DM, Nov. 26, 1916, ed. section, p. 4, c. 3-4.

99. "Buffalo Are Increasing," DM, Dec. 28, 1916, p. 10, c. 5.

100. "Louse Was Forecaster," DM, Dec. 30, 1916, p. 10, c. 2.

Chapter 9

1. CIA to Secretary of Interior, Sept. 25, 1905, U.S. Bureau of Indian Affairs, "Selected Records of the Bureau of Indian Affairs Relating to the Enrollment of Indians on the Flathead Reservation, 1903-08," NAmf M1350, reel 1, frames 282-291, pp. 44-53; U.S. Bureau of Indian Affairs, "Selected Records of the Bureau of Indian Affairs Relating to the Enrollment of Indians on the Flathead Reservation, 1903-08," NAmf M1350, reel 1, frame 52, #1884; U.S. Senate Committee on Indian Affairs, *Indian Appropriation Bill, 1919: Hearings* (Washington, D.C.: U.S. Government Printing Office, 1918), pp. 400-413; F. E. Brandon to CIA, Mar. 8, 1922, file 22,203/1922 Flathead 154, NA CCF; H. F. Peacock to Inspector in Charge, July 20, 1916, file 20,153/1916 Flathead 175, NA CCF.

2. U.S. Bureau of Indian Affairs, "Selected Records of the Bureau of Indian Affairs Relating to the Enrollment of Indians on the Flathead Reservation, 1903-08," NAmf M1350, reel 1, frame 2, #42; Maxime Barnaby to W. H. Smead, Apr. 21, 1904, FH Agency Papers, letters received.

3. Thomas R. Wessel, "Political Assimilation on the Blackfoot Indian Reservation, 1887-1934: A Study in Survival," Douglas H. Ubelaker and Herman J. Viola, eds., *Plains Indian Studies: A Collection of Essays in Honor of John C. Ewers and Waldo R. Wedel*, Smithsonian Contributions to Anthropology, no. 30 (1982) pp. 59-72.

4. "1841-1941: A Century of Catholicity in Montana: Souvenir Centenary Edition," *The Register* (Diocese of Helena, Helena, Mont.), vol. 17, no. 35 (Aug. 27, 1941).

5. Fred C. Morgan to CIA, Jan. 7, 1917, and CIA to F. C. Morgan, Jan. 22, 1917, file 1438/1917 Flathead 056, NA CCF.

6. DM Apr. 6, 1917, p. 2, c. 3.

7. DM, May 6, 1917, p. 6, c. 2.

8. Walter G. West to CIA, Sept. 6, 1918, file 71,378/1918 Flathead 150, NA CCF; "Request for Per Capita Distribution," May 28, 1920, file 72,408/1919 Flathead 054, NA CCF.

9. "St. Ignatius Woman Shoots a Large Elk," DM, Oct. 30, 1918, p. 4, c. 2.

10. "M'Donald Greets Friends," DM, Dec. 4, 1918, p. 3, c. 1.

11. "Montana Pioneer Dies at Home in Dixon," RP, Feb. 28, 1919, p. 5, c. 3.

12. "Duncan M'Donald Here for Health," DM, Mar. 9, 1919, p. 3, c. 1-2.

13. "Indian Colony Is Paid Visit," DM, May 11, 1919, p. 7, c. 1-2.

14. "Indian Legend About Missoula," DM, July 21, 1919, p. 5, c. 4; Margaret P. Ganssle, *The Selish: A Pageant–Masque* (Missoula, Mont.: Missoulian, 1919).

15. "McDonald Seems to Be Right on Weather 'Guess,'" DM, Dec. 16, 1919, p. 5, c. 5-6; "Duncan McDonald in City Says Spring Is Now Near," DM, Apr. 8, 1920, p. 5, c. 4.

16. "Large Attendance at Meeting to Aid Flathead Project," DM, Jan 4, 1920, p. 1, c. 5; p. 7, c. 1-2.

17. U.S. House of Representatives, Committee on Indian Affairs, *Indians of the United States: Investigation of the Field Service: Hearings* (Washington, D.C.: U.S. Government Printing Office, 1920), vol. 3, p. 1293.

18. Ibid.

19. U.S. Senate, Committee on Indian Affairs, *Indian Appropriation Bill, 1919: Hearings* (Washington, D.C.: U.S. Government Printing Office, 1918), pp. 400, 406.

20. U.S. House of Representatives, Committee on Indian Affairs, *Indians of the United States: Investigation of the Field Service: Hearings* (Washington, D.C.: U.S. Government Printing Office, 1920), vol. 3, p. 1287.

21. CIA to Theodore Sharp, telegram, June 14, 1920, file 109,764/1919 Flathead 056, NA CCF.

22. H. S. Taylor to CIA, July 3, 1920, file 55,158/1920 Flathead 154, NA CCF, p. 24.

23. H. S. Taylor to CIA, July 3, 1920, file 55,158/1920 Flathead 154, NA CCF, pp. 24-31.

24. H. S. Taylor to CIA, July 3, 1920, file 55,158/1920 Flathead 154, NA CCF, pp. 32-34.

25. "Sharp's Slayer Won't Discuss Fatal Quarrel," DM, July 25, 1920, p. 1, c. 7; p. 7, c. 2; "Self Defense Plea Wins for Perkins," DM, Dec. 8, 1920, p. 1, c. 6-7; p. 5, c. 1-4.

26. "Old Timers Talk of Pioneer Days," DM, July 28, 1920, p. 3, c. 4-6.

27. "St. Ignatius," DM, Sept. 14, 1920, p. 3, c. 3-4.

28. "'Round the Town," DM, Nov. 30, 1920, p. 5, c. 3.

29. CIA to Max J. Barnaby, Sept. 1, 1920, file 109,764/1919 Flathead 056, NA CCF.

30. "Minutes of Meeting of Business Committee of Flathead Tribe," Feb. 15, 1921, file 33,825/1921 Flathead 054, NA CCF.

31. "Minutes of the Business Committee of the Confederated Flathead Tribes," Feb. 24, 1921, file 33,825/1921 Flathead 054, NA CCF.

32. "Minutes of the Meeting of the Business Committee of the Confederated Flathead Tribes," Mar. 8, 1921, file 33,825/1921 Flathead 054, NA CCF.

33. Frank E. Brandon to CIA, Apr. 22, 1921, file 109,764/1919 Flathead 056, NA CCF.

34. "Old Flathead Chief to Hunting Ground," DM, May 1, 1921, p. 8, c. 3-4.

35. "Phantom Mine Lure of Old Prospectors," DM, Sept. 4, 1921, p. 2, c. 5; "Around the Town," DM, Oct. 15, 1921, p. 8, c .1.

36. Charles Coe to CIA, Nov. 25, 1921, 109,764/1919 Flathead 056, NA CCF.

37. "Flathead Boosters Hold Jollification," DM, Dec. 4, 1921, p. 8, c. 1

38. Charles Coe to CIA, Jan. 10, 1922, file 63,544/1910 Flathead 010, NA CCF; CIA to Philip Moss, Feb. 15, 1922, file 35,851/1921 Flathead 056, NA CCF.

39. Will Cave, "Cave Articles Explain Montana Names," DM, May 14, 1922, special features, p. 1, c. 5-7; p. 7, c. 1-3; Will Cave, "Will Cave Gives More Facts About Western Montana Names," DM, May 21, 1922, special features, p. 1, c. 6-7; p. 10, c. 3-4; Will Cave, "Will Cave Tells More Stories of Origins of Montana Names," DM, May 28, 1922, special features, p. 1, c. 6-7; p. 8, c. 1-2; Will Cave, "This Cave Article Tells of Our Names," DM, June 4, 1922, special features, p. 1, c. 1; p. 10, c. 1-5.

40. "Today Is Biggest in Arlee Pow-Wow," DM, July 9, 1922, p. 4, c. 4; "Arlee," DM, July 13, 1922, p. 3, c. 1.

41. Charles Coe to CIA, June 22, 1923, file 43,164/1923 Flathead 054, NA CCF.

42. "Indian Pow-wow Is lacking Old Punch," DM, July 11, 1923, p. 3, c. 3-4.

43. St. Ignatius Post, July 13, 1923, p. 4, c. 1-2 (2 items).

44. Compton I. White, "Old Trading Post Is Found Again: M'Donald Helps," DM, Sept. 16, 1923, ed. section, p. 1, c. 1-3; "Blind Indian Is Guide to Trading Post Ruins," The Washington Post, Mar. 23, 1924, p. 23, c. 8.

45. CIA to Chas. E. Coe, Sept. 11, 1923, file 16,957/1915 Flathead 057, NA CCF.

46. U.S. Statutes at Large, vol. 43, (1923-1924), part 1, pp. 21-22.

47. John Galen Carter Diary, 1924, SC 1978, MHS Archives, pp. 72-82; "Butte Attorney Is Named to Push Flathead Claims," DM, Apr. 22, 1924, p. 5, c. 2.

48. Harold L. Ickes to Elmer Thomas, Mar. 24, 1942, Charles Kappler Collection, series 4, box 4A, folder 2, Little Big Horn College Archives, Crow Agency, Mont.

Chapter 10

1. Duncan McDonald to Paul Phillips, Mar. 19, 1925, Paul Phillips Papers, UM 1, box 1, folder 22, Toole Archives, UM; John Owen, *The Journals and Letters of Major John Owen, Pioneer of the Northwest, 1850-1871*, ed. Seymour Dunbar and Paul C. Phillips. (New York: Edward Eberstadt, 1927), 2 vol.

2. M. E. Plassmann, "Duncan MacDonald Describes Trading Posts Where He Lived His Boyhood," RP, Sept. 11, 1925, p. 6, c. 2-4; Martha E. Plassmann, "Old Fort Connah, in the Missoula Country, Last of Hudson's Bay Post to Be Established in the State," *St. Ignatius Post*, Aug. 7, 1925, p. 7, c. 1-6; M. E. Plassmann, "St. Ignatius — The Story of One of Montana's Oldest Mission Towns," *St. Ignatius Post*, May 14, 1926, p. 2, c. 1-3.

3. "Indian Boy Lost in Snow...," *Spokane Daily Chronicle* (Spokane, Wash.), Oct. 30, 1925, p. 2, c. 6-8; "Flatheads Attracted by Indian Congress," DM, Oct. 30, 1925, p. 5, c. 5; *St. Ignatius Post*, Nov. 20, 1925, p. 4, c. 3.

4. "Indians of Montana to Attend Congress," DM, July 14, 1926, p. 3, c. 1; "Second National Indian Congress, Spokane, U.S.A., July 21 to 27, [1926]: Final Revised Program," "Spokane Indian Congresses, 1925 & 1926," vertical file, Spokane Public Library, Spokane, Wash.; "Colorful Scenes Mark Indian Congress," The Spokesman-Review (Spokane, Wash.), July 22, 1926, p. 1, c. 7-8, p. 2, c. 1.

5. C. M. Russell, *More Rawhides* (Great Falls, Mont.: Montana Newspaper Assoc., 1925), pp. 29-31; *St. Ignatius Post*, Dec. 18, 1925, p. 5, c. 2. Russell's drawing is reproduced in chapter 2 above.

6. "St. Ignatius," DM, July 30, 1926, p. 6, c. 3-4.

7. "Flathead Project Will Show in Movie Scenes," RP, July 30, 1926, p. 1, c. 2.

8. "M'Donald Opposes Will Cave's Claim," DM, Sept. 12, 1926, ed. section, p. 1, c. 6, p. 5, c. 6-7; "'Saleesh House' of David Thompson Found by Cave," DM, Mar. 8, 1925, ed. section, . 1, c. 4-7, p. 5, c. 1-5.

9. "Gather Historical Material," DM, Oct. 16, 1926, p. 9, c. 2; Ellen Nye, "Flathead Indians Exhibited Many Relics of Olden Days...," *Rocky Mountain Husbandman* (Great Falls, Mont.), Aug. 11, 1932, p. 3, c. 1-6.

10. "Flathead Sage Recalls Mystic Tribal Lore of Many Years Ago," DM, Feb. 3, 1927, p. 10, c. 2-3.

11. "An Old Landmark at Ravalli Is Burned to Ground," RP, July 28, 1927, p. 1, c. 1.

12. "Dixon," RP, Aug. 11, 1927, p. 4, c. 4.

13. J. H. T. Ryman, "Why Call the Selish Flatheads?," DM, Aug. 21, 1927, feature section, p. 1, c. 1-7.

14. "County Commissioner's Proceedings," RP, Jan. 5, 1928, p. 4, c. 3-6.

15. McWhorter Papers; L. V. McWhorter, *Hear Me, My Chiefs!: Nez Perce History and Legend*, ed. Ruth Bordin (Caldwell, Id.: The Caxton Printers, Ltd., 1952).

16. "Strange Indian Death of 60s Related by M'Donald," DM, Aug. 13, 1928, p. 1, c. 1-2.

17. M. E. Plassmann, "Moving Camp," *Rocky Mountain Husbandman* (Great Falls, Mont.), Oct. 18, 1928, p. 3. c. 1-5.

18. H. T. Bailey, "Flathead Indians Add Romance to Valley," *The Daily Northwest* (Missoula, Mont.), Dec. 22, 1928, p. 6, c. 1-5.

19. "Pioneer of Flathead Valley Is Summoned," DM, Nov. 27, 1928, p. 3, c. 2; "Pioneer Woman of Flathead Passes Away at St. Ignatius," RP, Nov. 29, 1928, p. 1, c.2.

20. Mrs. L. L. Marsh, "Duncan M'Donald, Resident of Montana 81 Years...," *Great Falls Tribune*, Mar. 25, 1930, p. 6, c. 2-5.

21. Al Partoll, "Historical Sketches," *The Montana Kaimin* (University of Montana, Missoula), Jan. 8, 1929, supplement, p. 4, c. 4.

22. "Hudson's Bay Post Sold," DM, Jan. 16, 1929, p. 10, c. 1.

23. "Duncan MacDonald," DM, Jan. 21, 1929, p. 8, c. 5.

24. "True Indian Names Given, Suggestion," DM, Jan 26, 1929, p. 3, c. 1.

25. "Polson," DM, Feb. 23, 1929, p. 8, c. 3.

26. Al Partoll, "Historical Sketches: Duncan McDonald," *The Montana Kaimin* (University of Montana, Missoula), Mar. 12, 1929, supplement, p. 3, c. 2-3.

27. "Charlo," RP, Apr. 25, 1929, p. 1, c. 5.

28. William S. Lewis, "Spent Boyhood Days at Old Fort Colville," *Spokesman-Review* (Spokane, Wash.), Apr. 28, 1929, unpaged.

29. "Eighty Years with Redmen of Flathead," *Great Falls Tribune*, Aug. 9, 1929, p. 11, c. 2.

30. "Old-Timer Visits Friends in Ronan," RP, Oct. 31, 1929, p. 1, c. 2.

31. "Indian Hunter," DM, Jan. 10, 1930, p. 12, c. 3.

32. L. L. Marsh, "Duncan M'Donald, Resident of Montana 81 Years....," *Great Falls Tribune*, Mar. 25, 1930, p. 6, c. 2-5.

33. "Polson Banquet Memorable Event," DM, June 23,1930, p. 3, c. 1; "McDonald Ronan Caller," RP, June 26, 1930, p. 1, c. 1.

34. "Flathead Woman Dies at Mission," DM, Aug. 17, 1930, p. 12, c. 2.

35. "Duncan MacDonald Meets Old Friends," DM, Jan. 2, 1931, p. 8, c. 6; "Duncan MacDonald Missoula Visitor," DM, Mar. 27, 1931, p. 5, c. 7.

36. "Duncan MacDonald 82 Years Old Now," DM, Apr. 1, 1931, p. 2, c. 3.

37. "MacDonald Recalls Old Burial Ground," DM, Apr. 7, 1931, p. 5, c. 1.

38. "Duncan M'Donald at St. Patrick's From Fall Early in Week," DM, May 14, 1931, p. 5, c. 5-6; "82-Year-Old Man Out of Hospital," DM, June 5, 1931, p. 3, c. 7-8.

39. "Pioneer," DM, Aug. 5, 1931, p. 5, c. 3; "Duncan MacDonald Was Only '49er at Meeting," *The Kalispell Times*, Aug. 20, 1931, unpaged.

40. "Duncan Mac Donald Now 83 Years Old," DM, Apr. 2, 1932, p. 3, c. 4-6.

41. "Montana Pioneers to Open Convention in City with Reception This Evening," DM, Aug. 4, 1932, p. 1, c. 2-3, p. 2, c. 3-4; "Registration Is Near 300 Mark," DM, Aug. 6, 1932, p. 2, c. 1-2; "Pioneers Are Rotary Guests," DM, Aug. 6, 1932, p. 3, c. 1.

42. "MacDonald One of the Oldest," DM, Aug. 6, 1932, p. 2, c. 4-6.

43. "Registration Is Near 300 Mark," DM, Aug. 6, 1932, p. 2, c. 1-2.

44. "Old Relics on Exhibit in City Attract Hundreds," DM, Aug. 5, 1932, p. 3, c. 6-7.

45. "Polson," DM, Aug. 8, 1932, p. 8, c. 5.

46. "Pioneer Stories to Feature Hour," DM, Nov. 25, 1932, p. 8, c. 4.

47. "Returns From Dixon," DM, May 16, 1933, p. 3, c. 3.

48. "White and Red Men in Harmony," DM, June 29, 1933, p. 10, c. 5.

49. "Duncan MacDonald Now Is 85 Years Old," DM, Apr. 3, 1934, p. 8, c. 4-5.

50. Fred J. Ward, "Duncan McDonald Endeavored to Find Site of Salish House...," *Rocky Mountain Husbandman* (Great Falls, Mont.), May 24, 1934, p. 7, c. 1-4.

51. Dick West, "Duncan McDonald Nearly Lost Argument When He Wounded a Buffalo...," *Rocky Mountain Husbandman* (Great Falls, Mont.) July 26, 1934, p. 7, c. 1-4.

52. C. E. Schaeffer to Clark Wissler, June 29, 1934, C. E. Schaeffer Collection, Department of Anthropology, American Museum of Natural History, New York, New York.

53. "State's Oldest Pioneer to Be Among Visitors," DM, July 1, 1934, Pony Express Section, p. 3, c. 3-4.

54. "Western Montana Well Represented at Pioneers' Meet," DM, Aug. 28, 1934, p. 3, c. 1.

55. "McDonald Is Visitor," DM, Jan. 1, 1935, p. 10, c. 3; "McDonald Is Visitor," DM, Jan. 20, 1935, p. 10, c. 3.

56. "Jubilee Crowd of 25,000 Expected at St. Ignatius," DM, Sept. 14, 1935, p. 12, c. 3.

57. "M'Donald Leaves Hospital," DM, Oct. 11, 1935, p. 5, c. 7-8.

58. "Duncan MacDonald In City," DM, Nov. 5, 1935, p. 10, c. 3; "Mac-Donald Is Visitor," DM, Feb. 8, 1936, p. 5, c. 4.

59. Ellen Nye, "Duncan MacDonald, Montana's Oldest Pioneer, to Observe Birthday at Dixon," DM, Mar. 29, 1936, p. 9, c. 2-4.

60. "MacDonald and Latimer Talk of Early Days," DM, Mar. 4, 1936, p. 7, c. 4-5.

61. Ellen Nye, "Duncan MacDonald, Montana's Oldest Pioneer, to Observe Birthday at Dixon," DM, Mar. 29, 1936, p. 9, c. 2-4.

62. "Prophet," DM, Jan. 8, 1937, p. 6, c. 7.

63. "MacDonald Will Celebrate 88th Birthday Today," DM, Mar. 31, 1937, p. 12, c. 3.

64. "Pioneer Picnic Well Attended at Jocko Camp," DM, Aug. 29, 1937, ed. section, p. 3, c. 8.

65. "Duncan MacDonald Believed Oldest of Paper's Readers," DM, Aug. 29, 1937, Progress Edition, Missoula Section, p. 11, c. 1-3.

66. "Duncan MacDonald Is Seriously Ill," DM, Oct. 16, 1937, p. 3, c. 8; "State's Oldest Pioneer, Duncan MacDonald Dies," DM, Oct. 17, 1937, p. 1, c. 6, p. 6, c. 1-3.

67. Joseph McDonald, interview, March 19, 2015; "MacDonald Rites Are Held Monday at St. Ignatius," DM, Oct. 19, 1937, p. 5, c. 5; "Choir at Funeral," DM, Oct. 24, 1937, p. 4, c. 5.

Appendix

1. One copy of the transcript can be found in the Carling I. Malouf Papers, MS 640, series II, box 18, folder 1, Toole Archives, UM.

Index